# The Teacher's Guide to Intervention and Inclusive Education

## 1000+ Strategies to Help ALL Students Succeed!

## Glynis Hannell

Skyhorse Publishing

# Table of Contents

**The Teacher's Guide to Intervention and Inclusive Education:**
1000+ Teaching Strategies for Students with Learning Differences

## Chapter Three:  Written Language

## Chapter Four:  Math

## Chapter Five: Concentration and Organization

## Chapter Six: Teamwork

## Appendix

# The Teacher's Guide to Intervention and Inclusive Education

## 1000+ Teaching Strategies for Students with Learning Differences

## Introduction

Has there ever been a student who did not have 'learning differences'? Probably not! Every single human being on the face of the earth is unique. That is something we take for granted. Out of all the billions of people in the world, no one has exactly your face, your way of walking or your way of learning.

As teachers, we know that the amazing diversity and variety of the human race is reflected in every group of students we teach. We wouldn't believe it if all our students looked and behaved the same and had the same way of learning! Working effectively with diversity, variety and differences is at the very foundation of what good teachers do best.

Some of the qualities attributed to a good teacher are that he or she:

- develops ways to reach all children
- teaches the way the student learns
- never forgets what it is like to be a learner—vulnerable, anxious or dependent
- is able to change communication techniques to meet various students' needs
- has a big HEART
- sets the foundation—makes a difference
- enables his or her students to live better lives

In the following chapters, you will find a wealth of information on **intervention** and **inclusive education** (or simply referred to as **inclusion**) as well as numerous specific strategies for implementing these approaches to teaching.

**Intervention** involves explicit teaching and targeted instruction. Intervention is when teachers teach in the way that the student learns.

**Inclusive education (or inclusion)** involves the use of a range of strategies to ensure that students with learning differences are full members of the classroom and school community. Inclusive education refers to how teachers can make a difference and enable all students to live better lives. It is not limited to students with special needs but includes all students with diverse needs.

Are intervention and inclusion *extra* things that teachers do *on top* of their regular work? No! Intervention and inclusion are what good teachers do *all the time*! Therefore, this book is a practical resource for all educators who want to be ***good teachers*** and ***make a difference*** to ***all*** the students they teach.

# Chapter One
# Effective Teaching

## Introduction

This chapter will explain some of the basic foundations of effective teaching. How does the brain actually learn? That, in itself, is a miracle. To be effective as teachers, we need to understand the gradual, biological process we call learning, because as teachers, we actually make a difference—a real, physical difference—in the way our students' brains develop.

We also need to understand individual differences in learning capability and learning style. Then, we can adjust our teaching to the unique capacities of the individual students in our classes. Teachers who can do this are not only working hard, they are working smart!

Apart from inborn intelligence, every student has a range of personal qualities such as curiosity, persistence, self-confidence and so forth. The effective teacher can nurture these qualities and make a substantial difference in the quality of their students' learning.

Take a moment to reflect upon your own school days. Which teacher had the greatest positive impact upon you? In all probability, it was the teacher who built your confidence, encouraged your persistence and excited your curiosity. This chapter provides a range of ideas for developing these positive learning characteristics in all of your students.

The chapter ends with some thoughts on creating an inclusive classroom. *Being* included in a group and *feeling* included can be two, quite different situations. The effective teacher does not just do inclusive things. The effective teacher builds a classroom community where inclusion is part of the social fabric of the group of students and adults who work together.

The following Appendix forms are referenced in this chapter in the order given:

#24 – Teacher Checklist for Successful Learning
#26 – Teacher Chart for Planning an Inclusive Program
#23 – Teacher Checklist for Mastery Learning
#30 – Student Guide to Making Changes
#33 – Student Guide to Setting Goals
#35 – Student Self-Evaluation
#39 – Student Notes: Getting Ready for a Meeting
#36 – Student: What I Think about School
#37 – Student Reward Cards
#38 – Student Guide to 'I Can Do'

# The Brain and Learning

## Teachers—part of the miracle

The human brain is a miracle. From the earliest days of life, the cells of the human brain are organizing themselves into networks that communicate with each other, store and process information and learn new things. As teachers, we are part of this miracle. What we do in class will have a direct influence on how the students' brains develop. How does this happen?

## The developing brain

The human brain has at least 100 billion neurons (brain cells). Each neuron has a cell body and a tree-like structure of branches called dendrites. The dendrites reach out and connect with each other at junctions called synapses.

The synapses are a very important part of the brain's information highway. Information is processed, stored and retrieved through the network of neurons and synapses. The more these networks are used, the more the connections build up, so things become easier and easier to do.

A child is equipped with many more neurons and synapses than they will ever need. The networks that are used grow stronger and more complex. Those that are unused may become lost. If teachers provide the right learning experiences, brain development is enhanced and accelerated.

Some brain systems, such as those for language and vision, have critical periods for development. Once the critical stage has passed, it is very difficult to fully develop the networks of cells needed for a particular function, such as language or vision.

For example, babies with amblyopia, or 'lazy eye,' are born with one eye weaker than the other. The good eye may become dominant, and information from the weaker eye may be ignored. If this happens, the synapses connecting the weaker eye to the brain will fail to develop, because the synapses are not being used. Permanently impaired vision may result. That is why doctors often patch the good eye. They are trying to force the pathways from the weaker eye to develop before the synapses are permanently lost. There is a window of opportunity in early childhood for this to happen. If it is not developed during this time period, often those particular synapses in the visual pathways are lost, and the sight cannot be restored.

However, within limits, some new synapses will form 'on demand' throughout life. As an adult, you may not have developed your 'piano playing' synapses, for example. But what happens if you take lessons and practice? Slowly and surely, you will find that your brain begins to build up a 'piano playing' network of neurons that was not there before. If you skip lessons and don't bother to practice, you will find that your synapses won't develop, no matter how much you want to be able to play!

Whether you are a concert pianist, a first grade student or even a rat on a wheel, the principle is the same. Learning makes a physical difference to your brain.

Scientists set up an experiment with four groups of rats.

Group 1:   Exercise on a wheel for a set time each day
Group 2:   Unlimited access to an exercise wheel
Group 3:   No exercise
Group 4:   Obstacle course in which the rats had to learn challenging acrobatic moves

When the rats' synapses were counted at the end of the four-week period, the outright winners were Group 4. All that learning on the obstacle course had built up new brain connections that had not been there before. Simply exercising without thinking had not made new connections.

Learning, then, is a gradual, accumulative biological process. Networks are activated and strengthened through experiences. The result is something we call learning. As teachers, we are in the front line of managing this remarkable process. That's quite a challenge!

Following are some questions frequently asked by teachers.

**Q. If brains develop through experience and teaching, why can't I get all my students to the same level?**

Brains are all unique, so your students will all have different starting points for learning. Some students are well equipped to learn new things quickly, others develop synapses more slowly. Some have good neural networks already established in, say, language, but less well developed networks in math.

**Q. Can't the students just learn things (like times tables) by heart when they do not understand?**

If they learn things by heart, they will develop a little mini-circuit. This might work quite well if all they have to do is recite the information. But the circuit probably will not connect into any other brain networks, so the memorized information will not be used in new situations.

**Q. Couldn't my students learn more quickly if they tried harder?**

Of course effort is important to 'turn on' the brain activity that is needed. But remember that if the underlying synapses are not established, then structured, gradual work is needed to build up the necessary pathways. No amount of trying harder will produce a surge in brain networks without the necessary learning experiences.

**Q. I have a student who finds the class work too difficult. Surely she just needs to practice the same as everyone else.**

Practice works really well when the connections at the synapses are just forming. Extra practice at this stage will strengthen the connections between brain cells.

If the student does not have the early beginnings of the connections, then she will not have anything to build on. In this case, you will need to go back to find an earlier, simpler network that is already beginning to function. Once this is strengthened, then you will be able to move forward to new learning, step by step.

**Q. I have another student who learns everything quickly. She seldom makes mistakes. Surely she needs to practice just the same as everyone else.**

When synapses are really well established, the brain networks function with high speed and accuracy. The students can perform tasks automatically, without the need for thinking or applying a great deal of effort. In this case, further routine practice is not needed and can be very frustrating to the student. The student needs to move on to activities that will begin to develop new connections and networks, building on the existing framework.

**Q. Once the networks of synapses have developed, will they stay forever?**

Good strong networks of synapses are quite resilient. Some areas of learning are more permanent than others. For instance, we never forget how to ride a bike, even though we may easily forget our high school chemistry. There is usually some fading away over time, although often the network can be restored quite quickly, if it is reactivated. For example, you could probably relearn your high school chemistry much more quickly than the first time you tackled it, because some of the old connections are still there. Occasional practice can be helpful to make sure that earlier networks are still in good condition.

However, networks that are barely established and still in a fragile state will easily fall into disrepair if they are not exercised enough and given the chance to build up.

**Q. What about 'left brain' and 'right brain' learners?**

While it is true that some functions are localized, the two hemispheres of the brain usually work in a closely integrated and highly complex way as a single unit. Indeed, even localization can vary. For instance, most of us have our language centers in our left hemispheres, but there are quite frequent exceptions to this rule. About 10 percent of us have language in the right hemisphere. All of us have different patterns of interests and styles of thinking, and usually both sides of the brain are involved in any type of complex thinking.

# Strategies for Working with the Developing Brain

★ Because some synapses are lost forever when they are not used, it is very important to identify developmental difficulties as early as you can. Always investigate concerns promptly, so intervention can start as soon as possible, if this proves necessary.

★ Look for the level of difficulty where the student can *almost* complete the task unaided but needs a little help to succeed. Plan your teaching to strengthen existing connections and networks, and gradually build up more complex ones.

★ Use prompting to help students use existing networks for thinking. Observe students as they work. Remind the students of the next steps, ask questions that will help them to think along the right track or provide clues so students begin to activate the networks that are needed for the task.

★ Provide guided practice activities to help your students develop the brain systems they need to complete the learning tasks. As they experiment with a new task or skill, provide guidance so they see for themselves how to proceed through the steps to successful achievement. Going through the correct procedures helps to make brain connections.

★ Watch for students who are developing incorrect habits, for example in handwriting, spelling or math calculations. It is often very difficult to develop a new network when an existing one is already firmly established.

★ Use questioning to activate the student's existing understanding. Ask more questions to help develop new connections: *"What happens to water left on a saucer in the sun? . . . Where does it go? . . . What do you think happens to the water in the ocean? . . . Where does it go?"*

★ Brains that are actively engaged learn. Structure your activities so that all students have to think and use their brains at the level that is appropriate to their development.

★ Be cautious when using activities such as coloring or copying words as teaching tools. These activities will not necessarily contribute to brain development unless some mental activity is required.

★ Improve the teaching value of coloring by stimulating thinking. For example, ask the students to color in only the things that can grow or make all the metal red and all the plants green.

★ Improve copying tasks with instructions such as, *"When you have copied it down, read it through and draw a line under all the description words,"* or, *"Copy the sentences, then highlight the most important words in each sentence."*

✱ Plan your teaching to provide all students with the appropriate level of input and support. Students who find learning difficult will need more structure and support with their tasks. For example, you might provide a framework of headings for an essay, or break the task up into small sections, so the work is manageable for the student.

✱ When students learn very quickly and easily, adjust your teaching so the students are working at their own 'boundaries of competence' and their brains are continuing to develop in new areas of learning.

✱ Provide a plan or diagram of how to work through a task, step-by-step. This road map of how to think things through will help the students to develop their own thinking and make real connections with their learning.

✱ Appropriate levels of practice are important to strengthen the brain circuits necessary for long-term learning. Students with special needs often need more practice than most other students to reach a reasonable level of competence.

✱ Continue teaching and reinforcing until the student has a strong grasp of new learning so you know that the underlying structures are well developed and are more likely to be resilient.

✱ If students forget new learning too quickly, they have not had sufficient consolidation during the period of instruction and practice.

✱ Accept that students will not be able to bypass foundation learning. Learning is an accumulation process based on neurological development.

✱ Remember that students cannot suddenly produce brain structures that have not been built up by earlier experience, teaching or learning.

✱ The term *left-brain learner* or *right-brain learner* can confuse and worry students and parents. It is probably better to describe how the student learns, such as, *"This student works best when we use demonstrations and pictures to teach,"* or, *"This student enjoys language."*

## Individual Learning Differences

### Innate learning capabilities

As mentioned in the previous section, learning depends on the gradual development of systems within the brain that can process information. Each individual has a unique pattern of mental development that is determined by innate capabilities interacting with the environment.

For the most part, the growth in mental ability follows a timetable that is reasonably predictable. For example, we can say that the norm is for children to begin using single words by the time they are about 12 to 18 months old. But we also know that wide variations are to be expected.

In school, some students seem to be fairly average at most things, others may have general learning difficulties, and some will be more advanced than the majority of students. Some students will excel in some areas and be delayed in others. Such a mix of patterns is normal. It would be very unusual to have a class of students in which there was not a wide variation of abilities. Only in classes where the students have been selected according to their learning abilities would you expect some similarities—but even in this situation, there will never be complete uniformity.

## Moving from concrete to abstract thinking

Infants begin life thinking only about the here and now—what they can see or touch and what is happening at that very moment. If a toy is moved out of view, it also seems to move out of mind, and the baby has no further interest in it. This type of thinking is called concrete thinking.

Concrete thinking can continue throughout life. Even as adults, we want a diagram to show us how to put a table together, we try on a hat rather than just imagine what it will look like, we find it easier to understand a recipe than a chemical formula and we are more interested in a news item about our own neighborhood than about a place on the other side of the world.

However as children mature, they begin to be able to think about things that are more remote and not necessarily based in their real and immediate world. They also begin to be able to think about 'what if' situations, ideas and values that may have little or no connection to real events or objects. This type of thinking is called abstract thinking, and it is a very important part of learning and life skills.

Teachers work with students to develop the students' capacity to move from the concrete to the abstract in gradual stages. For example, a student begins math with concrete objects to count. Gradually, the teacher introduces tasks where thinking replaces physical action. Several years later, the student may be working with math theories and calculations that are essentially mental and not concrete processes at all.

Every student will go through the same stages of development in exactly the same sequence. However, the speed at which individual students will achieve various stages of thinking will vary considerably.

Some students will move through the stages of development more slowly. For example, a 12 year old may be using thinking skills usually more typical of an 8 year old. Compared with most of his or her age group, this student will need to be taught using more concrete methods and will be less able to cope with teaching that requires abstract reasoning.

Concrete thinking also impacts socialization. The student who is delayed in the development of abstract reasoning may find it hard to keep pace with the thinking and ideas of the peer group. The student may seem slow to catch on to the rules of a game or to understand a joke. This student may take things more literally, rely more heavily on his own experience and be less able to use 'what if' thinking in social situations.

Students who develop significantly more slowly may remain at a very concrete stage of thinking right through late adolescence and into adulthood.

---

In IQ tests, children are sometimes asked to say how pairs of items are the same. The concrete thinkers give answers such as, *"An apple and a banana are the same because they both have skin,"* or *"A dog and a cat are the same because they're both fluffy."* Their answers relate to physical qualities and personal experience.

The students who are abstract thinkers give answers such as, *"An apple and a banana are both nutritious fruit."* Sometimes, they also can deal with even more abstract ideas, such as, *"Anger and joy are both feelings,"* or even, *"Thinking and dreaming are both states of mind."*

---

In contrast, some students will develop abstract thinking more quickly than the typical child in their peer group. For example, at 6 years of age, the student may be able to use thinking skills usually typical of 10 year olds. Compared with most of his peer group, this student will be less dependent on concrete learning and more able to use abstract thinking.

Students who have an advanced capacity for abstract thinking may be able to solve problems and think through situations without the need for tedious, physical calculation or practical approaches. Socially, this student may be a 'fish out of water,' if the student talks about abstract ideas that have little meaning or interest to fellow students.

The chart on the next page provides examples of the way thinking evolves, from ages 0-4 on through to age 15+. Although age ranges are given in the chart, it is important to remember that these ages are when this type of thinking usually begins to emerge and become possible. Older students (and adults) often use a combination of very basic thinking and more advanced abstract thinking. Right through to adulthood, concrete thinking plays an important part in how we deal with information.

## Developmental Sequence:  Concrete to Abstract Thinking

|  | Typical age range | Type of thinking | Example |
|---|---|---|---|
| Level 1 | 0-4 years | Thought is tied to the real world and the here and now.<br><br>Problem solving is often physical and not mental.<br><br>Cannot think about their own thinking. | Forget about a toy once it is hidden.<br><br>Bang on a jigsaw puzzle to make the pieces fit.<br><br>Get upset that 'tomorrow' does not happen immediately.<br>Think that what they *guess* is certain to be the right answer. |
| Level 2 | 4-8 years | Thought is still closely tied to real-life experiences.<br><br>Information from the senses has priority over ideas.<br><br>Reasoning is often based on a single, sometimes irrelevant criterion.<br><br>The child's own perspective often dominates understanding.<br><br>Reasoning can be unsystematic. | Think that a polar bear will be 'cuddly' like their toy bear.<br><br>Choose the brightest colored book, instead of the book that would be the most help to them in their task.<br><br>Does not put peas in the vegetable category "because peas are yucky."<br><br>Choose a child's toy for a parent's present. |
| Level 3 | 8-15 years | Thought does not have to be tied to real life.<br><br>Ability to select relevant criteria improves.<br><br>Ability to coordinate more than one aspect of a problem increases.<br><br>Language and thought can be used to replace action or real-life experiences.<br><br>Reasoning becomes more methodical and systematic. | Can think about 'what if aliens landed' and make some reasonable assumptions.<br><br>Can talk through a plan and make decisions on probable situations that might arise.<br><br>Can gather several pieces of information and work it into an organized summary. |
| Level 4 | 15+ years | Thinking can be completely free of real-life experience.<br><br>Ideas can be developed and thought about in a systematic way. | Can agree or disagree with other people's theories or opinions on the basis of thinking, not experience. |

## Making connections between ideas

One of the biggest challenges in teaching is to show students how ideas connect to create a meaningful whole. Being able to link ideas is one of the most important aspects of learning and thinking. Some students find it difficult to produce a piece of work that has a coherent structure and logical flow.

Students with learning difficulties often seem to learn in 'boxes.' They may learn addition but not think about how it relates to subtraction. They may get help putting together a project on one topic but are unable to reapply those same skills to the next assignment.

## The importance of memory

Memory is an important part of learning, and many students fail in school because of poor memory. There are two main types of memory.

**Short-term memory** is the brief storage system where information is held before it is fully processed. We 'hold' a telephone number that we have just looked up, we dial the number and then we forget it. This type of memory is fragile and can easily be disrupted. If someone speaks to us before we dial, we may have to look up the number all over again.

**Long-term memory** is where information is stored for later retrieval.

Moving information from short-term into long-term memory often takes conscious effort. Memory is not like a muscle, so you cannot improve memory simply by 'doing' memory tasks. The only way to improve memory is to work on the strategies that help you to store and retrieve information efficiently. These strategies include:

- Paying attention
- Rehearsing the information
- Organizing the information in chunks
- Organizing the information in patterns
- Making sense of the information
- Using memory aids (mnemonics)
- Allowing enough time for learning to consolidate

Even when information is stored in long-term memory, it is not always easily located when it is needed. We may have no recall at all, or only parts of what are needed may be recalled. Often, we have to partially reconstruct the information in order to recall the whole.

Recall is easier if:

- You knew the information or procedure thoroughly in the first place.
- You understood the information or procedure well to begin with.

- You have actively recalled the information or procedure quite frequently since it was first learned.
- You have prompts, clues or context to trigger your recall.

Recall falls into several categories.

**Matching.** The simplest form of memory is matching. Matching occurs when we can remember enough about one thing to say that another is the same or different. If the teacher says, *"This word is **dog**. Find me another card with the word **dog** on it,"* the student may well be able to match the word, even though they cannot read *dog* independently. (In fact, matching words is a really good beginning for reading, as you will read in Chapter 2.)

**Recognition.** The second form of recall is recognition. Recognition occurs when the student can find a given word when asked to do so—e.g., *"Find the word that says 'house'"*—even though they still cannot read the word *house* independently.

**Retrieval.** The third form of memory is the retrieval of information. Retrieval is when the student is shown the word *because* and can draw on his memory and read it right away.

---

Tess was preparing for an exam. She read her notes over and over again, until she had a comfortable feeling of familiarity. Everything she read made her confidence build. She thought, *Yes, I know all this. There is nothing here that seems new.*

If the examination had asked her to *"Check the sentences that you have read before,"* she would have been fine. She would have recognized every one, because she had exercised her ***recognition memory*** when she reviewed.

However, Tess failed the exam because she had to ***retrieve*** information. Retrieving information is much more challenging than simply recognizing it.

If Tess had reviewed using active strategies such as working though previous tests, creating diagrams to organize the information and testing herself on her retrieval, she would have had a much better chance of passing.

---

## Speed of learning

Some students learn slowly because they lack the foundation skills or concepts and have real difficulty mastering what is required. Their problem is not really with their *speed* of learning, but with the higher level of difficulty.

Other students are quite ready to learn and capable of the task itself but simply need extra time to go through the learning process.

The speed at which a student learns is sometimes called a learning curve. Some students have a very steep learning curve. As soon as the teaching begins, they take off, and before long, they have mastered the idea and may need only a brief period of practice to consolidate the learning.

Other students have a more elongated learning curve. They are equally capable of succeeding with the task, but take longer to develop the ideas or skills. They may arrive at full understanding later than most. Once they get it, very little further practice may be required, or they may need to have extended practice to firm up their learning.

One of the greatest frustrations for the student who has a slow, gradual way of learning is that general classroom teaching is often aimed at the students who learn more rapidly. Often this student does have the capability to learn to the same level as others, provided enough instruction and practice is given.

---

**Jack is now a successful business man, and he tells his story.**

*Even now, I know I need time. It's no good giving me information too fast and expecting me to take it in. I need to read it over, hear it again, think about it and then it's OK—I can handle it. Same thing at school. I was a poor student, never got good grades and though I liked learning, it just seemed to go too fast.*

*Then I had this teacher, Mr. Grisham. Best thing that ever happened to me. Mr. Grisham kept teaching the same thing until we knew it—no going on to the next thing until you were rock solid on the first. He wouldn't let you move an inch until he was sure you were rock solid . . . and I found I could learn, and learn pretty good if we stuck at it, Mr. Grisham and me.*

---

The student with the extended learning curve may never get to finish any piece of new learning. Just as they are beginning to pick up, the topic is closed and the teacher moves on to the next part of the program. As a result, the student may have only partial or very fragile mastery of the first topic. Often, just a few more sessions of instruction and/or practice would have been all that was needed for the student to really understand and master the new skill or concept.

Conversely, students who learn very quickly can easily get frustrated and bored if further instruction and practice is given after they have accomplished the required learning.

## Language development

Without doubt, language is critically important in the process of thinking and learning. Language is the way in which we most frequently transfer information between teacher and student. Internal language is an important part of thinking, learning and remembering. It is hard to imagine how we would think without using words.

It follows that a student who finds it difficult to understand language and to use it effectively will likely have learning difficulties within the classroom. Does the student understand the difference between *"Draw a line down the middle of your page"* and *"Draw a line to the middle of your page"*? Can the student use words to create hypothetical situations, such as, *"If the book costs $12.00 and four people were going to buy it together, they would each have to put in _____"*?

# Strategies for Working with Individual Differences

## Planning for individual differences

✱ Use **Appendix #24: Teacher Checklist for Successful Learning** as a reminder of the basics of effective learning, so that all of your teaching is designed to make sure that your students can learn successfully.

✱ Use **Appendix #26: Teacher Chart for Planning an Inclusive Program** to look at the needs of individual students and to plan accordingly.

## Providing for concrete and abstract thinkers

✱ Identify the students in your class who work best with concrete materials and ideas. Developmentally, they may still need to work with real objects and experience hands-on learning, so provide the necessary materials.

✱ Allow students to use physical learning aids (such as counting on their fingers or making tally marks), if they need them. Students should not be made to feel that the use of these learning methods and materials is wrong.

✱ When you teach, always move from the concrete to the abstract. Start with a real-life example or demonstration of the principle you are teaching. Then move onto the more abstract ideas. For example, if you're teaching fractions, begin with real objects, then move to diagrams and finally to the written symbols.

✱ When you think students are ready, give explicit practice in moving from the concrete to the abstract. For instance, show the shortcut of counting on from the bigger number when adding two numbers together.

✱ Students who find abstract reasoning difficult often do not extract general principles from a single example, so provide several examples of the same concept. For instance, if teaching about flight, use examples of planes, birds, kites and autumn leaves to illustrate the general principles. If you use only one example, the more concrete thinkers in your class will tend to isolate the information to one example. If you use the example *"Airplanes fly because the air lifts their wings,"* the student may relate the information to airplanes but still not have any idea about what makes birds, kites or autumn leaves stay airborne.

✱ Teach students to think in categories as a way of enhancing their ability to use abstract rather than concrete reasoning. Classify and cross-classify items, e.g.: *"Butterflies, bees, eagles, seagulls and wasps can go into one group, because they all fly. . . . Or, we could say bees and wasps go together because they can sting. . . . Or, we could make groups of insects and birds."*

✱ Thinking about similarities and differences also helps to develop skills in abstract thinking: *"How are a bird and an airplane alike? . . . How are they different? . . . What is the same about a table, a chair and a bed? . . . Which is the odd one out—a bee, an eagle or a wasp? . . . Which three of these pictures have something in common? . . . How many ways can we group these things?"*

✱ Introduce thinking in analogies: *"Brush is to hair as broom is to . . . . Ceiling is to room as sky is to . . . ."* Have students make their own analogies.

✱ Create a 'backward quiz,' where the students are given the answers, not the questions, and get them thinking in a less concrete way. For example, *"If 'Africa' is the answer, what is the question?"*

✱ Give true/false quizzes to stretch thinking skills. *"All bees are insects. . . . All insects are bees."*

✱ Brainstorm in class various ways to develop abstract thinking. What do students think about questions such as: *"Why does rain fall down and not float away? . . . How does hair grow?"* Ask students to create their own questions and think about how their ideas could be tested.

## Enhancing the ability to make connections between ideas

✱ Note those students who find it hard to see the connections between ideas, and provide them with additional, explicit instruction so they can participate equally in the classroom learning.

✱ At the start of a lesson or activity, provide plenty of background and review to prepare students for new learning. Let your introduction create the scene for the new learning so that all students can 'locate' themselves and understand the 'big picture.' This helps activate prior knowledge and establish links between old learning and new.

✱ Give the students a clear summary of what is going to be taught. Write the headings as bulleted points on the board, and work through the topic systematically. At the end of the lesson, review what has been taught by going over the bulleted points to summarize what has been covered. This helps the students to see how the whole lesson has been a series of connected ideas.

✷ Always try to link new teaching to the students' previous experiences. Demonstrate to students how what you are teaching relates to what they already know. This helps to develop the connections that, in turn, help learning to make sense.

✷ Make the connections between different sets of information or concepts part of your teaching. Give explicit instruction and demonstration of the links between one set of ideas and another. For example, if you are teaching subtraction in math, take time to demonstrate and practice how the subtraction process relates to addition. If you are teaching about Mexico, talk about the similarities and differences between Mexico and Honduras (or whatever other country you have studied in class).

✷ Ask students to constantly compare and contrast new learning with previous learning: *"How is this story like the one we read last term? . . . How is it different?"*

✷ Have students use a storyboard (a series of pictures) to create an orderly sequence of ideas.

✷ Use software programs designed to help organize ideas and information.

✷ Get students to draw a 'mind map' to put their ideas into a logical structure.

✷ Make 'recipe cards' for procedures that require logical thinking in a series of steps.

✷ Have a poster that gives students a glossary of words and phrases that help to connect ideas together: *Although, because, unless, even if, more than, before that, afterwards, if, when, instead of, but . . .*

✷ Give explicit instruction and practice in writing sentences that combine ideas together: *"We went to the park because . . . . I like to swim even though . . . ."*

## Improving memory

✷ Get the students to pay attention to what they have to remember. Make eye contact and, if necessary, use their names.

✷ Alert students to the fact that they need to consciously attend to what they are learning: *"Now listen very carefully. You need to remember this."*

✷ Do not teach while a student is doing something else (such as finishing off previous work).

✷ Have students repeat the directions you have given them.

✷ Review previous learning, and check the students' retention.

✱ Have students over-learn information (that is learn and rehearse intensively until mastery is 100 percent on several subsequent days). Use **Appendix #23: Teacher Checklist for Mastery Learning** to help with this.

✱ Support students who have difficulty remembering by giving them information in written form.

✱ Make the information interesting and appealing. Have students read a school notice and act out the instructions: *"Mr. Saw says we have to bring the forms back tomorrow."*

✱ Use humor where possible to engage the students' interest and make the information more memorable.

✱ Give the information in several formats. For example, do not just tell the students the information verbally, but also draw a diagram or chart.

✱ Give students explicit instructions about how to store the information: *"Say it over to yourself . . . again . . . and again . . . and again."* (Many students don't realize this is necessary!)

✱ Use the example of a computer: *"Okay now, 'save' that information and send it to your brain."*

✱ Take them through the rehearsal process by giving real rehearsal that you can hear or see: *"Let me see you write that over again four times. . . . Tell me that same thing in six different voices. . . . Let's say that through five times before recess."*

✱ Have students rehearse using several senses: *"Write it down and say it over at the same time. Visualize what you have written. Whisper it to a friend."*

✱ Teach students to use pencil and paper, electronic organizers, computers and other memory devices to store information that is hard to remember.

✱ Give them an overview of what they have to remember: *"I'm going to tell you three things to remember. . . ."*

✱ Create logical patterns in the information to assist memory: *"There are six things to remember—three kinds of food and three things to wear."*

✱ Encourage visualization: *"Imagine those six things. Three kinds of food in the basket—can you see them now? 1 . . . 2 . . . 3. Now three things to wear—imagine putting them on. 1 . . . 2 . . . 3. . . . Five times six. Think about five rows of blocks, with six blocks in each row. Now imagine a big sign with 30 on the top."*

* Show how the information links together to make sense. *"See, you spell **today** with five letters—two little words, **to** and **day,** put together."*

* Have students use diagrams to organize information and aid recall.

* Put information in context so it makes sense and connects with things that are already remembered. *"Remember, we learned about how rivers erode the soil. Today we learned about two other sorts of erosion—wind erosion and ice erosion—so now we have three sorts of erosion to remember. Water, wind and ice."*

* Encourage students to create 'tricks' to help them remember, e.g., *"You **hear** with your **ear,** but **he** is in **here**."*

* Memory works best when there is no competition. If students are trying to remember something, allow some quiet time for rehearsal and consolidation before introducing new information.

* Build up the ability to recall specific information by giving students practice at matching and recognizing before they have to recall. For example, ask the students to pair up written questions with the answer before they are asked to remember the answers independently.

* Get students to practice recalling information if they are preparing for a test or exam by using practice tests, quizzes or written assignments that will help them to retrieve information.

* Check how students are reviewing for a test or exam. Explain how reading the notes over and over may only be activating their *recognition* memory, which will not help them when they have to *recall* information in the exam. Show the students how to go over the information using active strategies that assist recall, such as making mind maps, writing summaries, making their own self tests, etc.

## Accommodating various speeds of learning

* Consider those students in your class who are learning slowly because the task is too difficult for them to master. Provide an alternative, achievable task for those students you're sure are in over their heads. If you are unsure, it is a good idea to provide additional instruction and time. Perhaps the student *may* be able to cope with the learning given a longer exposure time.

* Design your teaching to accommodate students on the fast track, who need less instruction and practice to achieve success.

* Identify students in your class who you think *could* be expected to master the work, provided they had sufficient time and instruction. Set up your teaching to accommodate

their need for more instruction, an extended period of time and/or extra practice. Continue teaching until mastery is complete.

★ If students need additional instruction and practice, arrange for them to have supplementary work. Provide worksheets for extra practice at home, have a lunchtime study group for students to go over the class work, or provide additional, in-class teaching and practice sessions for those who need them.

★ Vary the required finishing time for any given piece of work to allow students to consolidate their learning if needed.

★ Instead of having a date when work is due, have an exit test to decide when the learning is complete. For example, the work will be complete when the student can achieve 80 percent or above on the exit test. Students can take the exit test when they think they are ready to move on, and it can be repeated if necessary.

★ Aim for quality, not quantity, in learning. Give the student fewer topics or assignments to allow them to spend more time mastering the ones they are working on.

★ Avoid moving students on to new work unless they can demonstrate a firm grasp of what you have been teaching already.

## Supporting language development

★ Monitor the language you use in teaching so that students with difficulties can still access the information you are giving. Make clear statements, write down key points, and order and summarize what you are saying.

★ Provide everyday-language versions of technical terms.

★ Give clear explanation of the meanings of new words that are introduced in a subject.

★ Be consistent with the vocabulary you use. For example do not switch between words such as *subtract* and *minus,* or *soluble* and *dissolves,* unless you make it clear to the students that you are talking about the same thing.

★ If other adults (such as parents, assistants, or volunteers) are working with students, make sure that you all are using the same terminology.

★ Make classroom charts as memory aids to help students assimilate new language that is being introduced.

★ Supplement what you say with diagrams, graphics and demonstrations to give information in a form that students with language difficulties can understand.

* Provide an assistant to help students with language difficulties understand what is being taught.

* Allow students to demonstrate their learning in a variety of modes, such as drawing, drama, construction, etc., in place of spoken or written language.

* Be aware of students who persistently make mistakes when answering questions. They may have difficulty with the *language* of the questions rather than the underlying knowledge or concepts. Try rewording the questions or assessing their knowledge by observing them putting the concept into practice.

* Some students have difficulty formulating spoken or written answers, even though they understand the topic quite well. Offer alternatives, such as multiple choice answers and true/false tests.

## Individual Learning Styles

Although learning depends to a large extent on the intrinsic capacity of the individual, personality, aptitudes and interests are important, too. Much has been written about 'multiple intelligences,' first described by Dr. Howard Gardner in 1983. As teachers, our experience confirms that students perceive information and problems through their own, unique sets of filters. When students' learning styles do not match the way they are being taught, learning difficulties can very easily arise.

> **It is only effective to teach by talking if you have a student who learns by listening.**

Commonly recognized learning styles include:

**Verbal-linguistic intelligence (word smart)**
These students like to listen and to talk, read and write.

**Interpersonal intelligence (people smart)**
Group dynamics and person-to-person relationships are priorities for these students.

**Kinesthetic intelligence (body smart)**
Physical activity, tactile sensation and movement are important to these students.

**Naturalist intelligence (nature smart)**
These students are very in tune with the natural world around them.

**Musical, rhythmic intelligence (music smart)**
Music and rhythm have meaning and appeal to these students.

**Intrapersonal intelligence (self smart)**
These students show independent thinking and action and highly developed self-awareness.

**Spatial intelligence (picture smart)**
Patterns, graphics, drawing and construction are strong learning channels for these students.

**Logical mathematical intelligence (math smart)**
These students like logic, mathematical order and systems.

**Aesthetic intelligence (beauty smart)**
Sensory beauty (colors, shapes, textures, perfumes) have a strong appeal to these students.

# Strategies for Working with Individual Learning Styles

* Plan your teaching and assessments to utilize the student's preferred way of learning.

* Offer alternatives so that students with different learning styles can work in the way that suits them best within the same curriculum area.

  For example, students might all study the same geography topic but take different angles depending on their learning styles. The students with highly developed interpersonal intelligence might work on the social aspects of the district they are studying; the logical, mathematical students might collect data and statistics; spatially aware students could draw maps and build models; while other students might focus on the flora and fauna and weather systems.

* **Verbal-linguistic intelligence.** These students thrive in a traditional classroom where most of the teaching and learning is based on spoken and written language. These students may prefer to learn by reading, talking and thinking rather than through practical activities. They may like to use words and language creatively in stories, poetry or drama.

* **Interpersonal intelligence.** These students learn best when they are able to work in groups, share ideas and support each other. They may find it difficult to connect with abstract or theoretical learning. They will be more involved if there is a human interest component in the topic. For example, they may not be interested in math for its own sake but become very involved when working out math connected with social situations, such as fundraising for a good cause.

* **Kinesthetic intelligence.** These students may find sitting still in class very difficult and may need frequent opportunities to move around. They may learn best through practical, active learning. They may be talented at sports, dance and other physical activities.

✹ **Naturalist intelligence.** These students will learn most effectively when they can connect with the living world. They may find being indoors frustrating and much prefer to be outside. Their preferred reading and viewing is often factual (documentaries) rather than fiction. They may connect well with hands-on activities that involve the natural world.

✹ **Musical, rhythmic intelligence.** These students may be very sensitive to noise and be disturbed by unpleasant sounds, such as loud, harsh or high-pitched voices, background noises, such as air conditioners, or competing sounds, such as noise from the class next door.

Using music in their general classroom program may enhance their involvement. They may have a strong need for musical or rhythmic expression and may need a legitimate outlet for this, such as being part of a choir, band or orchestra or being a solo performer.

✹ **Intrapersonal intelligence.** These students may actively dislike group work and prefer to work alone. They may prefer tasks where they are asked to give their own views and develop their own ideas independently. They may have distinct personal opinions and be prepared to defend their own ideas. They may like situations where they can negotiate what is required of them rather than having to follow the rules exactly.

✹ **Spatial intelligence.** When learning can be approached through graphics, design, visual patterns, construction and the like, these students usually enjoy learning. These students may prefer practical subjects, such as art, craft, design, technology and mechanics.

✹ **Logical mathematical intelligence.** These students obviously enjoy math and orderly sequenced learning. Scientific enquiry, research and information technology may have strong appeal. They may find creative tasks, where imagination or expressive, creative language is required, more difficult to master.

✹ **Aesthetic intelligence.** Students with high aesthetic intelligence are very aware of sensory information. They will notice presentation of learning materials and enjoy books, worksheets and equipment that have an aesthetic appeal. They may dislike having to work with materials that are ugly or unpleasant to look at or touch.

## Characteristics of a Good Learner

Learning characteristics make a big difference to learning outcomes. Some students find learning very easy. Some students find learning difficult and may have special needs. However, the student's characteristics as a learner (curious or apathetic, persistent or easily defeated, overly cautious or willing to take sensible risks and so on) will make a very significant difference to the quality of their learning.

Significant learning difficulties can be outweighed by strengths in persistence, curiosity, risk taking and so on. The characteristics of a good learner will go a long way towards making sure that the student is fully integrated and included within the classroom, despite the fact that the student experiences some significant difficulties with learning.

Conversely, high ability can be negated by negative learning characteristics, such as apathy towards new ideas, poor self-reflection and lack of persistence.

Some students in your class may be passive consumers of television and computer entertainment and not have had opportunities to develop their natural curiosity or their capacity for flexible thinking. Others may want instant results and give up too fast when success does not come quickly. Yet again, some students may be so afraid of making a mistake that they will try only things they are certain of getting right. Such students' learning difficulties may relate more to their characteristics as learners than to any problems they may have with the learning process itself.

Many notable discoveries have been made by scientists who were no more intelligent or better qualified than their peers. Some succeeded because they were more persistent, others because they were more prepared to think flexibly or follow the lead of their natural curiosity. Some scientists have made brilliant discoveries that were confined to their laboratories until someone with better communication skills came along.

Addressing your students' learning characteristics and working towards positive qualities is an important part of inclusion and intervention for all students, but especially for those who are already challenged by finding some aspects of learning difficult.

# Strategies for Developing Good Learners

## Stimulating curiosity and enthusiasm for knowledge

*   Students with learning difficulties often seem to have little energy left over to be curious or enjoy learning for its own sake. Identify any of your students who lack curiosity or zest for learning. Plan to stimulate this important characteristic in these students as an important foundation for learning. Ask questions and bring in exciting or interesting resources to get the students interested and intrigued.

*   Show your own enthusiasm for information. Express your own curiosity. Share your knowledge and let your students see that there is an endless and exciting range of things to learn about. Welcome questions and discussions.

*   Give lots of opportunities for real-life, practical science. Explore your local environment, experiment in the classroom and try things out to find answers.

*   Give assignments that encourage research and exploration for new information.

✷ Team a student who seems to lack curiosity with a partner who can model willingness to explore and go beyond the basic task.

✷ Subscribe to science or nature magazines that stimulate your students' curiosity and interest in the world around them.

✷ Encourage students to become questioners and to find out the answers. Make sure your classroom has a good stack of attractive reference books. Change the books regularly to create new interest.

✷ Allocate class time for students to browse through interesting books, magazines and other resources. Encourage them to follow through on their own interests.

✷ Use interesting posters and displays, and change them often to introduce new ideas and information into your classroom.

✷ Have students create a class quiz on a wide range of chosen topics, such as insects, life in our town in the 1950s, South American animals, the human body, automobiles, the solar system and so on. Every student contributes at least one question (and has the answer to that question worked out).

✷ Ask students with special interests to follow them up in depth. Vary assignments to accommodate a special interest.

✷ Encourage students to set up their own interest groups or clubs. Perhaps arrange for a special place for meetings at recess and lunch breaks. They can make collections and 'museum' displays for the interest of others. They might collect rocks as a geology group, collect information about aircraft or start a gardening club. The possibilities are endless.

✷ Have general knowledge quizzes at regular intervals in your class.

✷ Encourage an interest in words and their meanings. Get students to research word meanings and the origin of words and sayings.

✷ Have students research the meaning of their own names.

✷ Get students to find out about their own family history by talking to their parents, grandparents, aunts and uncles.

## Encouraging flexible thinking

✷ Students with learning difficulties may find flexible thinking difficult. Notice those students in your class who rely on *remembering* what they have been taught, rather than producing new ideas. Plan to encourage these students to think by presenting questions that have to be worked out by thinking.

✱ Introduce puzzles that use visual sequences or codes to encourage thinking in logical sequences.

✱ Have fun with 'what if' ideas: *"What if it rained soup? . . . What if you could fly? . . . What if time went backwards?"*

✱ Introduce Venn diagrams to encourage students to classify and cross-classify their ideas.

✱ Use the **Six Thinking Hats** technique devised by author Edward de Bono to show students how to use thinking skills flexibly. With this technique, each hat color signifies a different style of thinking. This technique helps students to change their patterns of thinking. The student who frequently is a Red Hat thinker (intuitive process) may be asked to use White Hat thinking (using facts and figures). If the class devises a plan that everyone in class is enthusiastic to implement, students may be asked to put on Black Hats to be sure they have not overlooked potential problems. If the class becomes stuck on a problem, they may be asked to put on Blue Hats and think about how to move forward.

**White Hat:** Focus on the facts that you already have; look for gaps in the current information.

**Red Hat:** Look at the problem using your intuition and 'gut feeling.' Think about how other people will respond.

**Black Hat:** Look at all the negatives; look cautiously and defensively. Look for the problems.

**Yellow Hat:** Look positively and on the optimistic side.

**Green Hat:** Think creatively. Use your imagination.

**Blue Hat:** Control the process of thinking and problem-solving. Decide what strategies to use.

✱ Ask for flexible thinking in your classroom: *"What could we use instead of a ruler for this job? . . . Let's think of a different way of getting to the playground."*

✱ Value the diversity of ideas in your classroom. Always welcome different ideas, and be prepared to discuss the range of ideas that come from the class. Do not allow students to ridicule ideas that are suggested by others.

✱ When you brainstorm ideas with the class, write every idea up on the board. Show how even 'wrong' ideas can give information that helps to solve the problem: *"At first we thought we could use a paper bag. That was no good, though, because when it got wet, it fell to pieces. So we knew we needed something that stayed strong when it got wet."*

✻ Collect riddles and encourage students to make up their own.

✻ Get students to do crossword puzzles and other word puzzles.

## Pushing persistence and determination

✻ Many students who find learning difficult become discouraged. Look at the students in your class and identify those who seem to lack persistence and determination. Plan to work on these important learning characteristics with those students.

✻ Use **Appendix #30: Student Guide to Making Changes** to help students clarify where extra effort is needed.

✻ Avoid letting students leave work unfinished, as this develops a poor work ethic.

✻ Use flexible time limits so that work can be completed, even if it takes the student longer than others.

✻ Be honest with students, and when a task is challenging, tell them that it will need a high level of persistence. Celebrate when they succeed.

✻ Give tasks difficulty ratings. Give bonus points for tasks with high difficulty ratings: *"This task has a difficulty rating of nine, which means it's a tough one. You'll get a bonus of nine points for giving it a try, and then a maximum of five points for getting all five questions right. Or, you can try this one, which is easier and rated two, so you get two points and then a maximum of five points."*

✻ Give students credit and public recognition of persistence and determination as a valued learning characteristic: *"We can be so proud of Jess. It took her four tries to get her story the way she wanted it—but she did it!"*

✻ Help students to set personal goals and reward their achievement. Use **Appendix #33: Student Guide to Setting Goals** to help with this.

✻ Encourage self-talk and self-motivation to enhance persistence and determination. Have students tell themselves they can succeed, or have them make motivational notes to put on their desks.

✻ Collect and value stories of children and adults who have shown determination in the face of difficulties and use them as role models.

✳ Work with the idea of practice, training and application being important elements in success. Emphasize the way in which successful sports men and women put in many hours of training and practice to reach their goals.

✳ Show students that setbacks and failures are part of the process of success. Talk the students through difficult patches by showing them how they are gradually building up to eventual success.

## Fostering good communication

✳ Communication involves good listening. Encourage your students to be attentive listeners by making your teaching dynamic and involving. Expect your students to interact with you as you teach. Ask questions, invite ideas and foster active involvement.

✳ Model good listening. Teach your students about eye contact, taking turns when speaking and keeping to the topic of conversation.

✳ Provide experience in structuring communication so it makes sense. Students need to organize ideas into a logical sequence. They need to make clear statements at the beginning and the end of what they say, so the listener has a framework for what they hear. Have them prepare talks using prompt cards, numbering each card so their plan has a sequence.

✳ Try having the students role-play TV newscasts to get them thinking about telling a story in a clear and engaging way.

✳ Look at professional broadcasters. Ask the students to identify how these people make their communication clear to the listeners.

✳ Most professional communicators have an editor, producer or director to enhance what they do. Offer students the same support. Have an adult or fellow student take on the role of editor, producer or director when the student is preparing a presentation or speech. That person's role can be acknowledged: *"I would like to thank my producer, Tim Atkins, who worked with me on this presentation."* Or, *"Written by Frankie Khan, edited by Rosa Patagonis."*

✳ Give all students the chance to communicate with a range of audiences, such as the whole class, a group of younger students or visitors to the school. Give every student in your class an equal opportunity to take on roles such as showing visitors around the school and speaking in front of the class. If the student does not have the necessary skills, rehearse what is required.

✳ Some students will have difficulties in specific areas, such as writing, talking, etc. They may be able to get their ideas across using art, graphics, computer programs, drama, construction or demonstration.

✴ Keeping to the topic is an important part of good communication. Provide activities in which students have to sift out irrelevant information from a talk or reading passage.

✴ Answering questions exactly is another important part of good communication. Students often think long answers are always better than short answers. Let them discover that a good answer is one that relates exactly to the question that is asked. Give them a question and then sort out possible answers. Ask, *"Which answers were the best answers?"*

✴ Have the students rewrite long messages in as few words as possible to get them to communicate the essential facts clearly.

## Encouraging sensible risk-taking

✴ Many students with learning difficulties do not like to take risks, because they so often make mistakes. Make sure tasks are at the right level, with sufficient support, so there is only a small risk of making a mistake and a high chance of getting things right.

✴ Some students think that getting something right is the only thing that counts. Always emphasize that making an attempt is an achievement in itself, regardless of the outcome: *"That was a great try. . . . You gave that your best shot. . . . That was tough, and you nearly cracked the first part."*

✴ Show students ways of saying they are not certain: *"My guess is that . . . it could be . . . I am not sure, but I think that . . . maybe . . . perhaps . . . my hunch is . . . I don't think this is right, but I'll have a try."*

✴ Tell stories of people who have taken on challenges and tried, often again and again, to succeed. Many scientists and explorers only made breakthrough discoveries by taking some chances.

## Supporting self-reflection

✴ Use **Appendix #36: Student: What I Think about School** to help students identify their own learning profile and feelings about learning.

✴ Students with learning difficulties often fail to evaluate their own work. They may be passive learners, waiting to hear how they have done from the teacher. Encourage your students to evaluate their own learning ahead of teacher response. You can use the **Appendix #35: Student: Self-Evaluation** to help your students reflect on their own learning.

✴ Before evaluating student work, ask them to talk you through what they have done. Explore their thinking behind their work. Why did they decide on that topic? Would they make the same choice now? How did they find their information? Were there other sources they could have tried?

✴ Encourage students to take an active rather than passive role in meetings regarding their programs. Give students the **Appendix #39: Student Notes: Getting Ready for a Meeting** to help them prepare.

# Self-Esteem, Self-Confidence and Optimism

**Self-esteem** is the value that you place on yourself. If you lack self-esteem, you may:

- Assume that other people do not like or value you
- Disbelieve any positives that people say about you
- Feel uncomfortable with praise or success
- Be easily led and afraid to trust your own judgment
- Not feel entitled to fair or equal treatment
- Be defensive if people try to help you

**Self-confidence** has to do with your belief in your ability to succeed. If you lack self-confidence, you may:

- Expect to fail at a particular task
- Be low in motivation because you do not expect to succeed
- Find it hard to overcome setbacks, because you think that proves you have failed

**Optimism** is the belief that things will turn out well. If you lack optimism, then you may:

- Be certain that things will go badly, even before you have begun
- Notice the negatives more than the positives
- Place negative interpretations on the daily ups and downs of life
- See reasons why things will go wrong more easily than reasons why things will go well

Inclusion is a two-way street, and students themselves are an important part of the process. Of course the *community* has to believe in the principle of inclusion and have inclusive systems and strategies put in place. However, that is only half of the story. The *students* have to have enough self-esteem, self-confidence and optimism to believe in their own entitlement to equal opportunities. Without this sense of entitlement, they will not be able to accept and utilize the inclusive practices that are available.

. . . . . . . . . . . . . . . . . . . . . . . . . . . . . . . .

Sven has multiple difficulties in school. He thinks that because he is different, he is inferior. He assumes that his future prospects are bleak. Sven thinks that the strategies offered to him are "a waste of time," because he 'knows' that he can never succeed or overcome his difficulties. He does not feel that he is worth the effort that people put in. He expects to disappoint those who work with him. Sven does not cooperate with his teachers or with the services and support that they provide.

Juan also has multiple difficulties in school. He has good self-esteem and values his own, unique set of characteristics. He has a strong sense of entitlement to inclusive strategies that are offered and a high expectation that, working with his teachers, he will be able to reach his full potential. Juan believes that the inclusion program is his right and uses the opportunities to their fullest extent.

## Strategies for Building Self-Esteem, Self-Confidence and Optimism

### Boosting self-esteem

* Provide the student's inclusive provisions as rights not privileges. Deal with difficulties honestly and with an open approach.

* Build a warm and personal relationship with the student. This seems very obvious, but it is all too easily forgotten.

* Take time to listen attentively, with enthusiasm, sympathy or whatever is appropriate.

* Make positive eye contact.

* Refer to what the student has previously told you about herself: *"How's that new dog of yours doing, Marcia?"*

* Smile at the student—for real.

* Greet the student warmly—with heart.

* Share something about yourself with the student.

* Find points of similarity and connection between yourself and the student—the same pet, the same favorite color, mutual interests or favors: *"Let's hope our team wins on Saturday, John. . . . Cheri, could I borrow your pen for a minute? . . . I'll bring that book in from home to show you."*

. . . . . . . . . . . . . . . . . . . . . . . . . . . . . . . .

✹ Ask for information or advice from the student where you know they have expertise or knowledge: *"My friends are coming over this weekend. Do you know a good place for their kids to skateboard?"*

✹ Be honest with both praise and criticism, so the student trusts your opinion.

✹ Show respect for the student's ideas and feelings: *"What do you think about that? . . . How do you feel that would work? . . . I agree with you; that's a good idea. You go ahead and get started. . . . Should we do it in red? Or maybe blue would be better. What do you think?"*

✹ Have high expectations of the student: *"I know I can trust you with that. You are responsible."*

✹ Encourage the students to acknowledge their profiles of strength: *"You know you are good at sticking to the task. . . . You are such a friendly person."*

✹ Teach students to evaluate their own efforts and to give themselves credit when they know they have done a good job. Similarly, teach them to be honest with themselves, so they do not accept second best from themselves.

✹ Remind the students that they are each unique. *"There is only one me in this world, and only one Josh Neilson, and only one Cilla DeMaggio. No one else even comes close!"*

✹ Use **Appendix #37: Student Reward Cards** to provide positive messages about the students' behavior and attitudes.

## Strengthening self-confidence

✹ Set tasks with a realistic level of challenge so students can take pride in achievements.

✹ Give feedback about personal qualities as well as competitive achievements: *"You are such a kind kid. . . . Your smile makes my day. . . . I love the way you give everything a try."*

✹ Encourage students to showcase their achievements—taking pieces of work home or showing the principal what they have done.

✹ Show the student that making a good attempt is, in itself, a success. The outcome is less important: *"That was a really good effort. . . . You had some good ideas about how to tackle the task."*

✹ Show confidence in the student yourself: *"I bet you will give this a really good shot."*

✱ Give students choices about the level of difficulty they want to tackle. Give them opportunities to try out more difficult tasks once they have gained confidence at their starting point.

✱ Use **Appendix #38: Student Guide to 'I Can Do'** to help students think positively.

## Encouraging optimism

✱ Encourage students to plan for positive outcomes and to think their way around potential difficulties.

✱ Teach students to discriminate between problems in the here and now (which do need to be dealt with) and hypothetical problems in the future, which may never eventuate.

✱ Encourage positive thinking. If students are predicting 'worst-case scenarios,' get them to balance these with 'best-case scenarios.'

✱ Encourage problem solving, so the students learn that whatever might happen in the future (good or bad), there is usually a way to deal with it.

✱ Model optimism. Be positive and confident about the future yourself.

✱ Challenge catastrophic language used by the student and others. *"Would it really be a 'disaster' or just a bit of a nuisance?"*

✱ Use humor to defuse negative experiences or expectations and put them in perspective.

## The Inclusive Classroom

*Being* included in a group and *feeling* included can be two, quite different situations. We have probably all been in situations where we have felt as if we were outsiders, even when we have been invited or have an absolute right to be part of a particular group.

If the student feels that they do not really belong to the class, then inclusion has not really happened. Often the student with difficulties or differences feels marginalized or excluded from the social group, even when the teacher uses a wide range of appropriate inclusive teaching strategies. These inclusive strategies are unlikely to work well if they are given in a context where the student *feels* socially excluded. Once again, remember that often it is not *what* you do, but *how* you do it.

> *"The teacher says 'Good job' to us . . . like she's trying to make us feel better about being dumb."*
>
> *"All of us bad readers get 'Good Reader' badges."*

# Strategies for Creating an Inclusive Classroom

✶ Create a class identity where everyone belongs. Have a class name, motto, badge, color, code word, flag, song or anything else that marks *every* student as a rightful member of the group.

✶ Do things together as a class, organize a show for the rest of the school, go on a field trip, do community service or anything that involves *everyone* in the class on an equal footing.

✶ Refer to the class as a group: *"All of us in Room 3 . . . We all want to . . . We look out for each other on the playground. . . ."*

✶ Monitor how you deal with the students in your class. Do you have a 'special' voice or phrase that you use only with the students with special needs? If so, revise your style!

✶ Make sure that all students have equal responsibilities. You may need to modify how they meet their responsibilities, but this does not mean they are excused from them. For example, everyone has an equal responsibility to keep the classroom tidy. The student who uses a wheelchair may have different duties from the other students but still does his fair share of the work.

✶ Make sure that every student has equal opportunities. For example, if your class has a student representative, then every student is equally eligible to be chosen. Provide support and assistance if needed, so the student can meet the obligations.

✶ Make class rules that are inclusive, so everyone can keep them. For example, if a class has a student with autism who often calls out, the class rules might be adjusted: *"Listen quietly when the teacher is speaking or go to the quiet corner with Mrs. K."* The same rule applies to every student.

✶ Work with the whole class to look at inclusive strategies in play and socialization: *"How can you adapt the rules of the game so that everyone can join in? . . . What if one of us has no one to play with at recess? . . . Some students will need a buddy for this game."*

✶ Teach students to value diversity and individual differences by valuing them yourself: *"It's so interesting how you all thought of different ideas. . . . It's never boring with this group. . . . So many different people, all with something special."*

✶ Invite a range of guests into your class to speak to the students, so they can see that everyone has an amazing array of talents: *"Jack's father can bake bread and do ballroom dancing, Lilla's mother can drive a truck and fix a car, and Sam's sister wears really interesting clothes and draws great pictures."*

★ Use real-life stories to highlight the fact that many people with apparent disadvantages do exceptional things.

★ Intervention and inclusive practices should be an integral part of what you do, not an 'add on' or extra to 'normal' work. Reflect this in the way in which you plan, talk and write about your program. For example:

*"We will all be studying frogs this week, and you will all have your own tasks to complete. You can find your task in the tray with your name."* This is inclusive. Everyone has his or her own task to do.

Instead of:

*"We will all be studying frogs this week. Everyone will be doing the task that I have written on the board. Marcia and Cedda, you have your own special tasks to do on frogs."* This is not inclusive. Marcia and Cedda are not doing the 'real' work like the rest of the students. They have something different to do. Therefore, they are not included in "everyone."

## Concluding Chapter One

This chapter has presented numerous strategies for effective teaching and for creating and enhancing an inclusive educational environment. The variety of capabilities, skills, and learning styles that are inherent in any group of children can be a challenge. Intervention and flexibility are necessary to adjust teaching styles to the variety of levels, speeds and styles of learning encountered in the classroom—but it can be done! Yours is an awesome and much appreciated role to literally mold young minds and nurture young hearts. The specific ideas suggested here will help you to make every child feel welcome and a part of the group and help you to build on every child's strengths.

Remember, inclusion is first and foremost an attitude and approach that needs to be adopted in the entire school community to be most effective. As a teacher and one of the leaders in this community, you can provide a model of and support for this attitude and approach, making your school a happier place, where all children can achieve their personal potentials.

# Chapter Two
# Reading

## Introduction

We all know reading is an important life skill. Many students acquire reading skills easily. In a world where print is so important, these fortunate students are well equipped. They can use reading to learn and to gain information from the world around them. Reading can enhance their lives and be a source of great pleasure.

But what of the 15 percent or so of students who find reading difficult? In class, the student may experience a considerable disadvantage because of inaccurate or slow reading. Significant emotional and motivational challenges also may arise for the student who is struggling with such a fundamentally important skill.

For students with reading difficulties, intervention in school is vitally important to help develop their reading skills and minimize the risk of long-term disadvantages. Within the classroom, a wide range of modifications will also be needed to make sure that the students with reading difficulties can participate to the fullest extent.

The main subjects in this chapter follow the structure of the **Appendix #1: Reading Observation Chart.** The chart is divided into 11 sections, each focusing on a specific area of reading. The Reading Observation Chart may be reproduced and used to informally assess and record individual reading difficulties for students. As you assess individual students, specific patterns of difficulty may emerge. The sections in the Reading Observation Chart will provide a direct link between the recordings in the chart and the corresponding sections in this chapter that provide strategies to help the student in those specific area(s) of need.

The 11 sections of the chart have also been reproduced within the main text of Chapter Two. If you are interested in using the strategies without completing an informal assessment of the student, these sections will easily guide you through the chapter and provide a quick and easy reference tool for specific areas in reading. This will enable you to select from the intervention strategies, modifications and adaptations listed to help individuals and small groups of students.

The following forms from the Appendix are referred to in this chapter:

Appendix #1:    Reading Observation Chart
Appendix #40:   Parent Guide to Reading at Home
Appendix #38:   Student Guide to 'I Can Do'
Appendix #33:   Student Guide to Setting Goals
Appendix #23:   Teacher Checklist for Mastery Learning

The first section provides an understanding of and strategies for dealing with general negativity towards reading.

# Student Feels Negative about Reading

## Section 1 – Reading Observation Chart

| 1. Student feels negative about reading. |
| --- |
| Student is reluctant to read; will not read without prompting; complains when reading. |
| Student avoids reading, 'loses' book, tries delaying tactics. |
| Student becomes angry or upset with reading. |
| Student tries to avoid reading in front of fellow students. |

When we consider how important reading is within the classroom and everyday life, it is not surprising that students who find reading difficult often become embarrassed, frustrated, distraught or angry. Reading is a highly complex skill, and some students, even if they are intelligent and motivated, truly find the process very difficult.

Students with reading difficulties may be afraid that adults will be angry or disappointed with them. Adults do sometimes show irritation or frustration when a student stumbles through what seems to be easy reading or makes the same mistake over and over again. It is easy for adults to think that the student simply needs to put in more effort.

---

The parent or teacher may be thinking:

*If only he would try harder. . . . He can't be trying if he makes so many mistakes. . . . I can't believe how many times he has forgotten this word.*

On the other hand, the student may also be feeling very frustrated and anxious:

*I can tell Mom is getting mad at me. . . . I am trying as hard as I can. . . . This is so tough to do. . . . It all looks the same to me. . . . Why can't I get this? . . . I've forgotten it all over again!*

---

The student may be afraid that having difficulties with reading means they are 'dumb.' It is hard to believe in yourself if you can't read well, especially when most of your peers seem to be coping so easily. The possibility of ridicule from other students can be a very real fear.

> *What will the other kids say if they see I am reading a little kid's book?*
>
> *Will they laugh at me when I make a mistake reading in front of the class?*
>
> *Will they think I'm dumb if I get special help?*

Once a student is anxious, defensive or angry about reading, then the educator has a much harder task in addressing not only the reading difficulties but also the negativity towards reading that the student has developed.

# Strategies for Developing Positive Attitudes towards Reading

## Communicating with all teachers

* All teachers need to be made aware of the student's difficulties with reading. The teachers also need clear and concise information about what special provisions have been agreed to, such as modified assignments, tests read aloud, audiotapes of reading material, etc. For students who receive special education services, these will be documented in the Individual Education Plan (IEP).

* In some large schools, it is difficult to stay in contact with every teacher. The student can be provided with a laminated card that states that the student has reading difficulties and itemizes the special modifications that are required. This card can be discreetly shown to any teacher as needed.

* When students transfer from one grade level to the next or change schools, information about strategies that have been used successfully should be passed on to the new teacher before the student begins in the new class.

## Giving parents support

* Talk to the student's parents to ensure that they are being supportive. Some parents find it hard to understand their child's reading difficulties and may let their own frustration show.

* Parents need to know that reading is a complex skill and that reading difficulties are not unusual, even in bright, motivated students.

* Be aware that some parents may themselves have reading difficulties and find it difficult to support the student. In this case, arrange for alternative support in the school or community.

* Give the parents help with supporting reading and building confidence. You can use the parent information sheet **Appendix #40: Parent Guide to Reading at Home.**

## Respecting the student's self-esteem

* Respect the student's sensitivities about their reading difficulties. Some students are self-conscious about being excluded from reading in front of the class, even though they are anxious about making mistakes. Check with the student to see whether or not they are comfortable reading in front of the class.

* If the student chooses to read in front of the class, you can arrange to give the student prior warning so he or she can rehearse the reading ahead of time. Help the student prepare if necessary.

* If the student chooses not to read in front of the class, deal with this tactfully.

* Teachers will be strong role models in showing the class as a whole that students with reading difficulties are accepted and supported without criticism, put-downs or ridicule.

* If the student's program plan involves the student receiving support that is obvious to fellow students (for example if the reading specialist visits the student in the classroom or if the student leaves the classroom for special support), be particularly careful that this is handled sensitively. Talk to the student about what type of help he or she feels most comfortable having.

* Provide all students with information about individual differences. Seek out examples of successful adults who struggled with reading difficulties and introduce your class to their stories. Examples that you could provide include Tom Cruise, Whoopi Goldberg, Pablo Picasso, Thomas Edison and Leonardo Da Vinci.

* Ask a colleague, parent, student or well-known community member who has reading difficulties to talk to the class, so everyone understands that reading difficulties are part of life and can be managed successfully.

* Provide the student with honest information and supportive counseling. Talk honestly about the reading difficulties and reassure the student that this does not mean he or she is dumb. Explain that, like many complex skills, reading can take time to master, and that many very smart and successful people had reading difficulties when they were students and may still have.

* Give objective, quantified information about the student's reading abilities. Reassure the student that he or she will be able to make progress and will be given the necessary support.

★ Give objective, quantified information about the student's strengths to counterbalance the information about his or her reading difficulties.

★ Use the **Appendix #38: Student Guide to 'I Can Do'** worksheet to help students come to terms with their learning difficulties.

★ Students may need ongoing counseling and support to understand that, with effort, appropriate help and perseverance, their reading will improve.

★ Create a positive and personal relationship with students who require extra help with reading. If possible, maintain continuity of help if things are going well.

★ Be prepared to change the approach, setting or teacher if the student becomes or remains negative about reading. A poor attitude from the student indicates that the modifications already created are not effective in dealing with the interplay of reading difficulties and frustration/low confidence.

★ Remember that trying to bolster confidence by excessive praise is not helpful. Students soon become cynical about praise that is won too easily or is not honest. The student with reading difficulties may simply feel patronized when an adult praises them.

> *That was a really easy book for most kids in my class, so she must think I'm dumb if she thought my reading was fantastic. . . . I know she's only saying that to make me feel good. . . . She says that stuff about 'fantastic reading' to all the kids who can't read. She never says it to good readers.*

★ Praise needs to be genuine to be effective. Praise the effort, persistence, courage and determination the student shows in tackling the difficult task of reading.

★ Give honest feedback about the student's reading, so the student values compliments when they are given. (But make sure the reading tasks you give the student are appropriate, so you can give honest praise for real successes.)

★ Students often need to see tangible evidence of real positives before they can truly believe they are progressing. Keep good records of reading progress, and share these with the students so they can see for themselves the progress being made.

★ If there are good role models within your school, community or the student's family, ask them to mentor the student and show that even though reading can be hard, the difficulties can be managed and success achieved.

★ Provide students who have reading difficulties with opportunities to show their strengths in academic, athletic, musical, interpersonal, artistic or community-based areas of interest.

★ Provide positive affirmation by assigning the student special responsibilities or positions that add status in the school community despite reading problems.

★ If necessary, provide the student with administrative help. For example, a student chosen as class president could be asked to select a fellow student to act as secretary to the president to assist with reading tasks.

★ Publicly recognize the student's successes by celebrating such milestones as "most improved in word decoding," "personal best in reading word list," or "ahead of schedule in reading program." Emphasize effort and give credit for perseverance.

★ Include the student as part of the intervention process. Talk to the student about how you are going to work together to deal with the reading difficulties the student is experiencing. Show the student your record of the skills that have already been mastered. Follow through with a clear program of intervention, so the student can see for himself how your program will take him step by step through the stages of learning to read.

★ If the student is self-conscious about being seen with 'little kids" books, allow him to have two reading books on his desk. One book is for image and is typical of the books that other students are reading. Perhaps the student can listen to this book on tape or see a video of the story, if available. The second book is more appropriate for the student's reading level. This book must still be chosen to match the student's age and interest levels. A wide variety of high interest-low vocabulary reading books are available for the older student.

★ If a student wants to read aloud to the class, allow him to rehearse a new book before it is read. Let the student decide how he will prepare for his 'performance.' He can read it himself, listen to an adult read it and/or read it aloud to a helpful adult. Also, the student can read along with an audiotape as often as he likes. Allow him extra time to rehearse the difficult parts until he is confident and ready to read in front of the group.

★ Let the student choose when he is ready to read the book to an audience. In this manner, the student is not pressured to read without assistance until he feels sufficiently confident and well prepared to give it a try.

★ You may be able to allow the student to choose his own audience. Perhaps the student will read it onto a tape or read to a grandparent or a school friend.

✱ Although, as the professional educator, you will need to design the overall program, allow the student to make some choices in what to learn and how. Ask the student to make some choices within the teaching goals that you have identified. *"Next we have to study the 'oa' and 'ai' sounds. Which shall we do first?"*

# Student Is Disadvantaged by Poor Reading

## Section 2 – Reading Observation Chart

| 2. **Student is disadvantaged by poor reading.** |
| --- |
| Student demonstrates difficulty reading materials or textbooks suitable for age group. |
| Student needs additional time to complete reading tasks compared to peers. |
| Student does not finish reading assignments in the allotted time. |
| Student runs out of time in examinations because of slow reading. |

Students with reading difficulties are often substantially disadvantaged with school work. Information they can easily understand if it is spoken may be a mystery to them if it is presented in print. This means that they may not be able to learn at the same rate and level as their classmates, even though they have similar intelligence.

Researching a topic is very difficult when reading is slow and inaccurate. The student will not be able to scan through possible reference books to decide which ones offer the best information for a project. Just reading a few pages of one book may take hours and discourage the student right from the beginning. The student may not have time to read several, complementary texts and therefore have to rely on the first one selected, regardless of its merit.

Some students spend an enormous amount of time and effort trying to keep up with the reading requirements, although this commitment may not show in their results.

> *I spend hours and hours reading, even on weekends. It takes me forever to get through just one or two chapters! But the teachers always say, "More time spent reading would improve his results."*

When researching information on the Internet, the students with reading difficulties may become overloaded with too much information. The student may have trouble sifting through the numerous pages to find the key pieces of information. As a result, the student may resort to simply copying and pasting sections of information without much thought.

In tests and examinations, students with reading difficulties may misread questions. This can lead to the loss of many valuable points.

> *A very smart adult taking a realtors' examination lost 25 percent of his points writing about 'unfinished' apartments instead of 'unfurnished' apartments!*

Students may also read so slowly that they spend much of the available time reading the questions, leaving only limited time in which to write their answers. It is often a warning sign of reading difficulties when a capable student, who does well with class work and homework, constantly submits papers that are incomplete during timed tests or examinations.

Slow readers may miss out on part of the reading assignments. For instance, if the teacher asks the class to read three chapters of the class novel before Friday, the student who reads slowly may only be able to finish one or two chapters, even if he puts in a fair amount of effort. This means, of course, that this student also misses out on important information. If the class is reading a novel, then the student may lose the continuity of the story, because he has missed several chapters at intervals throughout the book.

## Strategies for Managing the Disadvantages of Poor Reading

### Using inclusive strategies

* Make inclusiveness a priority. Some bright students have reading difficulties, which may mask their underlying capabilities. Students who have the intelligence to learn a particular subject will need teachers to make special arrangements and modifications in the classroom so that they have an appropriate program of academic study.

* Create resource packs to support the student with lessons and projects. The packs should contain selected reference articles, highlighted text and condensed information related to given topics.

* Provide someone who can assist the student in locating appropriate resources for a project—for example, an adult who can go to the library with the student and offer guidance in the process of selecting suitable resources.

* Provide summary sheets of key points from textbooks or lessons that will help students digest the information contained in longer pieces of print.

* Provide students with reading lists ahead of time, and encourage them to get started with the reading earlier than other students who read more quickly.

* Use short or abbreviated reading materials that contain the same intellectual challenge as longer books. For instance, some authors produce short stories as well as novels. Some novels are shorter than others.

✶ For standards-based assessments, the student's learning difficulties may need to be evaluated and documented before special provisions are made available. For students with Individual Education Plans, these provisions will be listed in the IEP.

✶ Some students who have not qualified for special education services may still benefit from modifications and adaptations with tests and examinations. Invite students to nominate themselves for modified test or examination conditions (such as extra time) in situations where this is appropriate. For example, when testing a student's understanding of a topic in biology, the time taken to demonstrate the required knowledge is immaterial.

✶ With tests and examinations, it may be appropriate to provide the student with a reader. This adult reads the paper to the student, without any additional comment. The reader remains close by throughout the examination and is available to reread sections or clarify particular words if the student requires it.

✶ Some students will find it easier to read out loud. If this is the case, allow the student to take the exam in a separate room so as not to distract the other students.

✶ Allow extra time for quizzes and exams. The amount of time allocated will obviously depend on the individual student's needs. The length of the test is usually taken into consideration. For example, a student may be given an additional 10 minutes for each portion of the exam.

✶ Modify the test so it fits into the time available. In this situation, the student is graded on the work they have completed. They are not penalized for the questions that were omitted from the abbreviated test. If they have been given eight questions instead of 10 and get all eight correct, then they have scored 100 percent.

✶ Some exams start with easy questions, and the level of difficulty increases. Make sure that the students have the opportunity to tackle each level of difficulty. It is not appropriate to shorten the paper by removing only the last (difficult) questions. It is better to remove, for example, every fourth question from the entire exam, so the student receives questions in all areas, ranging from simple to more advanced questions.

## Using technology

✶ Show the students how to use "auto summarize" on their computers. The computer summarizes selected text from sources such as Internet downloads or scanned text. Key phrases can be highlighted throughout the text, or an executive summary can be written. The student can determine the percentage of reduction. Although not completely accurate, it is a useful tool for the student who can't cope with a large volume of print.

. ▪ . ▪ . ▪ . ▪ . ▪ . ▪ . ▪ . ▪ . ▪ . ▪ . ▪ . ▪ . ▪ . ▪ . ▪ . ▪ . ▪ .

✳ When the class is reading a book, provide an audiotape to the student who finds reading difficult. This will help the student to keep up with the pace of the reading so he will not be left behind or miss various chapters.

✳ Have an adult read all or part of the assigned book to help the student keep the same pace as his classmates.

✳ Consider using the computer program called Text to Speech for students with serious reading difficulties. It reads aloud any text that is scanned, copied or typed into it.

# Student Has Difficulties with Reading

## Section 3 – Reading Observation Chart

| 3. *Student has difficulties with reading.* |
| --- |
| Student needs additional time to acquire basic reading skills. |
| Student achieves less than other students in reading. |
| Student needs more support than others when learning how to read. |

Reading is a complex skill involving several different processes, all of which have to be integrated successfully before reading can occur. If you attempt to draw a diagram of the brain circuits involved in reading, you quickly realize that there are many steps between the eye seeing some black lines on the paper and the brain receiving and understanding a meaningful message.

Often students are expected to read a previously unseen book in its entirety without any preparation. Let's think about this. Do we expect a musician to pick up a new piece of music and immediately play it completely through? As adults, do we want to read to an audience in church or at a public meeting without having a chance to preview the reading material? Reading a new book, especially if you have reading difficulties or lack confidence, can be a really daunting challenge.

Given the complexity of the process, it is not surprising that some students find it very difficult to learn to read. Maybe the remarkable thing is that so many students learn to read quite easily!

> In total, about 15 percent of students have difficulties in learning to read.
> About 8 percent have mild to moderate difficulties.
> About 5 percent have significant difficulties.
> About 2 percent have severe difficulties.

Reading is a high-order skill that links language and visual processing.

. ▪ . ▪ . ▪ . ▪ . ▪ . ▪ . ▪ . ▪ . ▪ . ▪ . ▪ . ▪ . ▪ . ▪ . ▪ . ▪ . ▪ .

Developmentally, reading always comes after speech and language have developed. Students with severe developmental or language difficulties may never fully master reading.

Students with milder, general learning and/or language difficulties will be expected to experience some reading delay in line with their general developmental level. If, for example, a 12-year-old student's intellectual or language development is at the level we would usually expect from a 9 year old, then it is likely that their reading development will also be at around the 9-year-old level. Put another way, if a student is placed at the third percentile for intellectual or language skills. then it is likely that reading will also be at a lower than average percentile.

Some students will be disadvantaged by impoverished home circumstances where books are not available and reading is not encouraged. Their early experiences of books and print may be very limited in comparison to many other students.

However, many students of good (or even exceptional) intelligence, who have excellent support at home and at school, also experience specific reading difficulties.

Reading difficulties are a major barrier to success at school and beyond. To address this disadvantage, two key approaches are required.

*Intervention* is important. Intervention provides the student with appropriate instruction and supported practice over a sufficient period of time. This 'treatment' approach helps to reduce the severity of the reading difficulties, which in turn minimizes the disadvantage to the student.

*Inclusion* of students with learning difficulties is also vital. Difficulties that would disadvantage the student are minimized through a range of adaptations of teaching methods, the curriculum and assessment.

For students with reading difficulties, finding a good book to read can be a real problem. Books that are easy enough to read are usually written for younger children. The illustrations and the story line will often be well below the student's interest level. On the other hand, books that would be of interest to the student are often too difficult for the student to read. So it is not surprising that reading is not an enjoyable activity. For many students with reading difficulties, the effort of reading just does not seem to be worthwhile.

## Strategies for Working with Reading Difficulties

### Assessing reading development

* If it has not already been done, arrange for the student's reading to be assessed by someone with expertise in the assessment of reading difficulties.

* Use a test that gives both a standardized score and diagnostic information. It is useful to know the exact standard the student has reached and to have a clear picture of where difficulties arise. The testing should show you and the student where successes have been achieved and indicate where remediation needs to take place.

## Providing an effective intervention program

* Plan an intervention program (in collaboration with the special education department, if appropriate) that will improve the student's skills. Target the student's areas of difficulty, and if possible, build on existing strengths.

* Consider using one of the many structured reading programs available that teach phonetic word decoding in a systematic way. Programs based on the Orton Gillingham method are well regarded.

* Target the program based on the student's needs. All activities need to be critically evaluated for their instructional value. Is the cutting and pasting making a real contribution to this student's learning? . . . Is the student ready for this reading task?

* Make the program intensive. Instruction that is repeated or backed up on a daily basis has a much better chance of success than a program that is only given, say, once a week.

* Combine quality instruction with intensive practice. Many potentially good programs fail because the students are not given enough practice of what has been taught.

* Structure the student's program so that each session is part of a 'stepladder' of learning. Every activity links to previous learning and builds the skills that form the foundation for future learning. Ask yourself, What earlier learning is this activity based on? And, What future learning is this activity leading towards?

* Students forget when they have not consolidated learning well enough. Be sure that one level of skill is firmly established before moving on to the next level.

* Do not rely on reading practice alone to produce gains in reading. Always provide explicit instruction to develop the underlying skills. Reading practice without ongoing instruction may mean that the student rehearses inappropriate strategies and fails to develop new, more effective strategies.

* The tasks in your program will vary in difficulty. Let students know if a task is particularly difficult, so they can take pride in their efforts to reach the final goal. Some students like to be able to choose their level of difficulty. Offer a choice, and see how some students will prefer to opt for a more difficult challenge than you thought. Being able to choose to tackle something difficult can increase motivation. Success with a hard task boosts confidence.

★ Teach students to learn from their own errors by encouraging them to monitor their own performances and understand their own errors. Ask students to devise their own strategies, such as, *"I messed up on that word because I guessed and didn't think about whether it made sense. Next time I'll think about what it means."*

★ Set explicit, achievable reading goals. Break the student's reading program into small, achievable sections. Make each learning goal explicit, and describe how it will be assessed. Vague goals, such as "Bart will improve his reading," make the task seem endless. Bart and his teachers won't have any way of knowing whether or not they are achieving the goal.

The following chart provides a process for writing a specific goal for a student, setting a time limit and describing a plan for assessing the student's progress towards achievement of the goal.

## Writing Student Goals

| | |
|---|---|
| Specify what Bart will achieve. | Bart will be able to read 50 of the most commonly used words. |
| Set a time limit. | Bart will be able to read these words by the end of the term. |
| Describe your assessment plan. | We will write all 50 words on note cards. Each time Bart reads a word correctly, we will place a check on the back of the card. When a card has five checks, Bart will have finished with that word. He can tear the card up and throw it away. |

★ Show the student how much he is learning, not how much there is to learn. Create a chart so that both you and the student can see that progress is being made. You could use the **Appendix #33: Student Guide to Setting Goals** or the **Appendix #23: Teacher Checklist for Mastery Learning** chart.

★ Reward cooperation with reading practice. For younger students, create a chart that records the amount of time spent reading. You can use the **Appendix #8: 100 Minutes Reading Chart**, or make your own. Create a chart with 100 squares. Each square represents one minute of reading. If the student reads for four minutes, the student will color or stamp four squares. Give small rewards for reading a total of 10 minutes and a larger reward for reading for 100 minutes.

✳ For older students, negotiate a reward system in return for compliance with the reading program. Rewards that are meaningful to the student work best, so ask the student to select rewards from a predetermined list, which the student can add to if desired. Use the **Appendix #33: Student Guide to Setting Goals** chart for this.

✳ Add an extra incentive for good attitude. For example, the student might be paid $1 for completing the reading task and $2 for completing the task without complaining or wasting time. This, of course, needs to be arranged with the parent in advance. The **Appendix #33: Student Guide to Setting Goals** chart provides a section for this.

✳ Make sure definite time limits are set for how long the student has to work on reading skills. Some students feel overwhelmed thinking that the reading session is going to go on "forever." Knowing that there is a definite time limit helps the student to settle down and get through the required work in the allotted time.

✳ Celebrate the achievement of learning goals. Negotiate with the student the type of achievement celebration they would like. Perhaps the student simply would like a certificate to take home to show parents and grandparents, or possibly a special treat or privilege during the school day.

✳ Select reading materials that suit the student's reading ability and age/image. It is particularly important to make sure the books chosen are of interest to the student.

✳ If necessary, collaborate with the student to make sure the books have intrinsic interest for the student.

✳ Locate publishers that produce special books for older readers with reading difficulties and make these available. Enlist the help of the librarian or media specialist to find books that will suit the student.

✳ Read interesting and exciting articles and books to the students. This helps students to see that reading is interesting and is definitely a skill worth acquiring.

✳ Create a personal reading folder with the student. Select magazine and newspaper reports that interest the student. Photocopy and enlarge the articles and paste the articles into the folder. The student may have special interest in a favorite sports team or movie star and could accumulate articles of interest throughout the year.

✳ Create a group or class folder on a topic of shared interest, and encourage all students to look at home for articles that can be brought to school and placed in the reading folder.

✱ Choose an appropriate time for interventions. If possible, arrange it so the extra help occurs at a time that does not unsettle the student. Missing out on recreation, a favorite subject or an opportunity to have fun is a sure way to make the student feel negative about a reading program.

✱ For younger students or students who have major reading difficulties, look at the time of day that suits them best. The student with difficulties in learning may be very tired by the afternoon and may learn best earlier in the day.

✱ Keep a careful register of books that the student has read so you will know if the student is returning to the same book time and time again. You will also be able to monitor the difficulty level that the student is selecting.

✱ Remember to teach, not test. Teaching involves providing students with tasks that are at the margin of their competence. The books should not be so easy that the students feel bored or 'put down,' nor so hard that the students feel overwhelmed and anxious. The teacher should work in partnership with the students, providing as much help, support and coaching as needed to enable each to succeed with the task.

✱ If a student needs an excessive amount of help, then the task itself is too difficult. If the student needs little or no help, then the task set is too easy for new learning to occur. Easy tasks do have their place in consolidating skills and building confidence.

✱ If the student becomes mixed up or confused when reading a particular section, quickly and quietly join in to help him through the difficult part, and then fade out once the student is reading smoothly again.

✱ Try to avoid giving complex instruction in the middle of a student's reading. Allow him to continue (with your help if needed), and then revisit the difficult sections once the reading has been completed.

✱ Some students get very flustered reading out loud. Clarify what they should do if they encounter a word they don't know. Some students like to be allowed some time to try to work the word out for themselves, with a prearranged signal (such as tapping on the table), if they need the adult to help.

✱ If the student selects a book that's challenging, read the entire book in tandem with the student. With both adult and student reading along together, the student takes the lead for most of the time. The adult takes the lead when the student encounters a difficult section. It can take a little while to develop the skill of reading in tandem, but once established, this method is a good way to help an anxious student read with fluency and confidence. It also helps to provide the student with access to books that they could not read unaided.

✱ Move from the familiar to the new in small steps. Provide a structured set of reading books that are very carefully graded for difficulty. Introduce a slightly harder book to the student and show the student where the new challenges are. Help the student to tackle these new challenges by explicit teaching and support. *"See, this book is almost the same as your favorite. Let's see now. Here are a few new words. Let's learn them first so you can go right ahead and read the new book by yourself."*

✱ Take a familiar book and, with the student, rewrite it, adding more detail and dialogue than the original, using the student's own words. Print out the new and expanded version of the story, and have the student read the revised edition.

✱ Ask the student to dictate his own reading materials. First, the student tells the story and the adult types it. Then the story is printed and forms a new book for the student to read.

✱ Encourage rehearsal (or rereading) for improved confidence and skill. Introduce reading materials that have to be rehearsed, such as a speech to be given to the class or an acting part in a play. The student can rehearse (and reread) as often as he likes until he is ready.

✱ Some students are happy to read a 'little kid's' book, if it's for a genuine purpose. Check to see if your older student would like to read a play or a story to a group of younger students.

✱ Build a library of story tapes for the younger students in your school by having older students (who need the reading practice) create the tapes by using rehearsed reading. The students can add expression and sound effects and make up different voices for characters to add interest to the recording.

## Student Does Not Understand How Reading 'Works'

### Section 4 – Reading Observation Chart

| 4. Student does not understand how reading 'works.' |
| --- |
| Student thinks that reading happens automatically. |
| Student does not realize that skilled readers have to work hard at times. |
| Student does not think about own reading strategies. |

It can be difficult for students with reading problems to see the complete picture of what they are learning and how they are progressing. We know that *metacognition* (thinking about your own thinking) can be a very useful tool in learning.

Students progress more quickly if they understand what strategies they are already using successfully and which skills they need to work on. Many students with reading difficulties downgrade their own skills, because they misunderstand how good readers perform. They assume that good readers:

- Always know every word right away without sounding out or guessing
- Always understand something the first time they read it
- Never need to read anything more than once
- Can always read fluently and expressively
- Can read any book in a very short period of time
- Have total recall of every word they have read

> Paul, who was 13 and struggling with reading, explained: *"The other kids, they read a book and it's like they've just seen the movie. They just sit there, and then they've finished the book."*
>
> Frank, a successful business man but poor reader, said, *"I'd like to be able to do like the teachers do—go to a library and read all the books and know everything about everything in that library. Me? I pick up a book and read the first chapter, but I couldn't even tell you everything in that chapter."*

If poor readers believe that others can read a book in the same time it takes to watch the movie, or that people who can read transfer the contents of a library into their own minds, then it's not surprising they feel inadequate and frustrated by their own reading skills.

## Strategies for Helping Students Understand the Reading Process

### Talking about reading

✴ Have a class discussion about reading strategies that students who are good readers implement. It is helpful for students who are struggling with reading to understand that all readers, even those who appear skilled, do have to work at the process, and that strategies such as the following are a normal part of skilled reading.

- Sounding out unfamiliar words
- Using the context to guess at a word
- Reading something through several times
- Making notes on important points
- Using the index or chapter headings to select what is most important
- Skimming the text when searching for information
- Asking for clarification from others
- Taking many hours to read through a lengthy book

✱ Before a student starts to read to you, ask the student what strategies might be needed.

- *"Does this book look like you can read it through just once?"*

- *"It looks as if there might be some tough words in this book. What will you do if you come across a word you are not sure of?"*

- *"This is a big book, and you only want to find out about penguins, so what is the best plan?"*

✱ Ask the student to describe the strategies they are using. Discuss what other tactics they might be able to use.

- *"I was guessing because I knew the story. I could try sounding out the words."*

- *"That took too long. I should have used the index to find the information I needed."*

✱ Ask the students to listen to self-made tape recordings of themselves reading. What do they notice about how they read? Are they too hesitant? What could they do to fix this problem? Did they stumble on hard words? What could they do about that?

## Student Has Difficulties with Phonics

### Section 5 – Reading Observation Chart

| 5. Student has difficulties with phonics. |
| --- |
| Student has difficulties remembering letter shapes. |
| Student makes errors when sounding out single letters. |
| Student makes errors when sounding out letter blends. |

The ability to use phonics is a critical foundation skill in reading. The ability to sound out words allows the student to move beyond reading whole words by sight. Once phonic skills are firmly established, the student can become an independent learner. They can read new and unfamiliar words without assistance and steadily build the repertoire of words they can read with ease.

Even as adults, we use phonics to continue to extend our reading. When we encounter new words, such as *unchup* or *hinbeek,* we put our existing knowledge of letter patterns and their sounds into action and read the word. The process is quick and inconspicuous, because we are so skilled at it.

Students also have to be able to learn the connection between a sound and a letter shape. Even if they can recognize the *d* sound in *dog,* they still have to be able to remember that the sound only matches the *d* letter, and that similar looking letters, such as *b* and *p,* have their own sounds.

Quite a few letters can be easily confused with each other. Letters such as *b* and *d* may be reversed, or letters such as *u* and *n* may be inverted. Students also have to learn that every letter has an uppercase and a lowercase form—and that sometimes the lowercase is just a miniature of the uppercase, but sometimes it is not!

The students also have to be able to detect quite subtle differences between sounds. For example, say the sounds *c* and *g* to yourself and notice how similar these sounds are to one another.

Some students also get mixed up between letter sounds and letter names. Many children's books and computer programs use letter names and uppercase letters for preschool learning. Parents may also use letter names and teach capitals for the child's first reading and writing experiences.

Our alphabet is confusing. Every letter has a name and at least one sound. Some letters change sound depending on their position in a word and some letters make a new sound when they are combined with one or more other letters. Some letters have a name that starts with their own sound, some do not!

---

Go through the alphabet for yourself now, and see which letter names actually start with their own sound. For example:

Name the letter *W.*   This letter's name starts with the *d* sound!
Name the letter *B.*   This letter's name starts with the *b* sound!
Name the letter *Y.*   This letter's name starts with the *w* sound!

Confusing isn't it?

---

Many students with learning difficulties will not have completely mastered the phonic system when it was being taught in the general classroom. They may have learned enough to get by, and may have become skillful in bluffing their way through. However, these students tend to slip through the cracks once explicit instruction and overt practice have finished. We know that one of the hallmarks of a reading disorder is a slow response to appropriate intervention. Many of these students will have only a fragile hold on phonics and will need the skills to be regularly taught, practiced and revised over an extended period.

# Strategies for Teaching Phonics: Letters and Sounds

## Establishing the basics

* Teach the basics of letter names and sounds. Ensure that the student understands the difference between a letter name and a letter sound.

* Teach the upper- and lowercase form of each letter. Teach when capital letters are used.

* Encourage parents to use lowercase letters when teaching the alphabet to their children.

* For some students, this learning will need to be carefully structured and taken at a slow pace to make sure that each letter being taught is thoroughly known before the next one is introduced.

* Check that the student is able to give the sounds for all single letters before you expect them to be able to read using basic phonics. The **Appendix #6: Diagnostic Phonics Assessment** will help you to do this.

* Teach contrasting letters and sounds first to avoid confusion. It is easier to learn contrasting letter shapes and sounds such as *o* and *f* rather than letters that sound and look quite similar to each other, such as *t* and *f*.

* Teach parents the basics of phonics, so they understand and support what you are doing in school. Help parents to select early learning materials that provide practice in letter sounds and lowercase letters.

* Provide parents with suitable resources that they can refer to if they are not sure of letter sounds themselves—for instance, a chart that gives a letter and a word that prompts its sound: *a* as in *cat, d* as in *dog,* etc.

* Be prepared to teach and revise the same basics over and over again to students with reading difficulties.

* Check that older students still retain the basics, as often they will use letter names instead of sounds if they are not carefully monitored.

* Some students believe that sounding out is only for little kids. Reassure the students that adults often use sounding out too. It is one of the most important ways of reading new words, however old we are.

# Student Has Difficulties with Phonological Awareness and Word Building

## Section 6 – Reading Observation Chart

| 6. *Student has difficulties with phonological awareness and word building.* |
| --- |
| Student makes errors when trying to hear sounds in words. |
| Student makes errors when blending sounds together. |
| Student makes errors reading new words. (See Appendix #6: Diagnostic Phonics Assessment.) |

Many students with reading difficulties find phonics difficult at first. The student needs good phonological awareness (the ability to recognize segments of speech within words) before early instruction in letters and their sounds make much sense to them.

If you can't hear that *man* is made up of the sounds *m-a-n,* then being told that the letter *m* makes the special *mmm* sound doesn't make much sense. Things that don't make much sense are hard to remember and put into action.

Once the student does know all the letter sounds, they have to be able to blend those sounds together and make recognizable words. Again, this can be a real stumbling block for some students. The student will produce a string of sounds such as *t-w-i-s-t* but think that the word is *whistle* or *twin,* or even invent a word, such as *tittles.* These difficulties show us that the student has difficulty with the phonological skill of hearing the link between *t-w-i-s-t* and the word *twist.*

In most schools, phonics are thoroughly taught in the early years. Children with good phonological skills usually pick up the idea quickly and are soon successfully using letter sounds to work out words.

## Strategies for Developing Phonological Awareness and Word Building Skills

### Working with auditory discrimination

✻ If the student seems to have a lot of difficulty with discriminating the subtle differences between sounds, ask the parents to arrange for a hearing test. Some children (especially those with a history of recurrent middle ear infections) may have problems with auditory discrimination.

✻ Relate sounds to real words. When using prompts, such as *"s* is for *sun,'* always give several examples. This helps the student to understand that the letter *s* and its sound occur in many words, not just *sun.* For example, teach *"s* is for *sun, sand, sit . . . ."*

✱ Encourage students to think of their own words for sounds. If a student has trouble doing this, it's a warning sign that the student has difficulties with phonological skills.

✱ Some students will need additional prompts. You could put out some objects (or pictures) on the desk, such as a cup, pen, box, tin, hat, sock, and pin, and sound out the names. The student has to listen and say which item you are sounding out. For example, you sound out *p-i-n,* and the student points to the pin and says "pin."

## Linking listening with written words

✱ Teach letters in groups that can be put into words, so the students see the point of the learning and understand how to put their newfound knowledge into action. Teach all the letters in words such as *sun, bat and pig.* Then show the students how they can mix and match the letters they know and read words such as *sun, bun, gun, bat, pat, nut, bit . . . .*

✱ Teach blending skills once you are sure that the student can confidently give the correct sound for each letter. Some students find it hard to blend sounds together to make whole words. If this is a problem, then give them practice in listening to strings of sounds that you produce and guessing at the word you are reading. For instance, you read *c-u-p,* and the student says "cup." This is an easier task then having to sound and blend for themselves.

✱ Build phonological skills in graduated steps. Choose a reading program that has a phonic basis, so the reading materials provided will reinforce phonic skills. Books written in rhyme (such as the Dr. Seuss books) are often very good sources of phonic reading and can be lots of fun, too.

✱ Give students short, simple words that only contain one challenge. For instance, if you are teaching words with the blend *sh,* stay with short words, so that apart from the *sh,* all the other letters have single sounds. Good words would include *shop, ship, dish.* On the other hand, teaching *sh* in words such as *shopping, shoe, pushing* makes the word itself too hard. The students have several different phonic challenges to handle at the same time. This distracts them from the *sh* blend that they are trying to learn.

✱ Try to keep what you teach clear and carefully structured. Deal with the levels of difficulty systematically, so your students build skills and confidence by moving from easier phonic tasks to more difficult ones. Refer to the following chart for examples.

# Stages of Phonics Instruction

| | |
|---|---|
| **Stage 1** | Use words in the consonant-vowel-consonant pattern. For example: *set, pet, wet* or *pin, win, tin, bin* or *fat, cat, hat.*<br><br>Notice that often these words can be clustered in groups that share the same vowel-consonant ending (called the rime) but have different initial letters (called the onset). Teaching onset-rime patterns makes this first stage much easier, because the learning from one word can be generalized to the next. If you can read *pin*, it is easy to read *win*. |
| **Stage 2** | Use a maximum of four letters in each word, so the student only has to deal with one letter blend.<br>Two consonants sliding together: *trip, spin, stop*<br>Two consonants making a new sound: *ship, chop, thin*<br>Final *e: hope, take, like* |
| **Stage 3** | Two vowels making a new sound: *out, feet, boat*<br>Vowel and consonant making a new sound: *part, dawn, dirt*<br>Silent letters: *gnaw, knot* |
| **Stage 4** | Three consonants sliding together: *shrug, ring, strap, scream*<br>Four letters making a new sound: *ration, light, rough*<br>Words ending in *y* or *ing: happy, silly, tapping* |
| **Stage 5** | Words that combine two or more of the previously taught patterns: *combine, sprout, market*<br>Words that are compound words; words using prefixes or suffixes: *preview, unhappy, defeat* |

★ Use magnetic letters or letter cards (lowercase) to encourage students to play with word building and reading. Start with building three-letter words, and color code the vowels. Teach that these color-coded letters should be placed in the middle of the word for this early word building game.

★ Teach the students to recognize vowels and consonants.

★ Use reading analogies to show students how to use known words to read unknown ones. Write pairs of words that share the same pattern. Read the first word to the student and ask the student to work out the second word in the pair. *"If this word says 'seed,' what does this word [need] say? . . . How do you know that?"* Encourage the student to 'shortcut' sounding out by recognizing that by substituting one letter of a word with another, they can read a new word very easily.

✹ Ask the student to change a word one letter at a time and see how many words they can make. For example, they may begin with the word *give* and then change the word, one letter at a time: *live, line, lane, pane, pine, pink, wink,* etc.

✹ Provide the student an ample selection of letters, syllables and small words written on cards. The student can create both real and nonsense words by putting cards end to end and then reading the newly created words. This really helps to create confidence and can be lots of fun.

✹ Provide the student with multi-syllable words written on cards, and ask the student to cut the words up into syllables, prefixes and suffixes. Ask the student to use these word segments to make other words. The student can choose to use the segments he already has or write any new ones that are needed. For example, a student may take the word *caravan* and cut it up into three segments: *car a van.* They can then take *car* and turn it into *scar, carry, carwash* by adding new letters and words.

## Student Has Difficulties Recognizing Words at Sight

### Section 7 – Reading Observation Chart

| **7.   *Student has difficulties recognizing words at sight.*** |
| :--- |
| Student makes errors when attempting to read everyday words. |
| Student can read words in a familiar book but cannot read the same words out of context. |
| Student relies on pictures to get sense of story. |
| Student makes many errors and self-corrections when reading. |
| Student confuses words of similar appearance, such as *bread* and *bird.* |
| Student makes errors when copying words. |
| Student reads word by word. |
| Student puts in different words but keeps the meaning of the story. For example, reads *Jane got a present for her birthday* instead of *Jane got a parcel for her birthday.* |

All students need to be able to read using phonics (sounding out letters and blending the sounds together). However, students also need to be able to recognize words at sight. In English, some words are irregular and simply do not sound out. Other words occur so frequently that sounding out over and over again is just not practical.

Many students with reading difficulties have problems in remembering the appearance of commonly used words, such as *the, they, my, am, are, is, here* and *where.* Even though the student may see these words literally hundreds of times, they may still 'forget' them over and over again. Adults can get very frustrated when students constantly forget these apparently easy words.

However, we need to remember that print is easiest to recall if it has an unusual visual pattern and conjures up a picture or feeling for reader. Words such as *spaghetti, elephant, Barbie* and *Batman* have quite distinctive patterns and grab the young reader's interest. On the other hand, words such as *the, they, my, am, are, is, here* and *where* have no distinctive visual pattern and are often easily confused with one another. Some students find it very hard to remember these frustrating little words through exposure in everyday reading. For them, a more explicit and deliberate teaching approach needs to be used.

Accurate reading depends on the ability to make distinctions between words that look quite similar such as *beard* and *bread, trail* and *trial* or *king* and *knight*. Students who find this difficult often rely heavily on the context of the story, using a mixture of 'look and guess' and picking up some clues from the sounds of the letters. However, they may overlook the sequence of the letters or rely too heavily on context.

Traditional readers often had 'controlled' vocabulary. This meant that new words were introduced gradually and each new word was repeated several times over. The reading books were often in a numbered sequence, so the student moved through the levels of difficulty in a gradual way. The downside was that the readers were often repetitive and uninteresting. These readers are now rather out of fashion, but they still have their place, particularly for students with learning difficulties.

Students who have difficulty remembering the appearance of words often have trouble copying accurately. They may copy letter by letter because they are unable to remember whole words or phrases, or because the words they are writing are meaningless to them.

Looking at a printed word and saying that word automatically is quite a high-order skill. Fortunately, there is a ladder of easier tasks that can be introduced first to build up a student's ability to recognize key words by sight.

## Strategies for Developing Word Recognition Skills

### Using a hierarchy of learning

✱ Check that the student can read commonly used words automatically. Use **Appendix #5: 100 Most Frequently Used Words** to do this.

✱ Use a graded sequence of activities to develop word recognition. Select about 15 to 20 words that you are going to teach. For students who are struggling, it is a good idea to select some words that are high interest and visually distinctive. You could use names of the students' friends or families, favorite foods or animals. Reading a long and interesting word such as *tyrannosaurus* is much more exciting and confidence building than being able to read *when*. The student will never guess that the long word is actually much easier to recognize by sight!

★ Take just four or five words from your list to work on at any one time, gradually building up the word list as the student progresses. Write all of the words on separate cards. Make several sets of each word.

## Hierarchy of Teaching Strategies for Whole Words

| | |
|---|---|
| **Match to sample when the sample is in view.** | At this stage, the student is asked only to match the target word to an identical sample. The sample remains in view the entire time as the student searches for words that match. Keep one card as a sample. Place the word in the student's view. Ask the student to sort the other cards into groups to match the sample. *"Look . . . this word is **went**. See if you can find all the other cards that say **went**. Check with the sample if you are not sure. I'll leave it right here for you to see."* You can repeat the process with all the words you are teaching. |
| **Match to sample when the sample is hidden.** | This is the same as the previous step, except that once the student has been shown the sample word, it is hidden from view. *"This card says **went**. Have a good look before I turn it over. Do you think you can remember it? Okay, I'm turning it over so you can't peek. Now see if you can find all the other cards that have **went** on them."* |
| **Recognition** | Working with the same cards as before, the student is now required to recognize the words on the cards but does not have a sample to match. The cards are spread out, and this time the student is asked, *"Can you find me the word that says **went**?"* If the student is confused, allow the student to look at the sample card before it is hidden again. |
| **Reading** | At this stage, the student is reading the words without any prompts. Point to individual words and ask, *"What is this word?"* Work through all the words you have been teaching, presenting them in jumbled order. If the student is confused by this, then show four cards that all have the same word on them, one after the other. When the student becomes more confident, go back to presenting the word cards in jumbled order. |
| **Consolidation** | Stack all the words that have been taught into a pack. Shuffle the cards and deal them. Increase the speed as you go, until the student can read each word quickly as it appears. Games such as Word Snap and Word Lotto can provide additional practice, if necessary. |

★ Use real sentences to practice word recognition with an activity called transformations. This can easily be combined with the activity described above and is a very effective way of teaching whole word recognition skills. In this activity, the student learns to recognize whole words in a real language context.

## Transformations: Reading Words as Real Language

| | |
|---|---|
| **Say a sentence.** | Work with the student to produce a sentence. If possible, the sentence should be the student's own, although sometimes a combined effort works better. |
| **Write the sentence.** | Write the sentence clearly on a strip of paper or card. Read the sentence back with the student, so the student understands that the language is now in print form. |
| **Cut the sentence.** | With the student's help, cut the sentence into parts. Generally, cut each word apart from the sentence. Sometimes you might choose to keep a phrase such as "Once upon a time" together on a single strip of paper. |
| **Scramble the words.** | Scramble the words and phrases. |
| **Rebuild the sentence.** | Have the student reassemble the sentence in its original order. If the student finds this difficult, provide a sample sentence to work from, so the student can match the words one by one. |
| **Make a new sentence.** | Work with the student to see how the words in the sentence can be rearranged, and perhaps how new words can be added. |
| **Save the sentence.** | Have the student paste the sentence into a blank book made for this purpose as a reading resource the student can read again another day. |

✱ Make activities and games where reading words and phrases is all part of a game.

## Making learning fun

✱ Create a treasure hunt! Write simple clues (at the student's level), which if read correctly, will lead to a prize. *Look under the teacher's table. . . . Go to the back of the classroom. . . . Open the blue cupboard.* It's a good idea to read the options to the students first, so that when they play the game, they already know the range of words they are likely to encounter.

* Write the names of various edible and non-edible items on strips of paper. Put all the strips into a box, and have students take a "lucky dip" into the box to select one of the items listed. For example, students may create their own special pizza topping. Perhaps the student will end up with a *banana, ham, cheese* and *old sock* pizza!

* Ask students to select their outfits for the day by taking a lucky dip from a variety of clothing items. Maybe they will end up with *jeans, a wedding dress* and *a space helmet!*

* Write characters and their actions on slips of paper, and play charades. The student chooses a paper, reads the scenario and acts the out the part for the others to guess: e.g., *a horse jumping; a cook making a cake;* or *a dog hiding a bone.*

* Write names of popular heroes, family, friends and fictitious characters, and take a lucky dip to find out the guests to your next birthday: e.g., *Batman, Mom, a green jelly monster, Mrs. Nichols* and *a duck.*

* Encourage your students to use written language to communicate. Exchanging letters with students in other schools via the Internet or postal service is a great way to develop an interest in the written word.

* Use a classroom bulletin board as a communication spot where students can post information to be read by other students. Jokes, amazing facts, cartoons, announcements of school and community events, invitations to sign up for recess sports, etc. can all entice reluctant readers to read for information.

## Providing repetition and consolidation

* Make sure that there is enough repetition of hard-to-remember whole words to develop solid learning.

* Provide reading materials with a high level of 'scaffolding,' or support. For instance, create a set of questions. The question is read out loud by the adult, and the student reads the answer. The question and the answer contain many of the same words, so the student has a very strong framework for the words he has to read. For example:

**Question:** Which animal likes to catch mice?
**Answer:** The cat likes to catch mice.

* Some students who read a book once simply read and forget the new words over and over again. These students need activities where the reading vocabulary in one book is taught and reinforced in a variety of ways.

* Introduce a new reading book by doing some preparatory work, even before the book is opened. Teach new words that will be encountered, revise words that have proven difficult in earlier books and introduce the topic and related vocabulary.

★ The book can be used in a variety of ways. Of course the student will read the book, possibly several times. The words that present difficulty can be singled out for additional practice.

★ The student may create additional books that have the same reading vocabulary as the original. These books can provide additional practice with reading the difficult words along with the rest of the vocabulary.

★ Word games, such as Word Lotto, Word Pairs and Word Snap, are sentence building activities that can reinforce new words. These games can easily be created to use in the classroom. There are many variations for these three games.

**Word Lotto:** The teacher prepares four playing boards so that four players can participate. Each board is marked off as a grid. The teacher selects 24 words that are being taught and writes six of these words on each board. Any sections of the board that do not contain a word can be colored in. The teacher then writes the same 24 words on 24 small cards to fit the dimensions of the playing board. These small cards are shuffled and shown to the students one by one. If the card shown matches a word on a student's card, then that student can claim the card. The student must be able to read the word before it is given to him. The student places the card on top of the word on his board. The student who fills his or her board first is the winner.

**Word Pairs:** Use index cards to create pairs of words. The word cards are mixed up and placed face down on the table. The students take turns turning over cards to see if they can get two matching words. Spelling words, vocabulary words or any reinforcement words may be used. For a more difficult version, students must be able to define the word before winning the pair.

**Word Snap:** Select 10 words, and make four to six copies of each of the words (40-60 cards in all). The cards are shuffled and placed in the center of the table. Each player draws a card from the center pile and places the card face up in the discard pile. When the same word appears twice in a row, the players shout "Snap!" The first player to shout "Snap!" wins the pair of words. The player with the largest number of pairs wins the game.

★ Students should not begin a new book until they have mastered at least 95 percent of all the words in their present reader. If this takes too long to achieve, the book is too hard and the students will become too frustrated. A substitute book should be chosen.

★ Provide challenges in word discrimination. The students have to select one word from a pair of words that look quite similar. For example, the student may be asked to listen to a sentence that is read out loud and then underline the correct words: e.g., *"When Jack came home, he found a **parcel/packet** by the room/door." * Or, *"As the **king/knight** rode into view, the crowds all rushed to **greet/great** him."*

★ Preview or pre-read the book to the student to prepare him for the unfamiliar words.

★ Provide an audiotape of the book, so the student can read along with the tape.

★ Support the student who is slow to read and copy words. Provide a printed copy of the notes, and ensure that the student understands what is written. Either read the paper to the student, or support the student as he reads it through.

## Student Has Difficulties with Reading Fluency

### Section 8 – Reading Observation Chart

| 8. Student has difficulties with reading fluency. |
| --- |
| Student's oral language is hesitant and lacks fluency. |
| Student stammers when speaking and reading. |
| Student cannot find the right word when reading. |
| Student's reading is hesitant and stilted. |
| Student takes a long time to recognize words. |
| Student sounds out the same words over and over again. |
| Student does not use punctuation to guide reading. |
| Student reads so slowly that the amount of practice is limited. |

Some students have general difficulties with fluent speech, and this can have an impact on their ordinary speaking and on their reading. They may stammer or have difficulties producing a fluent sequence of words when talking and when reading aloud.

However, many verbal fluency problems are caused by 'word finding' difficulties. When the student attempts to answer a question in class, he may get stuck halfway through because he is unable to 'find' the right word. When the student is reading, the same thing happens. He sees the word but cannot name it quickly enough, even though it is recognized. In this situation, reading may be slow and disjointed because of the more general language production problems rather than a reading difficulty.

Students may also be self-conscious and nervous about reading out loud, and this, too, can have a direct impact on their fluency and expression. In particular, students may feel embarrassed to read with expression, fearing that they may sound silly if they read in an exaggerated or dramatic manner.

For some, early reading difficulties may have created the habit of reading word by word without expression. Sometimes, even when reading skills have improved considerably, the old habit of slow and disjointed reading continues.

Other students' reading may lack expression because they are not following the story line well enough to pick up the meaning. Perhaps they are working so hard to figure out individual words that they lose sight of the sentence, or perhaps they experience general difficulties with the comprehension of language.

Punctuation can make all the difference to the fluency of what is read. Punctuation gives shape and structure to the text and sometimes even alters meaning. For the student who finds getting through the words more than enough of a challenge, punctuation is often ignored. This can lead to poorer comprehension of the text, which in turn, results in limited expression and fluency.

Lack of 'automaticity' (the ability to recognize a word at sight) in reading is a very common characteristic of students with poor fluency. The student either has to study the word carefully and hope that he can retrieve its name, or he has to sound out the word to decode it using phonics. Both processes are slow and make the reading sound disjointed.

If a student reads word by word, then obviously he will be more likely to find the process tedious and less enjoyable. The student will also be more likely to miss out on the necessary quantity of practice that is essential for the development of reading skills.

Although explicit teaching is very important in the development of good reading skills, the old saying "Practice makes perfect" certainly also applies. For the student who reads very slowly, the amount of practice the student experiences may be significantly reduced in comparison with more skilled and speedy readers. This means that the student is doubly disadvantaged. First, he has poor reading skills, and second, he misses out on some of the practice that is really needed.

## Strategies for Developing Reading Fluency

### Understanding why the student lacks fluency

✳ Assess the student's reading through silent reading tests.

- Is the student able to read more quickly if he reads silently?

- Can the student cope with the challenge of reading comprehension if he reads silently?

- Is the student able to fill in missing words in the text accurately if he reads to himself?

If the answer to these questions is yes, then the student does not actually have a reading problem—only a difficulty with the verbal fluency needed for oral reading.

* If the student has poor oral fluency, allow the student to read silently rather than out loud.

* A speech pathologist will be able to give advice for improving oral fluency.

## Improving fluency

* If it is essential for the student to read out loud, allow the student additional practice before he has to do so.

* Rehearse fluent reading by reading in unison with the student. Read along with the student, setting the pace somewhat faster than the student's own natural speed, so that as he reads with you, he is forced to read a little more quickly. Then ask the student to read unaided, and encourage him to keep up the pace of the reading that was practiced together.

* Move a marker under the words slightly faster than the student's natural speed. Encourage the student to keep pace with the marker.

* Have the student move the marker, and encourage the student to read as smoothly and quickly as he is able.

* Ask the student to read along with an audiotape that sets a reasonable pace to help develop verbal fluency when reading.

* Offer the student options for audience and setting. Some students much prefer to read at home, some will read willingly to a supportive older student, and others may prefer one-to-one with a teacher or other adult.

* Show that fluent, expressive reading is not only okay, but accepted and desired. Good role models with fluent and expressive reading are very valuable. An adult, older student or classmate reading an exciting book with expression and fluency to the class can make a real difference to your students' understanding that it is okay to read with enthusiasm.

* Encourage theatrical reading, where the dialogue of the script encourages the readers to take on the personality of the characters and read with expression. Reading a script also allows for rehearsal, which is important in developing reading skills.

* Have students read and reread a passage until they are fluent, accurate and confident. Use a stopwatch to encourage students to speed up and decrease the amount of time it takes to read the passage. This helps to build 'automaticity.'

* Some students have a habit of sounding out words that they know perfectly well. Give the student rapid word reading practice with flash cards to change this habit.

* Run your finger or a pencil underneath the print as the student reads to encourage smooth, speedy reading. Encourage the student to do the same when he reads to himself.

* Make sure the students practice their reading daily, for at least 20 minutes, to build their skills. Nobody is fluent at a skill if he never practices.

* Highlight phrases to show the student which words should be read together in one breath: *Once upon a time / there was a wicked witch / called Bernadette.*

* Check the difficulty level of the book to be sure that the student can read it with a reasonable degree of fluency. If the book is too difficult for the student, he will read very slowly and feel frustrated. The student should be able to read at least nine out of every ten words to be able to read with understanding and fluency.

* Teach the student to use punctuation to aid fluent, expressive reading. Ask the students to go through the selected reading before beginning to read. Use a brightly colored highlighter to mark the punctuation marks. Discuss what the punctuation marks mean and how they are used during reading, and then encourage the student to apply these skills while he reads.

* Provide your students with printed text where all the punctuation has been removed. Read the text to the students, emphasizing the pauses and expression. Ask the students to fill in the punctuation marks as you read.

## Student Has Difficulties Making Sense of What Is Read

### Section 9 – Reading Observation Chart

| **9. *Student has difficulties making sense of what is read.*** |
| --- |
| Student puts in words that do not make sense. For example: *Jane got a playing for her birthday.* |
| Student makes up words. For example: *Jane got a purrel for her birthday.* |
| Student makes errors answering reading comprehension questions. |

Unfortunately for many students with reading difficulties, understanding the story is the last thing on their minds! They have such a struggle figuring out the words, that they are only too pleased to be able to stop as soon as the final word is reached.

Students may rely on working out and guessing words one by one. They insert nonsense words, or words that do not make sense, when they come to an unknown word. Being able to understand, remember *and* discuss the meaning of what has been read can be very challenging indeed.

There is an unusual group of students whose reading accuracy and speed are phenomenal, but whose reading comprehension is poor. While not many students fall into this group, it is important to be aware that such a pattern is possible.

Some students with general language difficulties will also have reading difficulties. Strictly speaking, they may not have a reading problem as such, rather they may have limitation in the way they understand language, whether it is spoken or written. However, such language difficulties are often most clearly apparent in the student's reading. Typically, they may find it hard to maintain the correct grammar of the sentences and superimpose their own, rather disordered, grammar in place of what is written on the page.

Some students with reading difficulties do manage to grasp the factual information they have read, but they fail to move on to make deductions, inferences and predictions.

It is often difficult for students with learning difficulties to formulate an answer in comprehension. They do not always understand that reading comprehension is quite different from the informal question-and-answer exchanges that occur in conversation. In conversation, it is fine to say "yes," but in written language, an expanded response is required.

## Strategies for Making Sense of Reading

### Finding the right level of difficulty for the student

✴ No student will understand reading material that is too difficult for him to read. So make sure that the student can read the story reasonably accurately and fluently.

✴ The language and ideas in the book must also be at an appropriate level to suit the student's own level of language and cognitive development.

✴ You may need to ask for a psychologist or speech pathologist to assess the student's general language or cognitive abilities, if the student experiences major difficulties with reading comprehension.

### Highlighting meaning

✴ Prepare some reading passages with every ninth word deleted. Ask the student to fill in the missing words so the passage makes sense.

✴ Give comprehension questions before reading begins. Encourage the students to monitor what they are reading in relation to the questions that will be asked. This will help students to develop their awareness of the need to follow the meaning of the words as they read.

## Visualizing

✱ Students may not even realize that they can visualize a story. Talk to your students about turning what they read into a 'movie' in their heads as they read.

✱ Read aloud to the students and ask them to listen with their eyes closed, imagining the story in their minds.

✱ Encourage the students to draw a series of storyboards that tell the story in picture form.

✱ Watching a video or movie of the story before beginning to read can substantially improve students' abilities to visualize the story, relate to the characters and follow the plot.

## Finding the right answer; formulating the right answer

✱ Ask your students to be detectives and locate where information is in the text. *"Find the words that tell us that the lion was getting annoyed. . . . Where does it give us a clue about what might happen next? . . . How do you know where the story is taking place? . . . What does the author tell us about Eloise and Harry?"*

✱ Give explicit instruction in how to formulate an answer. Teach the students that a *Why* question usually needs *because* in the answer; *Where* is followed by an answer that includes mention of a place; *When* has to be answered with an indication of time and so on.

✱ Teach students to use the words from the question when they formulate an answer. This not only helps students to understand the correct way to respond to a formal question, but also provides an excellent starting point for the answer. For example, let's say the question is, *"Why do you think Rex went away without saying anything?"* The student might respond in either of the following ways:

 *"He was scared."*

☑ *"Rex went away without saying anything because he was afraid of the boss."*

✱ Ask the students to read a passage and write their own set of comprehension questions. Students can exchange questions with each other or ask an adult the questions instead. It takes a strong understanding of what is read to be able to generate good questions.

✱ Give the students several possible answers to each comprehension question. Discuss with the students which answers work best and how poor answers could be improved.

## Making the connections

✶ Give the students a context for what they are reading. If the book that your students are reading takes place in an unfamiliar time, situation or place, provide plenty of information that helps to set the scene for the students. Provide pictures, video or teaching content as a starting point.

✶ Make sure students with poor general knowledge or understanding are reading books that relate to familiar topics and situations, so the students can connect their current knowledge to what they are reading.

# Student May Have Visual Difficulties

## Section 10 – Reading Observation Chart

| 10.  *Student may have visual difficulties.* |
| --- |
| Student rubs eyes when reading. |
| Student tilts head when reading. |
| Student uses finger to keep place when reading. |
| Student covers one eye with hand when reading. |
| Student complains of headache when reading. |
| Student skips words and lines when reading. |
| Student reads for only a short period of time before needing a break. |
| Student chooses books with large print. |

It is obvious that good eyesight is important for reading. Being able to read the doctor's eyesight chart doesn't mean the student has adequate vision for reading. The doctor's chart usually tests distance vision of single letters. To be able to read, students must be able to:

• See the words clearly when they are close, for example in a book
• See words clearly at a distance, for example on the board
• Scan along a line of print, accurately moving from one section to the next
• Drop down accurately to the beginning of the next line of print
• Get both eyes to work together, so there is one sharp image, not two
• Sustain focus on the print for a considerable period of time
• Alternate focus, for instance, if they are reading from the board and then writing in their books

One last point to remember! Not all visual difficulties are completely corrected by glasses.

# Strategies for Managing Visual Problems

## Getting information about possible or known visual problems

✶ Monitor all students for signs of visual problems. Beware of simply asking students if they can see well. They may not realize that their vision is poor, as it is all they have ever known.

✶ Arrange for any student showing signs of visual difficulties to have a full test of vision if you are concerned about the student's reading. Make sure the specialist knows that reading and school work are of concern.

✶ If students have known visual problems, do not assume that because they wear glasses, they can see perfectly. Check with the student's specialist and/or the advisory teacher for visual impairment so that you can understand the nature of the student's visual difficulties and the impact this might have on the student's reading.

✶ If students do have known visual difficulties, check that their needs with regards to print size, lighting levels and visual aids are known and accommodated.

## Making the classroom and school work vision friendly

✶ Make sure that the lighting in your classroom is good. Good illumination aids good vision and helps to prevent strain.

✶ Watch out for shadows. Even if the students are in good lighting, there is still a risk that shadows may fall on some work spaces.

✶ Make sure that your board has good lighting but is away from glare. Avoid using colors that have poor contrast with the background.

✶ Avoid seating students so they have to turn around 180 degrees to see the board and turn back to do their work.

✶ Make worksheets easy on the eye. *All* students benefit from worksheets, assignment sheets and test papers that are clearly presented. Avoid a visually cluttered sheet. Make sure that photocopying is clear. Choose a legible font. (Arial, 12 point is ideal.) Use clear graphics and formatting to make the page easy to understand.

# Student Has Advanced Reading Skills

## Section 11 – Reading Observation Checklist

| **11. Student has advanced reading skills.** |
| --- |
| Student's reading is advanced in comparison to peer group. |
| Student complains that reading is boring, even though the student reads well. |
| Student prefers factual books to fiction. |

In most classes, some students will have exceptionally advanced reading skills. Usually, their advanced reading skills will be a positive. Nevertheless, some consideration will also have to be given to these students' special needs. For example, the young student with advanced reading skills may not need to go through the series of graded readers that are necessary for most students. Preference for factual books rather than fiction may reflect some students' difficulties in finding intellectually stimulating material that does not rely on adult themes.

## Strategies for Supporting Advanced Reading Skills

### Individualizing the reading program

✱ If the student is already a competent reader, allow him to skip all (or some) of the graded readers.

✱ Students with advanced reading skills may not need to join in class or group instruction of skills such as word decoding using phonics. Give these students an alternative activity at this time.

✱ Provide a wide selection of books that are suitable for the student's reading level but which also match the student's emotional and social maturity. Allow the student to select freely from these books.

✱ Recognize that many students with advanced reading skills enjoy or prefer nonfiction reading. Make sure there is a wide range of nonfiction in the mix of books offered.

✱ Give the student with advanced reading skills reading lists that suggest clusters of reading arranged by genre, author, topic and so forth. This encourages the student to follow through from one book they have enjoyed to others of a similar type. For instance, the student might enjoy one biography and be interested in reading other biographies suggested on the reading list.

✱ Develop advanced reading comprehension skills and answering techniques. Encourage the student to move beyond a simple retelling of facts to interpreting, analyzing and comparing what he has read. For example, instead of asking the student to describe the characters in the book, ask him to compare and contrast two of the characters.

### Placing the student in a stimulating reading environment

✱ Put advanced readers together in a reading group. The teacher may select the book for the group to read, or the students may take turns selecting titles. One student may be asked to present the book, for example, talking about the author and giving the group background information before the group discussion. Multiple copies of the book obviously have to be made available.

## Concluding Chapter Two

This chapter has discussed difficulties that may arise for students as they learn how to read. It also has presented strategies for helping both students who are struggling and those who are unusually advanced for their age group. The awareness gained here should help in detecting the sources of reading difficulties, which will, in turn, help determine the strategies to utilize. Many of the strategies given are appropriate for any young reader. Appropriate interventions will help to include all students in classroom reading activities and will thus support their self-esteem and attitude towards learning this most important lifetime skill.

# Chapter Three
# Written Language

## Introduction

Difficulties with written language along with difficulties in reading are probably the two major reasons students feel discouraged and inadequate in the classroom.

Being able to produce good written language is, of course, a very important part of success at school and in the world beyond. What about the students who have difficulty putting their ideas on paper? Many are talented and knowledgeable, others less so. All, however, need to be able to share their ideas with others, both in speaking and in writing.

Some students may fail courses of study, or underachieve, because what they write does not reflect what they know. When assessment is based only on what a student can write, then of course students who find it difficult to express themselves in print will be disadvantaged.

> Bob is now a successful builder. He recalls: *"When I was a kid, I loved woodwork and metal work and all that sort of thing. I was talented too. I could make anything you wanted. But then there were the exams, they were another story. I could have told you the answers, I could have shown you the answers, but writing them down? No way! Then one year I got lucky and broke my arm so I had to do the test verbally—straight A—and then the teachers could see that I was pretty knowledgeable about it all—it was just writing it down that was my downfall."*

In this chapter, we look at the difficulties that can arise with written language.

The section headings in this chapter follow the structure of the **Appendix #2: Written Language Observation Chart.**

The Written Language Observation Chart may be reproduced and used to informally assess and record individual reading difficulties for students. This chart is divided into eight sections, with each focusing on a specific area of written language. As you assess individual students, specific patterns of difficulty may emerge. The sections in the chart will provide a direct link between the recorded Written Language Observation Chart and the corresponding strategies in this chapter that will help the student in the specific area(s) of need. The eight sections of the chart also have been reproduced within the main text of Chapter Three.

. . . . . . . . . . . . . . . . . . . . . . . . . . . . . . . . . .

If you are interested in using the strategies without completing an informal assessment of the student, these sections will easily guide you through the chapter and provide a quick, easy reference tool for specific areas in reading. This will enable you to select from the intervention strategies, modifications and adaptations listed to help individual and small groups of students.

The following forms from the Appendix are referred to in this chapter:

Appendix # 2:  Written Language Observation Chart
Appendix #37:  Student Reward Cards
Appendix # 9:  New Ideas for Writing
Appendix # 7:  Spelling Log
Appendix #10:  Punctuation Checker

# Student Feels Negative about Writing

## Section 1 – Written Language Observation Chart

| 1. Student feels negative about writing. |
|---|
| Student complains when asked to write. |
| Student avoids writing whenever possible. |
| Student's writing is very brief in comparison to peers' work. |
| Student expresses difficulty in knowing how to start or knowing what to write. |

Writing is a complex process involving ideas, language, spelling, handwriting, punctuation, etc. Students with difficulties often feel overwhelmed by having so many targets within one task.

> "If I make it neat then I won't get much done. . . . If I write this really great idea, I won't be able to spell the words. If I stop and fix the spelling, I'll forget what I'm writing about. I'll never get all that done. Maybe I'll write something short and get it finished."

Writing also has the potential to expose the student to ridicule and embarrassment. Students often feel more comfortable with a worksheet that has a lot of structure. This helps to reassure the student that they are working along the right lines. But a blank piece of paper?

> "What if what I write sounds dumb? Once I've written it down, I'm stuck with it. It might be wrong. I'm not so sure I know what she wants. . . . I might have to read out loud what I've written and it will be stupid."

. . . . . . . . . . . . . . . . . . . . . . . . . . . . . . . . . .

Some students cannot make up their minds between several competing ideas and end up not even starting, because they are not sure which is 'right.' Students need to understand that writing is not a closed subject where there is only one 'right' answer.

Students may put a lot of effort and time into writing only to produce disappointing work. Some may find it hard to know what to write or how to get started. Others may have good ideas but lack the skill to get their ideas down on paper. Students may then feel discouraged and negative about writing.

> A parent explained: *"I watch him sit there, sometimes for hours, working away . . . writing something down, scratching his head, chewing his pencil, altering what he has done. And after all that, he has—maybe—a quarter of a page of terrible writing that I can hardly make out. His teacher says that, at school, he often has to stay in at recess to catch up with the work."*

Being slow and experiencing difficulties with written work may mean that some students seldom get to finish any piece of work to a satisfactory standard. Their books may contain half finished, poorly done written work. This does not build confidence or positive feelings towards writing. It is also a poor work ethic to leave work unfinished and of poor quality.

## Strategies for Developing Positive Attitudes towards Writing

### Using multimedia

* Encourage all forms of communication in the classroom. Have students talk, draw, act, build and demonstrate to share knowledge, so they remain interested and positive about the task itself.

* Make writing part of an interesting task that has other, supplementary ways of covering the topic. For example, make a photo journal with written captions and explanatory paragraphs.

* Use technology, so students can use computer programs, cameras, recording and multimedia to help get their ideas across.

### Providing support and guidance

* Provide appropriate intervention to improve students' skills. (See following sections.)

* Ensure that you use a range of inclusive strategies to make sure that the student is not at a disadvantage because of writing difficulties. (See following sections.)

✱ Brainstorm the task with the class before the students start to write. This will help trigger ideas and set the scene for the required assignment.

✱ Show students how different writers tackle the same topic in different ways. There can be several, quite different but equally acceptable, ways of tackling a writing assignment.

✱ Help students to choose between ideas or approaches by reminding them that other ideas can be tried at a later date.

✱ Have your class do a 'writing dash.' Set a very short time limit for the writing, so students have to learn to write whatever comes into their heads without stopping to worry about whether they are right or wrong. *"You have one minute to write about your favorite type of weather. Tell me why you like that weather best. . . . Here is the start of a story. You have five minutes to write the rest of the story."*

✱ Many students find it hard to get started with written work. Provide a few words or a sentence to get them started.

✱ Provide students with a scaffold for writing, such as a set of headings or an outline, to guide their writing and support their confidence.

✱ Let the students know your priorities for the task, so they will know where to direct their efforts. *"Today I am looking for really imaginative ideas, so we will not worry about neat writing or spelling right now."* Or, *"This activity is for practice with handwriting and presentation, so take your time—and remember, I am looking for good handwriting and presentation as my number one priority."*

✱ Assign several short writing assignments for the whole class. Fast writers may complete several; slower writers just one or two.

✱ Allow time for slow writers to complete work over several days—not as a punishment, but as an acknowledgement that good writing is a process of evolution that may take time to complete.

✱ Do not display students' work to others unless they are comfortable with you doing so.

## Valuing effort

* Evaluate outcomes on the basis of the effort put into them. Value the best that students can do.

* Emphasize the concept of 'personal best.' Developing writing skills is an ongoing process, so a small improvement in comparison to previous work should be celebrated as a real achievement.

* Use **Appendix #37: Student Reward Cards,** or create your own cards with sayings, designs, stickers or the like to acknowledge students' efforts and further inspire them.

* Make explicit and realistic goals for improvement in writing, so the student can see that the target goal is within reach.

* Emphasize that, in writing, there can be many 'right' ways to do something.

# Difficulties with Written Language Impact Classroom Achievement

## Section 2 – Written Language Observation Chart

| 2. Difficulties with written language impact classroom achievement. |
| --- |
| Student's oral contribution in class is not reflected in written work. |
| Student does not do well on written assignments, tests and exams. |
| Student has problems in getting ideas down on paper. |
| Student writes sentences that are brief, incomplete, disjointed or hard to follow. |
| Student does not use a wide vocabulary to express ideas. |
| Student often repeats words and sentences over and over again. |
| Student often uses the same format in every type of writing. |
| Student has difficulties in sequencing sentences in logical order. |

Students may underachieve with school work, because they cannot fully show their understanding and knowledge when they write. They may be able to have a strong verbal discussion on a topic, answer questions well orally or give a good oral presentation to the class, but they fail to produce the same quality work when they write.

In tests and examinations, difficulties in getting ideas down on paper may be a major problem and seriously disadvantage the student.

The mechanics of writing may be difficult. The student may find it difficult to find the right words or put words together into a good sentence: *"We did went and Mom over the night."*

The student may rely on the same set of words over and over again: *"We went to the park we went to our friends we went home."* Or, he may repeatedly use the same sentence structure: *"Bo liked Jane. Dad came home. I played ball."*

Even when students have mastered the basics of writing sentences, they may have difficulties in putting sentences together to connect pieces of writing. Collecting information from several sources and pulling it all together into a coherent whole can be a very challenging task.

# Strategies for Managing Writing Difficulties in the Classroom

## Using alternative assessments

✳ Many writing assignments can also be done in other modalities. Look to see if the same assessment objective could be met in a different way, such as an oral presentation, a diagram or a chart.

✳ Some students may benefit from recording their own voices and then transcribing their own words.

✳ The use of voice recognition software can enable students to dictate directly onto a computer, while the computer types up their words. This usually requires the student to go through a training process with the software to 'teach' the software to recognize the student's unique vocal characteristics.

✳ If knowledge is being tested, a multiple choice test where students 'check the box' may be a good substitute for a written examination.

✳ If the task requires the student to give a persuasive argument, an oral presentation may work as the assessment.

✳ Straightforward reporting of facts is also easily turned into an oral exercise. (Think how much of our daily news is delivered to us by audiovisual means as opposed to print media.)

✳ A student might construct a model, draw a series of cartoon strips or give a demonstration to illustrate a scientific principle.

✳ Use a combination of modalities, so a student can create a presentation that has only a small amount of written language supplemented by graphics, spoken word and dramatization. For example, if the class has been given a history assignment on the Civil War, the student may create a series of imaginary news bulletins of the events as they unfold, with maps, captions, 'interviews' with key characters and so on.

## Providing support

* Allow students to work in small teams, so skills can be combined. A student who can write well may benefit from the ideas and innovation of a student with writing difficulties. On the other hand, the student who does not write well benefits from the writing skills of the team member. Together, the team can produce a good piece of work.

* Provide a writing mentor for the student with difficulties. The mentor is available to provide discussion, guidance and practical advice while the student writes.

## Using a scribe

* Have a scribe write down what a student wants to say as a substitute for a written assignment.

* Provide a quiet and private environment for the student to work with the scribe.

* Make sure that a scribe is available for tests and examinations.

* If students are to use scribes in an examination, make sure they are already familiar and confident with dictating their work well before the exam.

* When using scribes, encourage students to make notes, chart the ideas and prepare a framework before beginning. This helps to formulate their ideas.

* Allow students to use notes, charts, etc., in an exam as preparation for dictation to a scribe.

* When a student has dictated a piece of work, make sure he has the opportunity to read back what he has dictated and make appropriate corrections. If the student has reading difficulties, the scribe may read back the work to the student and insert the corrections as directed by the student.

* If scribes are to be used in a formal test or examination, make sure they take dictation without comment or input. They are acting as writing 'machines.' Obviously the scribe must be able to write or type quickly and legibly.

## Developing creative writing

✶ Some students find it very difficult to write from their imagination. Offer the option of factual writing. For example, the student may do well writing a report about a real event or on a topic of scientific interest.

✶ Help students who find imaginative writing difficult to develop a real situation into something more creative.

## Strategies for Developing Imaginative Writing

| Strategy to move from real to imaginary | Real facts | Imaginary or creative idea |
|---|---|---|
| Exaggerate | It was a hot day. | It was so hot that the road was melting. |
| Substitute | My sister went to church with me. | The dog came to church with me. |
| Reverse | Dad had to look for my little brother, who was lost. | Dad got lost and we had to look for him. |
| Elaborate | We ate a hamburger. | We ate a juicy, sizzling hamburger with ketchup and fries. |
| Hypothesize | She was smiling. | I wondered if she had discovered the secret treasure. |

✶ You can use **Appendix #9: New Ideas for Writing** to help the students expand their ideas for imaginative writing.

✶ Some students find creative writing very threatening. They are afraid that their ideas will sound silly. Brainstorm with a group of students to help them see that lots of ideas have merit and can work, even if they seem a bit far-fetched.

✶ Brainstorming can also help trigger ideas in those students who do not have great imaginations or many creative ideas.

✶ You can provide a story in cartoon form and ask students to retell the story in their own words. This is reassuring for those students who find it hard to create stories themselves.

✶ Provide structure and a framework for students who really find creative writing difficult. You may need to give them some 'factual' information about characters or events to get them started on their writing. For example: *"Write a story about three brothers who lived on a farm. The story should be about how the boys discovered something very unusual in the barn. Your story should include an exciting chase on horseback."*

✶ Assign a task where certain words and phrases have to be included in a story. For example: *"Write a story and include the following words. You can use the words in any order you like to make your story interesting and exciting. The words are: **house, hill, dark, storm, yellow eyes, river, bridge, police, amazing, chocolate cake, grandmother** and **biggest I had ever seen.**"*

## Developing written expression

✶ Develop the students' vocabulary. Take every opportunity to introduce new words and phrases. Read to your students and discuss unfamiliar words, talk to them and expand their vocabulary.

✶ Start a classroom list that contains new or unusual words. Ask students to look for words that will baffle their classmates—and even the teacher!

✶ Have activities where the students work with synonyms, antonyms and word meanings, and encourage them to use new words in their own writing: *"How many words can you think of to describe water falling down? It can gush, drip, pour, sprinkle, or tumble. How can you improve the sentence that says 'It was raining.'"*

✶ Ask students to revise early drafts to improve written expression. They can look for opportunities to vary sentence structure, replace simple words with more interesting ones and expand what they have written.

✶ Encourage students to look out for repetition of ideas. Often students are working with very few ideas, which are recycled over and over again. If this is the problem, ask questions, provide resource material and brainstorm in class to produce more ideas.

✶ Provide explicit teaching in sentence construction. Use formal activities to show students that language can be deliberately manipulated to make expression clearer. For example, ask students to try some of the following:

• Combine two simple sentences into one compound one.
• Split a long sentence into two shorter sentences.
• Turn a sentence into the past tense.
• Make an active sentence passive.
• Rewrite a story, changing from first person to third person.

✶ Have students experiment with 'voice': *"How would this story sound if the giant was telling it? What words would he use? What would it sound like if the old grandmother was telling it? How would she tell the story?"*

## Helping with planning and organizing ideas

✶ Teach skills in planning for larger pieces of work. Encourage students to create a plan or create an outline before the student begins to write.

✶ Look at available software that helps to organize ideas.

✶ Use mind mapping to help students learn how to gather ideas and put them into logical clusters.

✶ Give direct instruction and practice on the skills of linking one idea with another.

✶ Ask students to build a glossary of linking words and phrases, such as *other people think that . . . as a result of this . . . soon after . . . even though . . . however . . . eventually.*

✶ Provide students with a paragraph with the middle sentence removed. The students' task is to 'repair' the paragraph by writing in a sentence that will link the remaining sentences in a logical way.

# Student Has Spelling Difficulties

## Section 3 – Written Language Observation Chart

| *3. Student has spelling difficulties.* |
| --- |
| Student makes many spelling errors. |
| Student makes phonological errors in spelling, such as *beg/bec*. |
| Student does not use the correct letters for sounds, such as *train/tran*. |
| Student makes errors in the use of spelling rules. |
| Student has repeated spelling errors with common words, such as *what/wot*. |
| Student's work is full of spelling corrections made as the student writes. |
| Student successfully learns words for a spelling test but then forgets them. |

Spelling can prove to be a difficult and frustrating aspect of writing for many students. Good spelling depends on the student having:

- good phonological skills (the ability to break spoken words into a sequence of sounds)
- the capacity to remember the letters that represent sounds
- the ability to recall visual sequences
- solid knowledge in spelling rules and word construction

- good 'motor memory' for spelling patterns in handwriting and typing
- the ability to retain spelling patterns that have been learned by rote

We often give students spelling words at the beginning of the week and a final test on Friday. It is then assumed that the ability to spell those words will stay with the student forever. It is an interesting assumption that students need only four days to learn a spelling word and then will remember it forever!

Many students can do well on the spelling tests for which they have had time to prepare. However, the student may forget the words immediately after the test is over. The students may develop a 'learn and forget' cycle. The student learns new words for the next test but forgets the words that were learned the week before.

Students may be able to spell words in a list when the words are given slowly, one at a time. However, writing the same words correctly in context can prove to be much harder. Once the student's attention is diverted to producing good content, neat handwriting and so on, they may not be able to concentrate on spelling as well.

Skilled spellers have a repertoire of words that they can spell automatically. However, even very skilled spellers also use phonological skills surprisingly often, quickly making a mental reference to the way the word sounds and then adjusting the spelling accordingly.

Students with phonological difficulties may be unsure of the speech patterns in a word and so make errors such as writing *house* as *hals*. They may be able to work out some phonological patterns, but only with slow, careful analysis.

Remembering the link between letters and sounds can be very challenging, especially when the student has to remember groups of letters that make new sounds. Pairs of letters that create a sound identical to a letter name, such as *ai, ar,* or *ie,* can be particularly confusing.

Good spellers can often look at a word and know on the basis of its appearance that it is not right. Sometimes they can tell how to correct the error right away, and sometimes they need to keep writing versions down until they find the one that looks right. However, some students cannot tell that a word looks wrong. They can write version after version without coming across one that looks right.

Many students who have spelling difficulties find it hard to use a dictionary. They may not know the order of the alphabet well enough to find the initial letter. Perhaps their spelling is so off track that they do not know where to start to find the right word (for example, searching under *w* for the word *once*). Even if they determine the first letter, what is the next letter? And the letter that comes after that? Sometimes you really need to be able to spell the word to be able to find it in the dictionary!

Students who find it hard to remember the appearance of words may have persistent difficulty with commonly used words.

When teaching spelling, we need to remember that there are two types of words. Some words have a regular phonic pattern, and you can sound them out. Referring back to the sequence of sounds in the word helps students to remember these words.

Other words are irregular. These words will not sound out. A multi-sensory approach that reinforces a 'motor memory' helps students remember these words.

# Strategies for Working with Spelling Difficulties

## Encouraging quality writing

* Separate good and creative writing skills from the actual spelling of words. Give credit for interesting, creative writing, even when spelling is poor.

* Encourage students to write freely, using invented spelling, if necessary. Assist the student with corrections after the first draft has been completed.
* Encourage the use of a word processor to provide support with spelling.

* Ensure that the program is customized correctly, if there are options for spelling.

* For students with severe spelling difficulties, consider the use of a software program that has predictive text.

* For students with extreme spelling difficulties, consider the use of voice activated word processing.

## Providing support in the classroom

* In the classroom, provide a range of resources to assist students with spelling. Some examples include:

  * charts of commonly used words and phrases
  * posters of common spelling patterns
  * spelling rules (with examples) clearly displayed
  * lists of topic words for the current classroom project
  * personal dictionaries at a suitable level of difficulty
  * electronic spell checkers and dictionaries
  * classroom dictionaries

* Provide students with spelling difficulties with a personal "desk dictionary.' This is a single sheet or card, placed on the student's desk. The card has a list of all the commonly used words that the student cannot yet spell. The list changes regularly.

When words are mastered, they are removed from the list. Other words can be inserted. Reminders about spelling rules and other writing formalities can also be included on the card as needed.

✻ Arrange for a 'spelling buddy' to be available to help the student with spelling difficulties.

✻ Make sure that students with spelling difficulties develop good typing and word processing skills, so they can use a computer from an early age.

✻ Give students with spelling difficulties priority access to a computer for written language.

✻ Provide adult support for checking spelling during writing sessions.

✻ If the student has severe difficulties with spelling, have someone else type up the rough draft and make corrections in consultation with the student.

✻ Display a few irregular words in the classroom each week and give the students a challenge. Can they write for the whole week without ever making a mistake on these target words?

## Teaching dictionary skills

✻ Provide regular practice at alphabetizing words. Use a simple, illustrated dictionary to get started. Or, use a telephone directory to practice at working with alphabetical order.

✻ Use address books with clearly marked alphabetical sections in which to write words that are needed as the student writes.

✻ Arrange for the student to store alphabetical index cards in a box for individual spelling words.

✻ Place alphabet tabs on the edge of dictionary pages to help students navigate their way through the dictionary.

✻ Teach students with severe spelling difficulties how to use an electronic rather than a paper dictionary.

## Individualizing the spelling program

✱ Look at students' spelling difficulties in their free-style writing. Analyze the types of errors that occur. Look for the following patterns of error:

- The use of the phonetic version of irregular words, such as *hir* instead of *here*
- Spelling the same word a different way each time it is used
- Losing track of the phonological pattern of the word, such as *but* for *boat*
- Failing to use spelling rules

Plan your teaching program on the basis of the error patterns identified.

✱ More of the same is not always a good intervention strategy for spelling difficulties. If the student is finding it difficult to learn and retain spelling, examine your teaching method and the way in which the student is learning. See if an alternative approach might work better.

✱ If the spelling list is too difficult for the student to learn within a few days, then the words are too hard. Place the student on a modified program.

✱ Have differentiated spelling tasks for your class, so all students have words to learn that are appropriate to their own levels of achievement.

✱ If a student has difficulties with spelling, teach only new words that he is certain to use in his own writing within the next few weeks. Words that are not frequently used will soon be forgotten.

✱ No student should ever have to learn to spell words he cannot read. If a student cannot read a word on his spelling list, remove that word from the list.

✱ Follow through after words have been tested. Use dictation, review spelling activities and even retest several times over the next few months.

✱ Avoid teaching words grouped according to themes. Cluster words that have a relationship with each other because of phonic pattern, derivation or other logical link.

## Teaching irregular words (words that cannot be sounded out)

✱ Use rainbow writing. Ask the students to write the word in large letters and then use different colored pencils to go over and over the letters to develop a motor memory of the spelling pattern.

★ Irregular words often need a lot of over-learning before mastery occurs. So teach, practice, review and use the words over and over again. You can use the **Appendix #7: Spelling Log** form to keep track of spelling mastery.

## Sample Spelling Log

| Target word: **weather** | | | | | | | | | | | |
|---|---|---|---|---|---|---|---|---|---|---|---|
| **Daily practice and test until six consecutive ✓s are obtained.** | Date 2/3 | Date 2/4 | Date 2/5 | Date 2/6 | Date 2/7 | Date 2/10 | Date 2/11 | Date 2/12 | Date 2/13 | Date 2/14 | Date 2/17 |
| **✓ if correct** **□ if incorrect** | □ | ✓ | ✓ | □ | ✓ | □ | ✓ | ✓ | ✓ | ✓ | ✓ |
| **Weekly practice and test until four consecutive ✓s are obtained.** | Date 2/25 | Date 3/2 | Date 3/9 | Date 3/16 | Date 3/23 | Date 3/30 | Date 4/6 | Date 4/13 | Date | Date | Date |
| **✓ if correct** **□ if incorrect** | ✓ | ✓ | ✓ | □ | ✓ | ✓ | ✓ | ✓ | | | |
| **Monthly practice and test until three consecutive ✓s are obtained.** | Date 5/14 | Date 6/12 | Date 7/14 | Date | Date | Date | Date | Date | Date | Date | Date |
| **✓ if correct** **□ if incorrect** | ✓ | ✓ | ✓ | | | | | | | | |

★ Give individual students their own personal challenge words that they persistently spell incorrectly.

★ Have students say the letters out loud as they write them down, and give repeated practice in doing this.

★ Have students 'write' the words with 'sky writing.' They trace the spelling of the word in the air with a finger.

★ If students are using cursive writing, encourage them to write their spelling words in cursive, as this helps to build motor memory.

★ If students have handwriting difficulties, encourage them to type the words over and over again to consolidate the motor memory of the action of typing the word.

★ Combine spelling and typing practice, using spelling words in typing tasks.

★ Have students make a design of individual words, decorating the shapes.

✱ Talk to students about spelling patterns: *"Look at this word. It says **'who.'** Which letter is the silent letter? There is something weird about the **oo** sound. How is it spelled in this word? If we mix the letters around, can we make another word?"*

✱ Have the students make up their own memory prompts, or suggest some to them. For example, the first letters of the sentence *Big elephants can always understand small elephants* will spell the word *because*.

✱ Teach 'old way-new way,' if students are stuck with an incorrect spelling. *"You used to write **whent**. That was the old way. In the new way, you leave out **h** and write **went**.*

## Teaching phonetic and pattern words

✱ Work on phonological awareness, so students learn and understand how to break down words into sounds.

✱ Have students say the sounds before they write the word.

✱ Teach reading and spelling together, so learning in reading crosses over and helps with spelling. Always teach a phonic skill in reading before the same skill is taught in spelling.

✱ Teach words in a sequence, so that phonics skills build gradually. This is exactly the same sequence as teaching reading using phonics.

# Sequence for Teaching Phonic Spelling Patterns

| | |
|---|---|
| **Stage 1** | Use words in the consonant-vowel-consonant pattern. For example *set, pet, wet* or *pin, win, tin, bin* or *fat, cat, hat.* Notice that often these words can be clustered in groups that share the same vowel-consonant ending (called the rime) but have different initial letters (called the onset). Teaching onset-rime patterns makes this first stage much easier, as learning from one word can be generalized to the next. If you can spell *pin,* it is easy to spell *win.* |
| **Stage 2** | Use a maximum of four letters in each word, so the student only has to deal with one letter blend. <br> Two consonants slide together; for example, *trip, spin, stop.* <br> Two consonants make a new sound; for example, *ship, chop, thin.* <br> Final *e*; for example, *hope, take, like* |
| **Stage 3** | Two vowels make a new sound: *out, feet, boat.* <br> Vowel and consonant make a new sound; for example, *part, dawn, dirt.* <br> Silent letters; for example, *gnaw, knot* |
| **Stage 4** | Three consonants slide together; for example, *shrug, ring, strap, scream.* <br> Four letters make a new sound; for example, *ration, light, rough.* <br> Words ending in *y* or *ing*; for example, *happy, silly, tapping* |
| **Stage 5** | Words that combine two or more of the previously taught patterns; for example, *combine, sprout, market* <br> Words that are compound words, words using prefixes or suffixes; for example, *preview, unhappy, defeat* |

★ If students find it difficult to hear sounds in words, start by using plastic letters. Give only the letters they need for a word, and ask them to make the word. For example, give them the letters *i, g* and *p,* and ask them to put the letters together to make the word *pig.*

★ Once students can build words using the letters, it is time for a bigger challenge. Give the students all the letters needed plus some extra letters, so they have to discriminate the sounds and choose the correct letters.

★ Teach students to swap sounds to spell new words. For example, ask students: *"If this word says 'log,' how can you change it to say 'hog'?"*

* Use nonsense words to extend practice in listening to the sounds in a word and writing the 'word' down.

* Teach words together that share the same phonetic pattern, so students see the link. For example, introduce *beach, peach, teach, reach* as a group.

# Student Has Handwriting Difficulties

## Section 4 – Written Language Observation Chart

| 4. *Student has handwriting difficulties.* |
| --- |
| Student does not always form letters correctly. |
| Student's letters and words are often too close together, have irregular spacing or are too widely spaced. |
| Student prints instead of using cursive writing. |
| Student's writing begins neatly but quickly becomes messy. |
| Student takes longer than peers to complete writing tasks, and work is still untidy. |
| Student's hand gets tired or sweaty after a few minutes of writing. |

Some students experience significant difficulty with handwriting. This can cause considerable frustration by limiting the quantity and quality of the written work that the student can produce.

Handwriting is a complex neurological process. Messages have to travel from the brain to the hand in a continuous flow. The muscles of the hand have to respond to these messages with speed and accuracy, and in sequence. For some students, this process does not work well.

It is tempting to assume that the student can easily improve handwriting skills by taking more time or practicing more. However, this is often a false assumption. Most handwriting difficulties are neurological dysfunctions. These difficulties will not necessarily respond well to increased levels of practice, especially in the older student who has been practicing for many years.

Some students can write neatly for a short period of time, particularly if they can take their time and write at their own pace. However, sustained writing is quite a different matter. Some students will write the first sentence of the paper quite well, but their writing rapidly deteriorates as time goes by. A rest break may restore neatness for a few minutes before the cycle begins all over again.

Other students may always have difficulties with neatness, and second or even third attempts may be little better than their first efforts. Handwriting may not reflect the effort put in. A huge effort might produce a short piece of written work that is neater, but the cost in terms of time and effort may be very high.

# Strategies for Managing Handwriting Difficulties

## Modifying requirements and providing support

* Allow students plenty of time to write.

* Allow extra time in testing situations to compensate for slow writing.

* Provide a scribe to take dictation from the student.

* Allow the student to do an oral rather than a written assignment.

* Allow rest breaks, if sustained writing is a problem during class work or tests.

* Give credit for content of what the student writes, rather than handwriting or presentation.

* Accept that if work is done quickly, then it may be very untidy.

* Minimize unnecessary writing. Provide lesson notes, handouts, copies, worksheets and so forth to help reduce the amount of writing required.

* Modify tests to reduce the amount of handwriting required. For example, use a multiple-choice format instead of an essay.

* Allow the student to make corrections to a handwritten draft using an eraser or whiteout rather than have the student rewrite the complete paper.

* Remember that untidy writing does not necessarily mean that the student has been careless or lazy.

* Encourage the student to experiment with different types of pens or pencils. Allow the student to use the one that suits him or her best.

* Do not require students to rewrite work because it is untidy, unless you are certain that they can easily do better.

★ Recognize that students may be able to produce neat work under special circumstances, but that they cannot maintain that standard for all work every day.

★ The desk and chair should be the right height for the student.

★ Students should have good writing posture. The student should not be slouching and should have both feet on the ground and back supported by the chair.

## Using computers

★ Encourage the student with a handwriting difficulty to use a word processor instead of handwriting.

★ Do not ask students to do a handwritten draft before they type their work up. Encourage them to develop the skill of typing the first draft on the computer.

★ Some students with handwriting problems also find typing difficult. Try using voice recognition software as an alternative to typing.

★ Have an adult type the rough draft for the student.

# Student Finds It Difficult to Copy Accurately

## Section 5 – Written Language Observation Chart

| 5. Student finds it difficult to copy accurately. |
| --- |
| Student makes errors when copying words. |
| Student needs additional time to complete copying as compared to peers. |

Some students have quite marked difficulties in copying things down. They may write very slowly. They find it hard to remember the appearance of words that they cannot already spell. They may also have to constantly refer back and forth between the book and the paper.

# Strategies for Managing Copying Difficulties

## Providing support

★ Provide handouts instead of having the student copy large amounts of material.

★ Allow extra time when copying is essential.

★ Allow students to take photocopies or scan rather than copying things by hand.

✳ Ask a fellow student to make a carbon copy of the notes.

✳ Leave notes on display until all students have had time to copy them.

✳ Arrange the desks and tables so that students are facing the board. Avoid having students with their backs, or even sides, to the board during copying exercises.

✳ Place important information on the school or class website, so students can access it at any time.

✳ Provide worksheets instead of having students copy exercises from the textbooks.

✳ Check that the student has copied correctly when taking down important information (such as details of a homework assignment or a school field trip).

✳ Request to have a student's eyesight checked, if he or she seems to have trouble seeing the board.

✳ Have students use a strip of firm tag board or a ruler under the line of text they are copying.

## Student Has Difficulties with Punctuation

### Section 6 – Written Language Observation Chart

| **6. Student has difficulties with punctuation.** |
|---|
| Student makes errors in punctuation when writing spontaneously. |
| Student makes more errors than peers when doing formal punctuation. |

Punctuation is an important, but often neglected, aspect of writing. As adults, we know that punctuation is needed to give shape to what the writer has to say. Skilled writers use punctuation to add an extra dimension to what they write. It can even change the meaning of a sentence!

# Strategies for Working with Punctuation

## Improving punctuation and formatting

✱ Give explicit instruction about punctuation, and vary it at frequent intervals.

✱ Give instruction in how punctuation is used when reading out loud. Once students understand this, punctuating their own work is easier.

✱ Provide formal assignments that are focused on punctuation and formatting (using capitals and creating paragraphs).

✱ Provide the student with a checklist for punctuation, and go through the steps before the student begins to write. Highlight areas where the student has specific difficulties. You can use **Appendix #10: Punctuation Checker,** or create your own.

| Areas to look for: | Checked |
|---|---|
| Correct punctuation at the end of sentences | |
| Capital letters at the beginning of sentences | |
| Capitalized proper nouns | |
| Question marks | |
| Quotation marks | |
| Commas | |
| Paragraphs | |

✱ Nominate another student as a 'punctuation buddy,' who will give advice if the student has a punctuation question.

✱ Encourage students to read their own work out loud and check the punctuation where there are pauses, emphases, questions, or stops.

✱ Give students a printed passage that has all punctuation removed. Read the passage aloud, and ask the students to fill in the punctuation.

# Student Has Difficulties with Proofreading and Editing

## Section 7 – Written Language Observation Chart

| 7. *Student has difficulties with proofreading and editing.* |
| :--- |
| Student overlooks errors when proofreading. |
| Teachers often comment, *"Check your work carefully."* |
| Student may alter correct words during proofreading activities. |
| Student may replace one error with another one during proofreading. |
| Student is not able to describe or demonstrate strategies for proofreading. |
| Student's editing of drafts leaves a significant number of unresolved problems. |
| Student is not able to describe or evaluate personal writing strategies. |
| Student does not seek editorial advice or assistance. |

Students who experience difficulties with written language often fail to check their work once finished. Maybe they are so glad to reach the end of the task that they want to leave it then and there! However, these same students often have genuine problems in recognizing errors they have made.

Often the student may have checked his work but overlooked many of the mistakes. Sometimes a correct word has been deleted and replaced with an incorrect one.

Editing is an advanced skill that many students lack. Being able to review what you have written and correct not only spelling and punctuation but also expression, sentence structure and overall format is a demanding skill.

# Strategies for Helping with Proofreading and Editing

## Providing support

✶ Provide students with in-class proofreading and editing assistance.

✶ Allow enough time for students to submit work, have it checked, and rework it.

✶ Have each student nominate a home editor for their work. This can be a parent, friend, sibling, neighbor or teacher. The editor is asked to review each piece of written work. The work is signed including the editor's name; for example, *Written by Sacha Davies, edited by Louise Alpin.*

✦ Teachers should give the editors a workshop at the beginning of the school year. The workshop should clarify that editors are advisors and consultants. The editor should understand that the student is the author of the work. The editor should not write or rewrite anything on the student's behalf.

✦ Give plenty of time for work to be written, to allow for several drafts and rewrites.

✦ Encourage students to get started as soon as possible with a writing task. Many students leave tasks until the last moment, allowing no time write a draft or to edit or rewrite the paper.

✦ Ensure that all students understand that writing is a craft and that most work needs to be revised, polished and carefully edited before it is finished.

✦ Create writing groups, where students read each other's drafts and then discuss each piece of work as an editorial panel. A teacher may facilitate the discussion. Obviously, the group must understand that the purpose of the group is positive, mutual support.

## Building skills

✦ Look at the pattern of errors with the student, so the student understands the sort of mistakes that frequently occur. This helps the student become aware of the errors that need special attention as he or she writes.

✦ Get students to write themselves a note for the start of the next piece of work. For instance, if they have left out capital letters in today's work, have them write "Remember Capitals" on the top of the page where they will start tomorrow's writing.

✦ Provide a checklist for spelling and punctuation errors that will act as a reminder for the type of errors that frequently occur. The student will take particular care to watch out for these errors next time. **Appendix #10: Punctuation Checker** may be personalized for individual students to include specific check points.

| Watch out for these! | Checked |
|---|---|
| Ends of words | |
| *Said* not *siad* | |
| Capitals for proper nouns | |

✦ Provide copies of real students' work. (Exchange with a colleague in another school or class.) Remove any identifying marks so the work is anonymous. Have your students proofread and edit the work. It is much more fun finding mistakes in other students' work!

✱ Ask a professional writer to come and talk to the students about how to go about writing and editing.

✱ Have students maintain a log of the drafting process, noting the date, the stage the work is in (e.g., Draft 2) and the editor's name.

✱ Have students keep the drafts on file. They should number each draft and submit it with the final piece of work.

✱ Encourage students to use Track Changes in their computer program to show how their writing developed.

✱ If time allows, have students put the piece of work away and look at it again with fresh eyes a day or so later.

✱ Ask students to double space their work, so they (or their editors) have space to insert comments if necessary.

✱ Have students keep notes or a log on how editing changed their work. These notes can be used as a reference point for future writing. For example: *I made the long sentences into two shorter sentences. I added some more descriptive words to make it more interesting. I rewrote the introductory paragraph to make it more exciting.*

# Student Has Advanced Writing Skills

## Section 8 – Written Language Observation Chart

| 8. *Student has advanced writing skills.* |
|---|
| Student sometimes produces work of exceptional quality. |
| Student expresses a love of writing and will write by choice at home or at school. |
| Student has accurate and advanced spelling skills. |
| Student uses a wide range of vocabulary and expression. |
| Student uses punctuation accurately and to good effect. |
| Student can vary writing style to meet various requirements. |
| Student shows exceptional imagination and creativity in writing. |

Some students have exceptional writing capabilities, and they, too, will need special consideration so they are able to develop their talents to their full potential.

These students may have advanced vocabulary and background knowledge, they may be creative and imaginative, or they may love to research and write about factual topics, such as historical events or current affairs.

# Strategies for Developing Advanced Writing Skills

## Modifying the classroom program

✶ Differentiate the classroom tasks, so the student with advanced writing skills can develop skills at a more complex level. For instance, if all students are assigned to write an account of their weekend activity, the more advanced student may try writing in a style other than first person. The student may write the account in the third person, as a travelogue, as a news report or perhaps in a poem.

✶ Group together the students who enjoy writing. Encourage these students to collaborate on challenging writing tasks, such as writing a class newspaper.

✶ Many students who write well are quite ambitious about what they want to write. Allow students to work on the same piece of work for several days, if not weeks, if they are keen to do so. Maintain a working plan of what they are doing.

✶ Watch out for capable students 'dumbing down' to fit in with the rest of the class. Challenge and provide extensions and encouragement for these students, so they continue to develop their talents.

## Placing the student in a stimulating writing environment

✶ Set up a writers' group where students can bring their writing, learn new writing skills and enjoy each other's writing.

✶ Find someone who can mentor the students with advanced writing skills, so the students can explore the many exciting aspects of writing.

✶ Encourage students to submit their writing to literary magazines and competitions.

# Concluding Chapter Three

This chapter has pointed out the many aspects involved in writing, such as spelling, punctuation, handwriting and putting words together to create meaningful sentences—not to mention entire paragraphs. Writing can be even more daunting to some students than reading. They are asked to put their thoughts and efforts down in concrete form to be 'judged,' and many have a fear of being 'wrong.' The varied strategies suggested here provide support for students who have difficulties with writing as well as encouragement for those who are especially good at it.

# Chapter Four
# Math

## Introduction

Did you know there are 10 times as many books on literacy difficulties as there are on math difficulties? Why is this so? Math and literacy difficulties are equally common. So we would expect about the same level of interest (and book buying) in both topics. Perhaps mathematics is seen as less important than literacy. Or, maybe having difficulties with math is accepted as 'normal,' leading to less need for books on the topic. For whatever reason, math does seem to be a relatively neglected area of intervention. However, math is very important for inclusiveness throughout our lives.

In school, students who find math difficult may be disadvantaged in a number of ways. They may not be able to participate fully in the regular classroom mathematics program. Self-esteem and confidence may fall. The students' potential to succeed in subjects such as science and technical subjects may be reduced. In later years, they may be excluded from some courses of study because of poor math results.

Today's students will all need mathematics when they leave school and get a job. All work places have some need for math, such as timesheets, travel records, taking inventories and so on. Some students will need to have specific vocational math to work in jobs such as woodworking, metal work, cooking or banking. Others, of course, will need to use math at a high level for engineering, science and the like.

All students will also need a basic competence in math to cope with everyday adult life. Without an understanding of math, the students will be disadvantaged to the end of their days. They will always need the skills and the confidence to make good decisions about wages, insurance, loans or any number of other financial transactions.

This chapter deals with the teaching of basic math concepts and skills. Building interest and confidence in math is also seen as an important element in intervention and inclusion.

The section headings in this chapter follow the structure of the **Appendix #3: Math Observation Chart.** The Math Observation Chart may be reproduced and used to informally assess and record individual math difficulties for students. The Math Observation Chart is divided into seven sections, each focusing on a specific area of mathematics. As you assess individual students, specific patterns of difficulty may emerge. The sections in the chart will provide a direct link between the recorded Math Observation Chart and the corresponding strategies in this chapter that will help the student in the specific area(s) of need. The seven sections of the chart have also been reproduced within the main text of Chapter Four.

If you are interested in using the strategies without completing an informal assessment of the student, these sections will easily guide you through the chapter and provide a quick, easy reference tool for specific areas in math. This will enable you to select from the intervention strategies, modifications and adaptations listed to help individuals and small groups of students.

The following forms from the Appendix are referred to in this chapter:

Appendix #3:    Math Observation Chart
Appendix #41:   Parent Guide to Math at Home
Appendix #12:   Addition Chart
Appendix #13:   Subtraction Chart
Appendix #15:   Math Checklist: Addition (single-digit numbers)
Appendix #19:   Math Checklist: Addition (two, two-digit numbers, no regrouping)
Appendix #20:   Math Checklist: Addition (two, two-digit numbers, with regrouping)
Appendix #16:   Math Checklist: Subtraction (single-digit numbers)
Appendix #21:   Math Checklist: Subtraction (two-digit numbers, no exchanging)
Appendix #22:   Math Checklist: Subtraction (two-digit numbers, with exchanging)
Appendix #17:   Math Checklist: Multiplication
Appendix #18:   Math Checklist: Division
Appendix #11:   Counting Chart
Appendix #14:   Multiplication Chart

# Student Feels Negative about Math

## Section 1 – Math Observation Chart

| 1.  *Student feels negative about math.* |
|---|
| Student expresses dislike of mathematics. |
| Student lacks confidence in own ability to solve math problems. |
| Student does not think mathematically in everyday situations. |
| Student expresses having difficulty with mathematics. |
| Student's math difficulties impact the student's classroom achievements. |
| Student needs additional time to complete math tasks compared to peers. |

## The language of math may seem confusing.

Literacy surrounds children in their everyday lives. The writing on a birthday card, the words on the television screen and many other forms of print prepare even the youngest child to understand that written letters represent words. Often children have an easy transition into school-based literacy learning.

But what about mathematics? Although children will often learn about counting and written numbers before they start school, once in school, they are introduced to a whole new set of ideas, words and symbols. Math can often seem much less familiar and less user-friendly than the written word. The words and symbols used can be difficult for students to grasp, and many misunderstandings can occur. For example, one student was quite sure that her teacher had said that the = sign was called *eagles* instead of *equals!*

## It may seem 'normal' to find math difficult.

We often accept that math is 'hard' and that it is quite 'normal' for a student to have difficulties with the subject. In turn, this may mean that some parents and teachers are quite complacent about the students' difficulties. It may also be that we do not expect students to enjoy math.

If we assume that the difficulties are natural, we may not consider the need for appropriate intervention or special arrangements for inclusion.

Sometimes it is even felt that math is a boys' subject. Expectations of what girls can achieve in math may then be lowered. Girls may not be offered support to increase their math performance.

## Parents may find it hard to help with math at home.

Parents are often eager to help their children learn, however they may not know how to build math into their child's daily routine. Often they understand math as counting and learning basic math facts. They may try to introduce their young child to formal algorithms in the hope that this will give them a head start in math at school. Inappropriate 'help' at home can have a negative impact on a student's confidence in math.

## Math is less flexible than literacy.

In literacy, you can often get by with only partial understanding or mastery. For instance, you might be able to make some sense of a story even if you can't read all the words, or you could try to write a letter even if you're not sure how to spell all the words. Mathematics is often less flexible and less open-ended. Often, very definite levels of understanding and skills are required for satisfactory completion of the task.

Students can become defensive, defeated and distressed when they are not sure of what to do in math.

## Understanding difficulties in math can be a challenge.

It can be hard for students to say what is puzzling them. Asking for help or identifying what needs further explanation depends on the student having a reasonable grasp of the topic to begin with. One of the students' biggest challenges in math is to explain what it is that they need help understanding. *"I don't know what I don't understand. All I know is I just don't get it."*

It can also be hard for the teacher to work out what is wrong! One of the teacher's biggest challenges is to locate where, within the concept or process, the student's understanding has failed. *"I went over the whole explanation again, and he still didn't get it."*

## Math skills build like a pyramid.

Each step in mathematical understanding often builds on the previous one in a pyramid fashion and links into other concepts in a logical way. Obviously, it is essential that these math concepts and methods are taught and understood in a definite sequence. A student can easily lose track of an entire sequence of connected ideas. A few days away from school, a few inattentive minutes or difficulties understanding one concept or skill can break the student's grasp of a sequence of connected ideas. What was becoming clear can suddenly become incomprehensible, when just one, perhaps very small, piece of the puzzle is missing.

> *"I only missed a week from school, but when I got back they were doing decimals, and it seemed like they were on a different planet. It was years before I really understood what it was all about. I lost my confidence and went from a good math student to an average one."*

Students vary in their position in the 'pyramid' of math skills. Some students will find math easy to learn, and others will find it much harder. Some will have had excellent groundwork from previous teachers; others may not be so fortunate. Your inclusive classroom will, of course, make allowances for a wide range of individual differences in math experience and ability.

## Good teaching is important.

Good teaching is particularly important in math, because the subject is so dependent on hierarchies of learning. Clear instruction and supervised practice at each stage is vital in laying down the foundations for successful learning. Even students with natural ability can become confused and frustrated by poor teaching. It is not unusual for students to do poorly one year and to excel the next, depending on the quality of the teaching they have received. Although some students do find math easier than others, math is a curriculum area where good teaching can make a substantial difference in the level of performance that students achieve.

## Students may find some math easy, other math difficult.

Although we refer to math as if it were a single subject, it is a collection of diverse concepts and topics. Students who may have an aptitude for one type of math, such as problem solving, might have difficulty in another area, such as mental computation.

## Having difficulties with math can create anxiety and undermine performance.

Anxiety and frustration disrupt clear thinking. Negative emotions, such as anxiety, anger and frustration, can have a very damaging impact on math learning.

Calm, systematic thinking is essential for success in math. Unfortunately, this type of thinking is very quickly disrupted by anxiety or frustration. The student can very rapidly fall into a negative spiral. A small difficulty creates an emotional response, which disrupts thinking and compounds the problem. This leads to more emotion and an ever-widening spiral of difficulty.

> *"I knew I had made a mistake, but when I tried to check my work, my head went into a whirl and I couldn't think straight. I looked at the numbers, but they didn't make any sense at all. I knew it all so well, but I couldn't think clearly."*

## Students 'switch off' when math does not seem relevant.

Perhaps the greatest barrier to successful math learning is lack of apparent relevance and connection to everyday life. Many students will say they only do math in a math lesson in their math books.

We all learn best when we see the relevance of what we learn. Learning is even easier when we find it interesting and reasonably easy. For many students, math seems irrelevant, boring and difficult. Math can often be done without any understanding of the process or its relevance to anything else. We have probably all known students who can calculate pages and pages of correct addition without having any idea of how this skill would be of use or interest to them in their daily lives. Many students develop a negative mindset, because they fail to see the purpose and value of math in school.

Students have different interests and mindsets. Some are naturally drawn towards math, other prefer social topics, art, sports, creating, music and so on. Making connections between math and the students' personal interests is often the key to making math relevant and interesting.

Some students find it difficult to relate the math skills and concepts learned in school to real-life situations. For example, a student may use counting blocks in school to work out the answer to a problem but never think of using blocks or counters in a real-life setting.

Belle's mother explained: *"You know, she has the numbers right up to 100 in the classroom, up there on the wall, and she seems OK with them. But when I tried to show her how to use my tape measure at home, she just didn't get it."*

# Strategies for Making Math a Positive Experience

## Teaching the language of math

✱ Use everyday language and real-life examples alongside the technical words and formal methods when you teach math. Help your students understand that math is an extension of ordinary, everyday activities.

✱ Use math concepts and language whenever you can. Make opportunities for the students to think mathematically in general classroom activities. Use the words and ideas from the math curriculum in other settings, too. Here are some ideas to get you started:

- *"We have used up half the paint. That's 50 percent used up and 50 percent left for the next job."*

- *"Two students are absent today, so 28 minus 2 is 26. That means we have a total of 26 students here today."*

- *"We have five boys and nine girls. That's not equal! How many girls have to go over to the boys' side to make the numbers equal?"*

- *"Let's divide these up equally between you."*

✱ Take extra care that all students understand new mathematical words and symbols. Discuss the new words and symbols, and ask students to show their understanding with practical demonstrations.

- *"What other words do we know that mean the same as 'plus'?"*
- *"Take these beans and show me what three times four looks like."*
- *"Put the total number of balls in the basket."*
- *"Show me half of your counters. . . . Show me half of your page."*

## Treating math difficulties seriously

✱ Identify students who are finding math difficult, and provide appropriate intervention.

✱ Consider whether you need to upgrade your resources and support for students with difficulties in math.

✱ Treat difficulties with math with the same seriousness as you treat difficulties with literacy.

✱ Demonstrate a belief that difficulties in math, like all other subjects, can be effectively managed by appropriate teaching and sufficient practice.

✴ Discourage your students from 'talking down' their math abilities.

✴ Look at the vocational needs of older students. Relate math teaching to real-life math. Do everything you can to assist students to achieve the necessary standard of math to meet their aspirations.

✴ Challenge stereotypes, such as math being too difficult to master or girls not being good at math.

## Making math a positive experience

✴ Be a good role model. Show positive anticipation and enjoyment of math activities yourself.

✴ Provide interesting math games, computer activities and puzzles as part of the range of free-choice activities to promote the idea that math can be fun.

✴ Match the math taught to the student's capabilities, so that all students enjoy success.

## Helping parents to help with math at home

✴ Encourage parents to involve their children in real-life math. You may like to use **Appendix #41: Parent Guide to Math at Home** as a parent information sheet.

✴ Invite parents into your classroom to observe math lessons in action. This allows parents to see the diversity of activities that form part of understanding math.

✴ Run a hands-on math session for the parents, so they can try out the math skills that their child is learning.

✴ Send math work home with clear guidelines, so parents know what is required and how it relates to the development of skills in class.

✴ Create attractive and interesting math displays in school with class samples, so parents are aware of the learning taking place.

✴ Make a list or create activity boxes of practical math activities covering a wide range of areas. Families can read through the lists or borrow the activity boxes so they can do the activities together at home.

✴ When you are putting together a show for the parents to watch, include an item that relates to math, such as some amazing math facts or math puzzles along with the songs, readings and other activities.

✴ Have a wide range of math books that students can borrow from the class library and take home.

## Encouraging risk taking and exploration in math

✷ Emphasize that experimenting and exploring are good ways of doing math.

✷ Show your students by example that you often need to make several attempts at finding a solution. Think aloud, so your students can hear how you think things through and have several possible ways of doing something.

✷ Invite students to suggest alternative working methods or approaches, presenting the clear message that often several correct solutions are possible. For example:

• *"Now how are we going to do this? We need to find out how many sheets of paper we have. Any ideas of the best way to count them?"*

• *"We need to leave some space for the big poster that is coming next week. How shall we estimate how much space to leave?"*

• *"We'll need to keep the scores. Any suggestions on how we could do that?"*

• *"Now how could we do this question in our math book? I think there are two or three good ways to do it . . . maybe more. Any suggestions?"*

✷ Have your students ask older students and adults to solve a set of problems that you assigned. Ask your students to talk about all the different ways that people have used to solve the problem. For example: *"Work out how much water there is in the classroom fish tank; or, calculate how many people there were at the stadium for the game; or, work out the budget for a family trip."* Your students will see that there is often guesswork, approximation and risk-taking involved.

✷ Make a classroom display to demonstrate the range of ways that different people will tackle the same math task. Following are ways that different people would determine how much water the fish tank holds:

• Todd's dad would take the water out of the tank in buckets, and he would count how many buckets he used.

• Tahlia's brother would measure the tank and then figure out the volume.

• Benjamin's mom would look to see if the tank had any writing on it to tell how much it held.

• Sam's grandpa would guess it held the same as three cans of oil from the garage, and so that would be about 30 gallons.

✱ Ask students to explain how they worked something out. Invite other students to describe their methods. As the teacher, you may be able to suggest different ways, too. *"If we are adding 13 + 8, I could count on after 13 for eight numbers, like this: 14, 15, 16, 17, 18, 19, 20, 21. Or, I could figure 3 + 8 = 11 and then add 10 to get 21."*

✱ Look through newspapers and magazines with your students, and discuss which figures were probably exact (a sports score, a date) and which were probably estimated (the size of the crowd at the game, the cost of a new airplane).

✱ Teach students to recognize when an approximation is all that is necessary. Practice estimating answers.

✱ Encourage students to estimate before they begin to calculate as a way of checking their final solutions.

## Understanding how difficulties occur

✱ Students will often think they have understood when they have not, so avoid saying things such as, *"Everyone okay with that? If you are not sure, then come up to my desk."* Some students will not realize they need help!

✱ Students may be self-conscious about having difficulties and feel reluctant to ask for help. Check how well students understand by watching them work. Observe whether they are following the correct procedures.

✱ Avoid asking, *"What don't you understand?"* Being able to explain what you do not understand is very difficult. It needs insight into the task or concept to be able to identify what is confusing or unclear.

✱ Ask a student to think aloud as he works through a troubling task. Listen to the way the student thinks through the problem, and note what procedure he used. Frequently, you can discover the cause of the problem. You will then have an idea of what to do. Often the student is confused with some of the information or rules, or he is using an incorrect method to arrive at the answer. *"I said to myself, six take away nine you can't do. So pretend it's nine take away six, and that's easy."* Or, *"If I start with 203, zero is nothing, so it's just 2, 3, and that's 23."*

✱ Ask the student to explain the method used to arrive at the answer. You may use the following approaches:

- *"Tell me, what did you do first?"*
- *"What did you say to yourself next?"*
- *"Show me how you used the blocks to work that out."*
- *"Let me hear you counting that again."*

* Look at the student's work to see if you can find any systematic errors in how they work. For instance, what is the pattern in these errors?

$$12 + 3 = 14 \qquad 11 + 9 = 19 \qquad 15 + 4 = 18$$

The correct answer is one more than the student's answer. In this example, it would be a good idea to check how the student is working with counters or fingers, if used. Chances are, these students are using the first number as the starting point for counting: $12 + 3 = 12, 13, 14$

* Use tests or independent class assignments, so you can be sure the student is doing the work correctly. Look at the errors that occur to find out exactly what the student is doing wrong. Obviously, if you find students have not mastered the topic you have just taught, provide additional teaching, support and practice.

## Using inclusive strategies

* Individualize instruction, so all students have work they understand.

* In any classroom, there will be marked individual differences in students' math abilities. It is essential that your classroom program have a range of levels of instruction to ensure that all students are included in a program that meets their individual needs.

* A student's difficulty in math could be due to missed schooling or poor teaching at an earlier stage. Keep an open mind about the student's capabilities until you have seen how he responds to good teaching at his level.

* A difficulty in one area of math does not mean that the student will have difficulties with other areas. For instance, a student may have problems with mental computation but be brilliant at problem solving. Allow for flexible grouping according to the type of math activity.

* Monitor students' progress in math very carefully. Learning math is very easily disrupted by small gaps in understanding. Take particular care to make sure that students really have grasped the work they are doing before you introduce new work.

* Take into account the different rates of learning in your class. The students who understand a topic quickly can move on to the next stage as soon as they are ready. Other students who learn more slowly will need a longer period of instruction and a more extended period of consolidation of skills and understanding.

* Although your students will be working on various levels of difficulty in your math program, it is usually possible to have the whole class work together on the same topic or area of study—for example, timetables and schedules.

# Differentiating a Math Activity to Suit Varying Levels of Math Development

| All students | General discussion on when and where students have seen or used timetables and schedules. |
|---|---|
| Level 1 | Students are making a timeline of their daily routines, from getting up to going to bed, including their school schedule. |
| Level 2 | Students are reading simple timetables to find departure and arrival times. |
| Level 3 | Students are planning trips, using timetables to coordinate several modes of transportation. |
| Level 4 | Students are planning trips across different time zones and over the international date line. |

## Providing plenty of practice

* After providing clear instruction and demonstration, have a guided practice session. While students work through the task, monitor their performance and prompt them as necessary to help them stay on track.

* The development of good math skills is very dependent on practice. Allow enough practice time for all students to feel confident applying what you have taught them.

* Students who find math difficult often make mistakes and work slowly. These students are especially at risk of missing out on the practice they really need. Make sure these students receive extra practice material, and allow enough time for them to work through all the practice items.

* Select similar exercises from several parallel books, and make booklets for intensive practice. This means the students will have enough opportunity to practice but will have new activities as they work through the booklet.

* Always make sure that students who have been absent from school have adequate time for catch-up learning and sufficient practice to enable them to absorb what they missed.

* Before introducing a new topic, provide all students with a thorough review of previously taught foundation concepts and skills, and provide some practice time. If any students do not understand the preliminary work, revise their program so they have an opportunity to master the prerequisite material before moving to the more difficult levels.

★ Use computer math programs for extra practice in basic skills. Programs can be used to reinforce an activity that has been done in class.

## Monitoring and supporting

★ Make sure students understand that the assignments match their level of competence. *"See, this is great work you did yesterday, but today you have some different shapes to work with."*

★ Arrange for a classmate to be a 'math buddy' to provide help when needed.

★ Provide appropriate intervention based on students' individual needs so they don't have to leave tasks unfinished or incorrect because they did not understand the assignment.

★ Use sketches to turn math problems into pictures.

★ Provide an example of an almost identical problem alongside the new task.

★ Write the steps in the process as part of the worksheet.

## Building confidence in math

★ Build confidence and understanding by supportive coaching, which provides the student with feedback in areas where they are succeeding: *"You are great at getting your ruler right at the beginning of the line."*

★ Celebrate what the student can achieve, and work on what he/she has found difficult.

★ Suggest that students write a note next to items or concepts they do not understand. As you are grading their assignment, you can see where they knew they had a problem.

★ Avoid using worksheets or books that look like 'little kids' stuff.' Select materials that have illustrations and examples that suit the student's age and interests. It is just as easy to add up hamburgers or baseball scores as it is to add up toy bears or little ducks!

★ Provide a reference sheet with examples of all the previously taught skills. Label all the examples. Also label all the items on the student's worksheet, so they can match up the example with the current task. For instance, label an example of *Subtraction with Regrouping,* and also label the new questions on the assignment *Subtraction with Regrouping.*

★ Be sure that a student with a reading difficulty can read the math worksheet. Provide extra support if necessary.

✱ Keep the atmosphere as relaxed as possible. Avoid using timed tests or rushing students to finish work.

✱ Let the students select the level of work they feel they can handle.

✱ Avoid making the students say their grades in front of their peers.

✱ Set up extra, optional math activities to support class work, and allow students to determine whether or not they would like to join the group doing them.

## Making math relevant

✱ Be creative in the examples you use when teaching math. Relate math to topics such as the environment, social issues, family, sports, art, construction, music, pets, food and so on, so students can visualize and relate to the math you are teaching.

✱ Have students look for any math-related information in their homes and community: a shopping advertisement, a sports announcement, a label from a container, a postage stamp, etc. Collect the items at school, and then discuss them, create collections and draw out math understanding.

- *"What weight is a regular box of cereal?"*
- *"What other things weigh about the same?"*
- *"How come the cereal box is so big compared to a packet of cheese?"*
- *"How much does it cost to go to the game?"*
- *"How much would it cost for everyone in the class to go?"*

✱ Create links between math and real-life interests. With math calculation worksheets, talk to the students about how the calculations relate to real life: *"Today we are doing this math sheet of multiplication. For 13 x 12, you could imagine that you were a farmer putting new chicks into their cages. You have 13 cages with 12 chicks in each. Or, maybe you are making cookies, and you have 13 trays with 12 cookies on each. Or, you have 13 bags with 12 suckers in each bag."*

✱ Relate math work to your students' individual interests by creating parallel worksheets. The math is exactly the same in each version of the sheet. Sheets can relate to the environment, creative activities, favorite sports, money or whatever interests them. For instance, most basic word problems can easily relate to the number of birds in a rain forest, measurements for a craft project, scores in a game, or the balance of a savings account.

✱ Use every opportunity within your classroom to show how math is used over and over again in many different situations that are useful and interesting.

★ Ask the students to talk to their families about how they use math. Make a classroom display of the results.

- Gina's grandmother counts her stitches when she knits.
- Teddy's sister gives change in the supermarket.
- Sunni's Dad measures the wood for the houses he builds.

★ If you have a math corner or an area where you keep math materials, use it as often as you can, right across the curriculum.

- *"Jack, could you get the counters from the math shelf to help us keep the score in this game."*

- *"Hey! We can use the math tape measure to measure and see if we can get the new art desk through the door."*

- *"If we use the math blocks, we can figure out how we can all fit in the school bus for our trip."*

★ All learning is more interesting if it links into everyday interests. Encourage your students to keep interesting math information in journals, charts or a database.

- Keep track of your local team's baseball scores.
- See how accurate the local weather forecast is.
- Develop a database on the students. Make a spreadsheet of the information.
- Make a timetable of favorite TV shows.

★ Encourage the students to think mathematically, and highlight when they have done so.

- *"I liked the way you used math to see if you have written enough for your journal."*
- *"That was good math thinking to get all those things packed away in that box."*

★ Suggest activities that involve several areas of the curriculum.

- *"Write a story. You must include some counting and measuring in the story."*
- *"Plant several different types of seeds. Make a chart to show how they grow."*
- *"Make a score sheet for your personal spelling tests. Track your performance for four weeks."*

★ Ask your students to look around the classroom and challenge each other.

- *"Find six things with acute angles in the classroom."*
- *"Find patterns of three."*
- *"Find examples of symmetry."*

- *"Find something that has over 1,000 parts."*
- *"What is the largest written number in the room?"*
- *"Find 20 things that are less than one inch long."*

★ At the end of each school day, give the students a summary of the day's learning. Include not only formal math lessons but any other math that occurred incidentally. *"We did quite a bit of math by figuring out which students are old enough to sign up for the new athletic team." . . . "In designing our class newsletter, we had a lot to fit on the page. All that measuring and trying out the sizes was good math work."*

# Student Has Difficulties Understanding the Number System

## Section 2 – Math Observation Chart

| 2. Student has difficulties in understanding the number system. |
| --- |
| Student makes errors when counting. |
| Student makes errors when working with place value. |
| Student makes errors in addition and subtraction. |
| Student does not understand the relationship between addition and subtraction (e.g., cannot use the missing addend to solve subtraction). |

## Counting

Remembering a long sequence of numbers can be difficult for many young students, or for older students with significant developmental disabilities. Counting is a foundation skill, and many students with difficulties need explicit teaching of the basics before they can move on to more advanced work.

Just saying the numbers in order is not of any real value. You must be able to apply this in a useful way. You need to be able to:

- Recite the numbers and relate them one by one to objects.
- Match a written number to a spoken word.
- Stop at the right place in the counting sequence.
- Count in reverse.
- Make a decision about what sort of counting to use. When is it better to count by 10s? What if there are so many that you can't count every single one?)

## Place value

As a very young student, you learn that the number 3 refers to three single items. Later you come across the numeral 37 or 3,931 and find out that the 3 in these examples is not three single items at all, but a far larger quantity. Understanding place value is, of course, an absolute foundation of math. The only difference between 109 and 901 is the position of two of the numbers.

Place value is a clever system, because it allows us to use just 10 symbols to represent an infinite range of numbers. However, students with learning difficulties often find the system very confusing. Without understanding place value, even basic counting is much more difficult. As an adult, you know the number that comes after 3,729, even though you have never learned to count by rote to that number.

Zero is particularly confusing for some young learners. Usually children learn that zero is nothing and think that whenever they see a 0, they can ignore it, remove it or pretend it doesn't exist. Although 0 is used to represent nothing, it is also used as a place holder in numbers such as 203 and 190, and as such, cannot be ignored. This is a hard concept for some students to handle.

## Addition and subtraction of numbers and application of missing addend

Understanding the addition and subtraction of numbers is a fundamental concept that supports later development in math. Once students understand that a number can be made up of two or more smaller numbers, they can begin to manipulate that knowledge. If you know that 3 + 4 = 7, then you also know that 4 + 3 = 7. If you know that the number 12 is made up of 4 + 8, then 12 - 4 is a simple matter of deduction that does not require counting.

Understanding halves and doubles is a very useful part of addition and subtraction and can lead to skilled mental computation.

# Strategies for Building Math Skills in Understanding the Number System

## Working with counting

* Counting real objects is very important, as well as using counting rhymes, songs and stories. Provide young students with plenty of practice counting real things.

* For older students who are still learning to count, make sure you frequently count out loud in the classroom as you distribute books, count students and organize activities.

* Discourage rapid counting before the student can touch count. Some young students can recite the number sequence without understanding. It is better to count slowly and clearly.

* Get students to notice numbers all around them. *"What is your street number? . . . What is the number of the house next door or across the street? . . . How many TV channels do you receive? . . . How many miles has the family car traveled?"*

✱ In the classroom, number the desks, chairs, coat hooks, shelves, worksheets, books and any other objects that can consolidate the students' awareness of numbers.

✱ Count objects of different size; some students think that there are more objects if they are large in size. Teach that the number 5 is the same, regardless of whether you are counting 5 elephants or 5 ants.

✱ If students find touch counting (touching and counting items one by one) difficult, introduce the easier activity of saying names and touching. Provide students with toy items, and ask them to touch and name each one in turn: *"Duck, cat, dog, cat, duck, duck, dog . . ."* You can do the same with colored dots or shapes. The student touches and names the color: *"Red, blue, blue, yellow, red . . ."*

✱ The easiest form of counting is to count all items in a set. So start at this level. Provide various objects to count, and encourage accurate touch counting. Gradually build up the number of items the student can count, always adding just one more. Do not suddenly shift from counting, say, three items to counting 12 items.

✱ Counting and stopping at a given number is a more difficult task than just counting everything in a set. Once the student can accurately count an entire set, ask them to count out a specific quantity from a larger set. For example, put 25 counters on the desk, and ask the student to count out only 12.

✱ Provide plenty of explicit teaching, relating the link between written numbers and the spoken sequence. Give the students number sets written on separate cards. The students can put the cards in the correct sequence and count the sequence.

✱ Always have a clear number line in view in your classroom or on the students' desks. Students will be able to check the number sequence when they need to.

✱ For older students, provide a number line for their math books. A clearly marked, metric measuring ruler can be used as a reliable number line.

✱ Encourage students to notice the numbering system in books: *"How many pages does this book have?"*

✱ Ask students to number every page in their workbooks.

✱ Show students how to use the word count in their computer software when they write and work towards specific word totals.

✱ Encourage students to recognize small quantities without counting. Many students with difficulties count each item in any display. Students should be able to look at up to five items and know how many there are without counting.

✱ Counting in reverse is an important skill. Model this type of counting as you check off students leaving the room: *"28, 27, 26 . . . ."*

✱ Have students do 'space takeoff' counting, where they count backwards to lift off.

✱ Use counting in 2s and 10s as you work with the students to show them how to vary the way they count.

✱ Have students help with classroom inventory to develop an awareness of different types of counting. Is it important to count every piece of paper, or can the students use the knowledge that the paper is packaged with 100 sheets per ream?

✱ Number the days of the year from 1 to 365, and keep track in your class of where you are in the year, day by day. For example, *"Today is the 96th day of the year."*

✱ Talk about the position of numbers on a number line: *"Which number comes right after 39? What number comes before 99?"*

✱ Make a number line and omit some of the numbers. Provide the missing numbers to the students, and see how quickly they can determine their correct positions.

✱ Teach estimating skills. Encourage students to guess large quantities, and then check their guesswork with some serious counting. Have students check how close the estimates are to the actual count.

✱ Give the students two clear jars, partly filled with beads, beans or other small items. Tell them how many beads are in one jar, and ask them to estimate how many in the other. Do the same with beads on a string, grains of rice on a plate and so on.

## Working with place value

✱ Give plenty of counting activities, where items are grouped into 10s and clearly marked. Have boxes, bags and jars and lots of different types of real objects to count, such as paperclips, ribbons, shells, pencils, beads, etc. At first, just count in tens and label your groups: *"We have six bags of shells, so that's 10, 20, 30, 40, 50, 60 shells altogether. We'll put 60 on the desk to show how many we have."*

✱ Put together sealed packets of items in sets of 10, 20, 50 and 100. You also could look in hardware stores for prepackaged small items (such as screws, nails, or hooks), which often come in 10s, 50s and 100s. Ask the students to put together various quantities without opening any of the boxes. This means they have to work without counting one by one. (*"Put 250 screws on the table. . . . Give me 320 buttons."*) The students should write the numbers to consolidate their understanding of place value.

* Because students cannot 'see' the 10s in a number such as 35, they are often confused and think that they have a 3 and a 5. Show them how the number is built up from the number 30 + 5 by using two layers of cards. (Fig. 1)

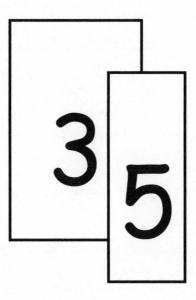

**Figure 1: Using card layers to build two-digit numbers**

* Continue to use the layer system to teach three- and four-digit numbers. (Fig. 2)

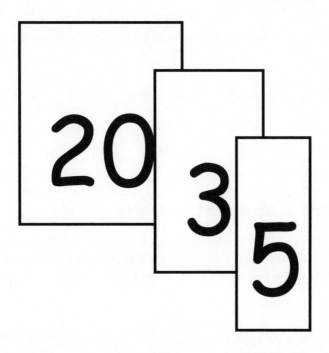

**Figure 2: Using card layers to build three-digit numbers**

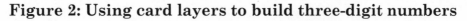

✴ Have students watch a counter (such as a pedometer or odometer) as the numbers increase, for example, from 49 to 50 or 99 to 100, and talk to the students about how the place values change. *"We had nine tens and nine ones, and now we have one hundred."*

✴ Encourage students to navigate through books using the index and page numbers. Use indexes and page numbers as a teaching tool for place value. Ask students to say where a certain page number will be found: *"Page 103 will be just after 100 but way before the 200s. ... If I am on page 44 and I want page 85, I have to go forward about 40 pages."*

✴ Use page numbers and indexes in an informal assessment of the students' grasp of place value. When asked to find a page, do they search at random for the number? Can they explain how to look for a particular page?

✴ For older students, have a line that goes up to at least 1,000, with the changes in place value clearly marked.

✴ Make a collection of whole numbers. Have students find and bring in any numbers from any source and write the numbers clearly on strips of paper. Pin the numbers on a board in order of size, rearranging the display as new numbers are introduced. Encourage the students to decide where a new number has to be positioned. *"Bobbie has found the number 150 on his lunchbox. Where does it go? That is correct; it comes in between 120 and 275."*

✴ For younger students, create a number line 1-100 with numbers missing. Have the students fill in the missing numbers.

✴ For older students, create a column of numbers in chronological order with some digits missing. Have the students fill in the missing numbers.

2321
2322
2*23
23*4
232*   and so on

## Working with addition and subtraction of numbers

✴ Accept that some students with learning difficulties will not be able to memorize the number facts. Encourage these students to use the number charts. You can copy the **Appendix #12: Addition Chart** and the **Appendix #13: Subtraction Chart** for your students.

✴ Teach students to use a calculator correctly. Many students with learning difficulties struggle endlessly with basic number facts, when the use of a calculator would allow them to succeed with more interesting work.

* Have a number of the week, and have students really focus on this number. For example, if 5 is the number of the week, some of the following activities may be appropriate.

  - Make patterns of five with pebbles, shells, bricks, cups, pencils or any items available.
  - Photograph or draw your patterns of five.
  - Make more patterns of five with markers, ink stamps or paper shapes.
  - Find patterns of five around you: five fingers, five toes, five petals.
  - How many different ways can you arrange five things?

* For students who are finding math difficult, *Number of the Week* can be a good exercise right through to large numbers such as 25, 100 or even larger.

* Make a class poster of every number that you focus on. This remains posted so that in later weeks, students with difficulties can refer to it.

* Encourage students to recognize number patterns without counting. Hold up various number patterns, and ask the students to say how many things they see. (Fig. 3)

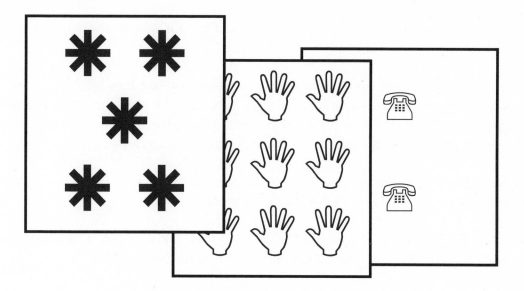

**Figure 3: Recognizing number patterns**

* With the students' help, develop a number chart showing all the possible number combinations up to 10. The two forms **Appendix #12: Addition Chart** and **Appendix #13: Subtraction Chart** can be reproduced for individual students to use.

* Show students how the addition chart can be used to find the answers to subtraction problems. *("If 2 + 5 = 7, then what is 7 - 2?")* For students with learning difficulties, you may need to demonstrate this with real objects over and over again.

✷ Play matching games for students to practice basic number facts. Write single numbers and symbols (+ - =) on small note cards. Give each student about 20 cards. Then write a whole number up on the board. Can the students make the number with their cards? For example, if you write 9, students can show cards 3 + 3 + 3 or 10 - 1. Once the student uses the cards, they are discarded. Continue the game until at least one student has discarded all of his cards. This student is the winner.

✷ Count in 3s or 4s or any other number to teach the intervals between numbers. For more able students, vary the starting point to make it harder. For example, start from 2 and count in 3s: *2, 5, 8, 11, 14 . . . .*

✷ Make doubles of numbers using paint. Fold a piece of paper in half. Use wet paint to make dots on one half only. Immediately fold the paper over so that the wet paint makes an equal number of dots on the other half of the page. Have the students build a chart of double number facts: The number 6, when doubled, is 12. . . . The number 7, when doubled, is 14.

✷ Halves are harder to learn than doubles. Teach doubles and halves together: *"The number 11 doubled is 22, so half of 22 is 11."*

✷ Make a classroom chart of doubles and halves and keep it where students can refer to it as they work.

✷ Teach odd and even numbers. You can show students how odd numbers are the numbers that do not have equal halves, so there is always an 'odd one out' when an odd number of things is shared. Use sets of beads or other small items to share between two containers, and record whether you can split the number of items equally or not.

✷ Ask the students to make patterns using odd and even numbers of buttons. What sorts of patterns won't work with an odd number of buttons?

✷ Make an individual or classroom chart of odd and even numbers, so students who do not yet understand the concept can still use the information when needed.

# Student Has Difficulties with the Four Operations

## Section 3 – Math Observation Chart

| **3. Student has difficulties with the four operations.** |
| --- |
| The student uses tangible objects to count without real understanding. |
| The student has difficulty applying standard algorithms. |
| The student makes errors in addition. |
| The student makes errors in subtraction. |
| The student makes errors in multiplication. |
| The student makes errors in division. |

## Using tangible objects to count

Many students are confused by counters, chips, blocks and other manipulative materials that are frequently used in school for curriculum support. Students often do not realize that these items are supposed to represent real objects and are not ends in themselves. This makes math work abstract and uninteresting. Does it really matter if you have ten counters?

> *"It was only when I started teacher training myself, that I realized those wooden blocks were only meant to stand in for real objects. I don't think we ever thought about it at the time. Didn't we ever wonder why the teacher was so interested in how many blocks we had, day after day?"*

Many of us sometimes use our fingers to count, or we make tally marks as adults as an aid in calculation. In itself, this is not a problem. However, students with learning difficulties may become confused as they use their fingers, or they may scatter tally marks, so the marks are difficult to count accurately.

## Understanding algorithms

Students frequently find written algorithms difficult to understand, because often they don't understand that what they are seeing when they look at 6 + 5 or 10 - 3 is a coded set of instructions that requires physical or mental action.

## Addition

Addition is the easiest of the four operations to understand, because it is very concrete. If you see 6 + 5, then you do have a real 6 and a real 5. It relates directly to earlier work that the students should have done on composition and decomposition of numbers.

There is a developmental sequence in the addition methods that students use. These methods range from concrete, physical counting through to mental deduction or recall of known facts.

The following chart appears in the Appendix as **Appendix #15: Math Checklist: Addition (single-digit numbers).** You may reproduce it and record your observations of individual students.

## Developmental Sequence for Addition of 4 + 5

| Strategy | Student's response | ✓ |
|---|---|---|
| Counts each, counts all | 1, 2, 3, 4    1, 2, 3, 4, 5    1, 2, 3, 4, 5, 6, 7, 8, 9 | |
| Counts whole group once | 1, 2, 3, 4, 5, 6, 7, 8, 9 | |
| Counts on from first number | 5, 6, 7, 8, 9 | |
| Counts on from largest number | 6, 7, 8, 9 | |
| Works from a known fact | 4 + 4 = 8,  8 + 1 = 9 | |
| Retrieves known fact | 9 | |

Students with learning difficulties may well prefer to stay with the safest, most concrete methods long after their classmates have moved on to more abstract strategies. They may need explicit instruction to learn how to use the more advanced strategies.

The format of the math problem can also challenge students. Math problems begin with horizontal positioning, which like reading, is read from left to right.

> *2 + 3 = 5*
>
> *In this example, you start on the left and literally read across, taking each symbol in turn.*

Later, the math problem changes to vertical positioning, and to solve this problem, the calculation starts on the right and moves towards the left.

$$23$$
$$\underline{+\ 42}$$

*In this example, you start on the right, adding vertically. Then you move one place to the left and add vertically again.*

You can use Appendix #19: Math Checklist: Addition (two, two-digit numbers, no regrouping) and Appendix #20: Math Checklist: Addition (two, two-digit numbers, with regrouping) to record your students' working methods.

## Subtraction

Subtraction is much more abstract than addition. Many students are tricked by the fact that the numbers they see written on their sheets are not two separate quantities. For example, with 8 - 2 you start with a real 8, but the 2 is already there, 'hidden' within the 8. Many students with learning difficulties will get out eight blocks and then another two to start this calculation off.

As with addition, there is a developmental sequence in the way subtraction is handled.

The following chart appears in the Appendix as **Appendix #16: Math Checklist: Subtraction (single digits).** You may reproduce it and record your observations of individual students.

## Developmental Sequence for Subtraction of 8 - 3

| Strategy | Student's response | ✓ |
|---|---|---|
| **Counts all and then counts back** | 1, 2, 3, 4, 5, 6, 7, 8 ,      7, 6, 5 | |
| **Counts back from largest number** | 7, 6, 5 | |
| **Counts up from the lowest number** | 4, 5, 6, 7, 8 | |
| **Works from a known fact** | $8 - 2 = 6,\ 6 - 1 = 5$ | |
| **Retrieves known fact** | 5 | |

Many students do not apply existing knowledge of addition facts to subtraction. Instead, they slowly and carefully count to work out number facts that they already 'know' in another form. For example they may know that 3 + 7 = 10, but they work out 10 - 3 by counting. Subtraction is much more effective if the student understands the composition and decomposition of numbers.

Vertical subtraction requires the student to work from right to left, but also to remember to take the bottom number from the top number. Subtraction with regrouping introduces some further challenges in the process of having to 'borrow' between columns. All of this can really confuse the student.

You can use **Appendix #21: Math Checklist: Subtraction (two, two-digit numbers, no exchanging)** and **Appendix #22: Math Checklist: Subtraction (two, two-digit numbers, with exchanging)** to record your students' working methods.

## Multiplication

Multiplication is most easily understood by students with learning difficulties as repeated addition. Obviously, this can involve very tedious repeated calculation to arrive at an answer. However, for some students this is the best option, if they find rote learning difficult.

Often the student will assume that all the numbers they see are tangible quantities, so that looking at 4 x 3, they will get out four blocks and then three blocks.

Students may also get confused between + and x, as the two symbols look similar apart from their orientation.

There are several ways of arriving at a multiplication fact such as 4 x 5 = 20. The following chart appears in the Appendix as **Appendix #17: Math Checklist: Multiplication.** You may reproduce it and record your observations of individual students.

### Developmental Sequence for Multiplication of 4 x 5

| Strategy | Student's response | ✓ |
|---|---|---|
| **Counts up in fives** | 5, 10, 15,  20 | |
| **Counts up in fours** | 4, 8 ,12, 16, 20 | |
| **Recites times table** | 1 x 5 = 5, 2 x 5 = 10,  3 x 5 = 15, 4 x 5 = 20 | |
| **Works from a known fact** | 5 x 5 = 25,  25 − 5 = 20 | |
| **Retrieves known fact** | 20 | |

## Division

Division can be understood as repeated subtraction, although many students are comfortable with the 'sharing' concept through real-life experiences. The relationship between multiplication and division is a very important link for the students to grasp.

The symbol ÷ can cause confusion, as it is very similar to the subtraction sign.

The following chart appears in the Appendix as **Appendix #18: Math Checklist: Division.** You may reproduce it and record your observations of individual students.

### Developmental Sequence for Division of 15 ÷ 3

| Strategy | Student's response | ✓ |
|---|---|---|
| **Counts off groups of three** | 1, 2, 3,   1, 2, 3,   1, 2, 3,    1, 2, 3 | |
| **Counts in threes** | 3, 6, 9, 12, 15 *or* 15, 12, 9, 6, 3 | |
| **Works from a known fact** | 5 + 5 + 5 = 15 or 3 x 5 = 15 | |
| **Retrieves known fact** | 5 | |

## Strategies for Understanding the Number System

### Using tangible materials

* Encourage all students to use concrete supports, such as blocks, charts or fingers, if needed. Remember, many adults still use their fingers to count or calculate!

* Provide students with a range of interesting materials, such as shells, buttons, small toys, pebbles and colored papers for support in math work.

* Continue to use familiar counting aids, such as Cuisenaire rods and Unifix cubes, from one school year to the next, so students have continuity of support and learning materials.

* For older students, provide more discreet forms of support, such as a ruler or number line, which can be used for counting, or a printed 'abacus' for support with addition. You can copy the **Appendix #11: Counting Chart.**

* Make your teaching explicit and clear for those students who have difficulty. Model the task. Provide a practical demonstration and a verbal commentary. Invite the students to participate to hold their interest. Aim to have students contribute about 50 percent of the thinking and action.

*"Now let me see. What do I have to do? Yes, I have to do some adding. We have a 6 and a 3. So let's get out the blocks. Can you do that?*

*Straighten the blocks, so they are easy to count. Can you handle the counting? That's looking good. Now can you write that number down?"*

✱ Make sure that your students understand that the counters, blocks, etc., used in class are simply convenient substitutes for real objects. *"It would be very hard to count the pigs in the farmyard. Let's pretend these blocks are the pigs. Now see how easy it is to count them? They don't run away like real pigs!"*

✱ Use concrete classroom situations that occur outside of the math lesson. *"We have eight students running, six swimming, and five at music class. Take out the blocks, and figure out how many students are at activities."*

✱ If students use fingers to count, watch to make sure they are using them correctly. For instance, some will double count the same finger or always call their thumb number 1.

✱ If students use tally marks, check to see that they are arranging them neatly, so they can count them accurately. Encourage older students to tally in groups of 10 to make counting easier.

✱ Some students will make a fresh set of tally marks for every calculation. This takes up a lot of time. Provide a copy of **Appendix #11: Counting Chart,** so students do not need to constantly draw and count their tally marks.

## Understanding algorithms

✱ Be sure that students are confident with the number system and have had the experience of composition and decomposition of numbers before you introduce formal recording of algorithms.

✱ Teach the concept and the sign of equivalence (=) as a starting point. Have the students match up pairs of cards and use the equal sign (=) to show equivalence. (Fig. 4)

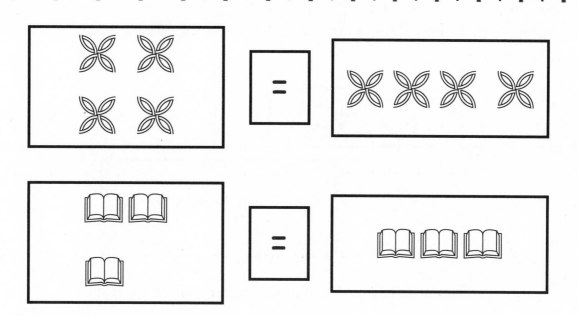

**Figure 4: Matching up equivalent picture cards**

★ Make sure your students understand that the symbols +, -, x and ÷ are codes for action. Every time they see one of these signs, they have to do something, either physically or mentally.

★ Explain to the students that each of these signs has several names. For example, *"We call this symbol (+) add or plus. . . . We call this symbol (-) minus, take away or subtract."*

★ Make a classroom chart of the symbols and the words that can be used to describe their functions.

★ As each symbol is introduced, provide students with practical activities, where they have to physically add, subtract, multiply or divide.

6 + 3     The students may get six books and then another three books.
12 - 5     The students may lay 12 counters on their desks and then hide five counters.

★ Have one student manipulate some objects, such as placing six pencils on the table and then adding two more. Have the other students write down the algorithm for what happened: 6 + 2 = 8.

★ Teach the students that the first number they see in an algorithm is the number (a real quantity) where they need to start. *"I have to start with 12."*

★ Teach the students that the symbol and the number that follows the symbol describe the 'job' that has to be done. Ask students to circle the symbol and the number and tell you what job must be done. *"I have to take away 7. . . . I have to divide it into 3. . . . I have to multiply it by 4."* (Fig. 5)

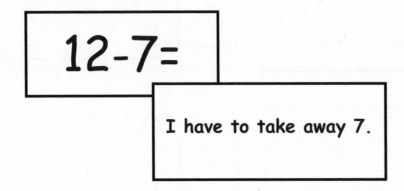

**Figure 5: Reading the symbol as the 'job' to be done**

* When working with a vertical calculation, teach the student to recognize that the number at the top is the starting point and the sign and the number at the bottom is the job to be done. (Fig. 6)

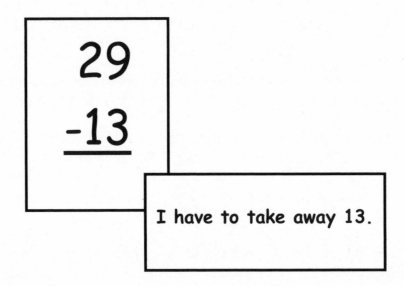

**Figure 6: Reading the 'job' in a vertical calculation**

## Understanding addition

* Observe the students to see which methods they are using for addition. **Appendix #15: Math Checklist: Addition** may be used to document the strategies a student uses and any observations. Look at the list of methods, and see if it is possible to introduce the student to a more advanced level.

✱ Teach addition facts in class. Take a few minutes each day to rehearse quick recall of number facts.

✱ Provide students with a copy of the **Appendix #12: Addition Chart.**

✱ For students with persistent difficulties with addition, allow the use of a calculator in place of mental computation.

✱ Many students with learning difficulties always use a concrete counting method, even when they know some number facts. Have the students complete an addition facts worksheet and use a highlighter to highlight the addition facts they know for memory. Encourage the students to work through the sheet, simply entering the numbers in the places they have highlighted.

✱ Teach the students 'counting on' to replace the 'counting all' method. Tell the students, *"We are going to do some counting. I am going to start, and then when I stop, you are going to continue on with the counting."* For example, you count *"one, two, three, four, five,"* and the student picks up *"six seven, eight, nine, ten."*

✱ For a group of students, place a pile of buttons in the middle of the table. Each student takes a handful of buttons. The counting goes around the table, with each student counting on from the previous total, until they have determined the total number of buttons. For example, the first student counts *"one, two, three,"* the next student continues *"four, five, six, seven, eight, nine,"* and so on, until all the buttons have been counted.

✱ Prepare some picture cards with various items. Write the number of items on each card. Give each student two cards, and ask the student to work out the total, by saying only the number on the first card and then counting the rest of the items on the second card one by one. So, for example, the student will look at the first card and say *"six"* and then continue by counting the rest of the items on the second card: *"seven, eight, nine, ten."*

✱ Encourage the students to use the 'trick' of counting on from the largest number to make the task easier.

✱ Give the students a sheet of simple addition and ask them to underline the largest number in each algorithm. Then provide supervised practice with counting on from that number. They may need to make tally marks for the smaller number to assist with counting on. (Fig. 7)

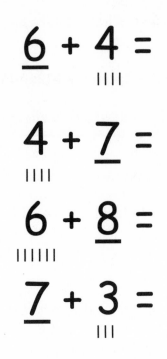

**Figure 7: Using tally marks for 'counting on'**

✻ Use the **Appendix #11: Counting Chart** to support students who need something tangible to count.

✻ Teach students to look for known addition facts and to work from there.

If $6 + 6 = 12$, then $6 + 7 =$
If $5 + 5 = 10$, then $5 + 4 =$

✻ Before introducing the concept of vertical addition, thoroughly review place value, as students may have forgotten the basics. In particular, practice making sets of 10. For example, have the students count out beads into groups of 10 and record the number: *"Three groups of 10 and four left over is 34."*

✻ Use concrete materials to support early work on vertical addition with regrouping.

## Understanding subtraction

✻ Observe the students and see which subtraction methods they are using. **Appendix #21: Math Checklist: Subtraction** can be used to note the strategies a student uses and your observations. Look at the list of methods, and see if it is possible to introduce the student to a more advanced level.

✷ Teach (or re-teach) how to interpret written algorithms: *"Start with the first number. The sign and the next number tell you what to do."*

✷ Teach subtraction facts in your class. Take a few minutes each day to review quick recall of number facts.

✷ Do not introduce subtraction until your students are confident with the concept of composition and decomposition of numbers (see previous section). Teach number facts in clusters of four related facts. For example:

$$4+5=9 \qquad 5+4=9 \qquad 9-4=5 \qquad 9-5=4$$

✷ Provide students with a copy of the **Appendix #13: Subtraction Chart.**

✷ For students with persistent difficulties with subtraction, allow use of a calculator in place of mental computation.

✷ Teach students to think about differences between numbers to aid in subtraction. Prepare cards with one pair of numbers. The students look at the differences between the two numbers and sort the cards into piles: *"The numbers on these cards all have a difference of 3. This pile has numbers with a difference of 5."* (Fig. 8)

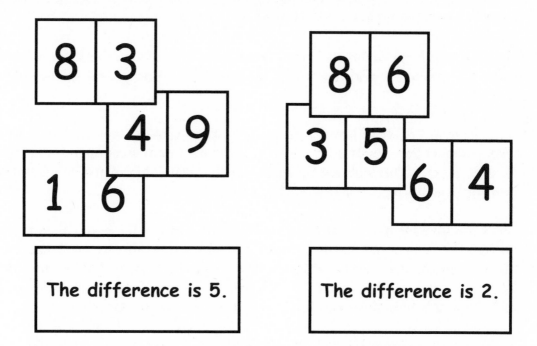

Figure 8: Grouping cards with the same differences

✴ Provide students with structured worksheets, where they are encouraged to use reason (not count) to arrive at the answer.

If 9 - 6 = 3, then 9 − 5 =

# Understanding multiplication

✴ Observe the students and see which multiplication methods they are using. **Appendix #17: Math Checklist: Multiplication** can be used to note the strategies a student uses and your observations. Look at the list of methods, and see if it is possible to introduce the student to a more advanced level.

✴ Familiarize your students with the meaning of the symbol x by making simple instruction cards for them to follow.

Jump x 4.
Draw 5 dogs x 2.
Show me 8 counters x 3.

✴ For students who find it difficult to sort out the difference between the symbols + and x, teach them that x is like + 'rolling along.' Students can often relate the idea of addition 'rolling along' to the repeated addition needed for multiplication. The sign tells them how many times the addition has to be repeated, or 'rolled.'

✴ Have the students create their own charts of multiplication facts. Start with a small chart, for example a grid of 5 x 5. Then introduce larger charts as the students gain competence.

✴ If students are ready to learn their multiplications tables, encourage them to recite the whole number fact: *1 x 2 = 2, 2 x 2 = 4, 2 x 3 = 6* . . . and discourage simply counting up: *2., 4, 6, 8* . . . . The counting up method is of little value in real-life situations when immediate access to the information is needed.

✴ Show the students how answers are repeated. If you learn 5 x 6, you already know 6 x 5. So once the student has learned some of the tables, they already know part of the other tables. For example, once the students have learned the 1s, 2s and 3s times tables, they know 51 of the 100 facts from the table below!  By the time the student learns the 8s table, they only have three new facts to learn (8 x 8, 8 x 9 and 8 x 10).

The following **Appendix #14: Multiplication Chart** may be reproduced from the Appendix. (Fig. 9)

|    | 1  | 2  | 3  | 4  | 5  | 6  | 7  | 8  | 9  | 10  |
|----|----|----|----|----|----|----|----|----|----|-----|
| 1  | 1  | 2  | 3  | 4  | 5  | 6  | 7  | 8  | 9  | 10  |
| 2  | 2  | 4  | 6  | 8  | 10 | 12 | 14 | 16 | 18 | 20  |
| 3  | 3  | 6  | 9  | 12 | 15 | 18 | 21 | 24 | 27 | 30  |
| 4  | 4  | 8  | 12 | 16 | 20 | 24 | 28 | 32 | 36 | 40  |
| 5  | 5  | 10 | 15 | 20 | 25 | 30 | 35 | 40 | 45 | 50  |
| 6  | 6  | 12 | 18 | 24 | 30 | 36 | 42 | 48 | 54 | 60  |
| 7  | 7  | 14 | 21 | 28 | 35 | 42 | 49 | 56 | 63 | 70  |
| 8  | 8  | 16 | 24 | 32 | 40 | 48 | 56 | 64 | 72 | 80  |
| 9  | 9  | 18 | 27 | 36 | 45 | 54 | 63 | 72 | 81 | 90  |
| 10 | 10 | 20 | 30 | 40 | 50 | 60 | 70 | 80 | 90 | 100 |

**Figure 9: Multiplication chart to 100**

★ Give students regular practice reviewing the times tables, so the response becomes automatic.

★ Give students a multiplication chart with some numbers missing. How quickly can they fill in the empty squares? (Fig. 10)

| | **1** | **2** | **3** | **4** | **5** | **6** | **7** | **8** | **9** | **10** |
|---|---|---|---|---|---|---|---|---|---|---|
| **1** | 1 | | 3 | | 5 | | 7 | | 9 | |
| **2** | | 4 | | 8 | | 12 | 14 | 16 | | 20 |
| **3** | 3 | 6 | 9 | 12 | 15 | | 21 | | 27 | |
| **4** | | 8 | | 16 | | 24 | | 32 | | 40 |
| **5** | 5 | | 15 | | 25 | 30 | 35 | | 45 | |
| **6** | | 12 | | 24 | | 36 | | 48 | 54 | 60 |
| **7** | 7 | | 21 | | 35 | | 49 | | 63 | 70 |
| **8** | | 16 | | 32 | | 48 | | 64 | | 80 |
| **9** | 9 | | 27 | | 45 | | 63 | | 81 | |
| **10** | 10 | 20 | | 40 | | 60 | | 80 | | 100 |

**Figure 10: Completing the multiplication squares**

★ Play a form of 'math bingo.' Each student creates a card with 10 numbers on it. (Fig 11)

| | 12 | 36 | | 18 |
|---|---|---|---|---|
| 8 | 27 | | 16 | 54 |
| | 42 | 55 | 21 | |

**Figure 11: Math bingo card**

The caller has the numbers 1-10 written on separate cards. The cards are shuffled. The caller selects the top two cards, and the numbers are called out as a multiplication problem, such as *6 x 3*. The students look for the product on their cards, and if they have the correct answer (in this case *18)*, a counter is placed over the number. The first student to get every number covered with a counter wins the game.

* Learning to recite tables by heart is frustratingly difficult for some students. Allow these students to use **Appendix #14: Multiplication Chart** or a calculator to compensate for memory difficulties.

## Understanding division

* Observe the students and see which division methods they are using. **Appendix #18: Math Checklist: Division** can be used to note the strategies a student uses and your observations. Look at the list of methods, and see if it is possible to introduce the student to a more advanced level.

* Only introduce division when you are certain that the students understand composition and decomposition of numbers and multiplication. Show how division is only an extension of decomposition. A number can be decomposed into several smaller numbers of equal value, with or without a remainder.

* Give explicit instruction about the relationship between multiplication and division, and encourage the students to use existing multiplication knowledge to solve division problems.

  If $8 \times 4 = 32$, then $32 \div 4 =$

* Provide real materials, such as a box of cookies, and show how the cookies can be divided into equal portions. *"If we give each person three cookies, how many people can we serve? . . . If we share these cookies between the six of us, how many cookies will each person get?"*

* Teach the $\div$ symbol as a special kind of subtraction, where you can keep subtracting until there is nothing left.

* Show the students how division relates to multiplication by using the **Appendix #14: Multiplication Chart.**

* Make sets of division and multiplication facts. Ask the students to match up each division fact with its corresponding multiplication fact.

# Student Has Difficulties with Recall

## Section 4 – Math Observation Sheet

| 4. Student has difficulties with recall. |
| --- |
| Student relies on calculator for basic number facts every time they are needed. |
| Student makes errors when saying multiplication tables. |
| Student forgets algorithms. |
| Student does not solve math problems mentally. |

Many students have difficulties with memory. Perhaps they understand the concepts but find it hard to remember the detailed facts. It is important for teachers to determine which students fail to provide correct answers because of general difficulties and which fail only because of memory problems.

Memory difficulties alone should not be used as an excuse to hold back otherwise capable math students.

## Strategies for Managing Difficulties with Recall in Math

★ Do not assess a student's math capabilities purely on the ability to recall number facts.

★ Provide as many reference charts as possible around the classroom and in the student's personal learning resources to help them remember number facts.

★ Make practice of number facts a part of your daily classroom routine.

★ Computer math games are infinitely patient teachers and may help some students learn math facts.

★ Do not hold a student back in math because of memory difficulties, if the difficulties can be overcome with the use of a calculator and/or number charts.

★ When reciting multiplication tables, some students get 'lost' in the sequence. Provide a card with the sequence written down (without the answers), so the students can keep their place as they work on their times tables.

★ Some students are able to calculate but not recall. Allow these students to calculate the facts that others can remember. If it is a slow process, allow the student to use a calculator as an important learning aid.

★ Students with memory difficulties often find mental math very difficult. They forget the question before they have had time to figure out the answer. Provide a written version of the test for the students to look at while they mentally figure out the answer to the problem.

★ For tests that are given orally, often the rate of the questions is too fast for some students to mentally process the answers. Ask an adult to give the test individually, so the pace can be adjusted.

★ Put mental arithmetic tests onto audiotapes, so students can work at their own pace and listen to questions several times over.

✱ Create a reference book of working methods. Write down a step-by-step description of the process to complete a problem, and provide a completed example to demonstrate the process.

✱ Have students keep a personal log of the number facts that they know and add to it as more facts are learned.

# Student Has Difficulties with Math Problems

### Section 5 – Math Observation Chart

| 5. *Student has difficulties with math problems.* |
|---|
| Student can solve basic math facts but makes errors when choosing which operation to use in a word problem. |
| Student gets confused about what method to use to solve a word problem. |

Some students do fine when they have a set of numbers in front of them, but once the math problem is changed to a written story problem, they find the work tough. Maybe the student panics at something that looks unfamiliar, or perhaps the student finds it difficult to turn a sentence into a math problem.

Sometimes the difficulty is caused by the fact that math has been taught as an abstract process using written numbers, and therefore the students are not used to linking math with real, everyday situations.

# Strategies for Working with Math Problems

✱ When teaching any math process, always use practical, real-life examples so the students understand that the math they are learning is used in everyday situations.

✱ Encourage students to use blocks, counters, tally marks or the like to represent a word problem: *"A farmer had six sheep, so let's get six blocks and pretend they are sheep. Okay, now what happened next? The farmer went to market and sold four of the sheep . . . so we can move the blocks along to the market and take four away, because they are sold. Now the farmer bought 10 new sheep, so we get 10 new pretend sheep."*

✱ Have students draw simple sketches of the math problem as an aid to visualizing what they have to do.

✱ Teach students to pick out key words that provide a clue about the operation(s) that will be used. Words such as *more, as well, together, bought* and *found* are usually associated with addition; words such as *gave away, lost* and *left* usually suggest subtraction and so on.

★ Provide students with two very similar word problems—one that shows a completed example and one for the student to complete. Explain how the first word problem was solved, and ask students to model their reasoning for the second word problem based on the example.

# Student Has Difficulties with Spatial Reasoning

## Section 6 – Math Observation Chart

| 6. *Student has difficulties with spatial reasoning.* |
| --- |
| Student does not use concrete math materials effectively. |
| Student's written numbers and symbols are untidy. |
| Student's math work is unorganized and difficult to follow. |
| Student expresses confusion when working with spatial math skills. |

While we often think of math as connected with numbers and numerical operations, many types of math depend on spatial awareness and problem solving.

Students with poor spatial skills may have problems in laying their work out neatly, or they may find it hard to use concrete counting materials accurately. For instance, they may use tally marks for counting but arrange the marks in a scattered pattern so that counting is difficult.

Some areas of the math curriculum, such as symmetry, tessellation (mosaics) and geometry, deal directly with spatial skills, and this may challenge some students.

## Strategies for Working with Spatial Reasoning in Math

★ Show students how to lay out tally marks or counters neatly, in tidy columns or rows. For older students, encourage grouping in 10s to make counting easier.

★ Provide explicit teaching and extra practice for writing numerals and symbols for students who find it difficult. Give a verbal commentary on figure formation, so the students have a script to guide them. *"Let's write the number 2. Start at the top and swing out, then swing in and then straight across the bottom."* Left-handed students will swing in first and then out.

★ Allow students to use the **Appendix #11: Counting Chart** if they have trouble with setting out their own tally marks.

★ Use graph paper to help organize the layout.

★ Lined paper on its side can help older students keep columns straight.

✷ Use a calculator with a printout to help students who have difficulty recording their work neatly.

✷ Have students verbalize the geometric shapes and problems. This may help the students to interpret what they see. *"It's like a square, but the bottom has been pulled out wider than the top, so there are still four lines. The top line is shorter than the bottom line, and the lines on the sides slope outwards."*

✷ Avoid having students copy math problems from the board before they can begin the assignment. Instead, provide handouts, so they can start work right away.

✷ Visually crowded worksheets can overwhelm and confuse. Provide clear and concise layouts with teacher created materials.

# Student Has Advanced Skills in Math

## Section 7 – Math Observation Chart

| 7. Student has advanced skills in math. |
| --- |
| Student demonstrates advanced mathematical thinking. |
| Student finds standard class work too easy. Can handle more difficult work. |
| Student expresses an interest in math and seeks out interesting math challenges. |
| Student makes negative statements about class math. |

Some students are very talented in math. They are capable of advanced mathematical thinking in comparison to their age group. Such students may seek out mathematical challenges and thrive in an environment where they are able to tackle complex and engaging math work.

However, these students may 'hate' math if they find the class work too easy and boring. With a natural aptitude in math, these students will have mastered the basic concepts very quickly. They will not need the same amount of practice and will be able to progress quickly through the math program. If they must follow the same math program as other students, they may become bored. Bright students are often unwilling to work through tedious work to earn the right to more interesting and appropriately challenging work.

## Strategies for Developing Advanced Math Skills

### Individualizing instruction

✷ Individualize instruction to include students with high math ability. Bright math students need a curriculum that matches their ability level, so they are stimulated and challenged.

* Assess these students regularly to identify their math skills.

* Be prepared, as bright math students may be one or two year levels ahead of their peers.

* Advanced students generally need a lot less practice in math. Modify the program to allow these students to shortcut the practice phase of learning, if they have clearly mastered the topic or skill.

* Look for math activities that provide the students with extra challenges in the application and interpretation of math. For instance, ask the students to each devise a budget for a school trip. Provide them with brochures and price lists required for the task. Ask the students to compare their various approaches and solutions. *"How can the difference in final costs be explained? How could the trip be made as inexpensive as possible?"*

* Encourage the students to identify the patterns in the work they are doing and use those patterns in their work. *"This one is just double the one I did before."*

* Students may be able to draw some conclusions from the work they have done. *"None of my answers are over 100 because . . . . All of these are right angles because . . . ."*

* Math challenges do not always have to involve more advanced concepts or techniques. Applying and interacting with basic math in innovative ways can also engage the bright student's interest and extend learning. These activities can involve other areas of the curriculum. For example:

  * a project related to an environmental issue involving graphs and statistics
  * a practical construction task involving math in the design and evaluation
  * a school trip where the student manages the time table, cost and so on
  * evaluation of a classroom plan, such as rearranging the furniture

## Allowing the student to skip basics they can already do

* Be careful to avoid simply giving the bright math student more of the same. For instance, adding up five-digit numbers is really no more challenging and engaging than adding up two-digit numbers for the bright student.

* Do not expect bright math students to prove they can do easy work. Most likely, they will be bored and perform poorly if they have to do work that is uninteresting and does not challenge them.

* Many students with high math ability cannot show their work or the process of basic arithmetic, because they simply 'know' the answer without working it out. *"I know that 72 is half of 144; it's just sort of in my head."* Observe carefully how the student arrives at answers. Require work to be shown only when the student does not arrive at the correct answer.

## Placing the student in a stimulating math environment

✳ Consider placing the bright math student in an upper grade level for math, or alternatively, create an accelerated math group in your class or school.

✳ Develop a math club or math interest group, where capable students can enjoy math-related activities as part of their free choice time.

✳ If possible, find an older student or adult to mentor students of exceptional math ability, to encourage math talk and exploration.

✳ Watch for national or international math competitions that your capable math students could enter.

## Concluding Chapter Four

In this chapter, you have seen that mathematics is a language unto itself and, like reading, can present a variety of challenges to the learner. Students in one class can range from those who don't 'get it' to math whiz kids. What is very confusing to one student may be perfectly clear to another, and neither can explain why. The strategies presented here provide ways to adjust the levels of learning math in the classroom and make it engaging with games, charts, rulers, physical objects and 'tricks of the trade,' while emphasizing its relevancy to the students' interests and everyday lives. Using these tips and strategies will encourage all students to advance their skills and feel included in 'the world of math.'

# Chapter Five
# Concentration and Organization

## Introduction

Have you ever stood in front of your class, ready to teach and waiting, waiting, waiting for one last student to settle down? Have you ever had to go over the same thing again and again because some students were not concentrating? Have you ever had to spend time helping a student search for a missing assignment sheet or an essential piece of material?

Your answer is almost certainly a very loud *"YES!"* to these three questions.

Poor concentration and organization contribute to frustration and wasted time for the teacher, the class and the individual student. In some classes, a significant percentage of time may be spent helping students who have difficulties in concentration and organization.

The ability to concentrate and to be well organized is linked to the overall development of the child. We would not expect a 5 year old to be able to concentrate or be organized in the same way as a 10 year old. However, there are also wide individual differences. Indeed, we all know adults who are poorly organized, or who find it really difficult to concentrate for any length of time!

Students with concentration difficulties may be just as intelligent and motivated as other students. But they may find it genuinely difficult to pay attention and sustain concentration. As a result, they may be seriously disadvantaged and unable to achieve their learning goals, simply because they find it difficult to connect with the classroom program.

Similarly, the 'executive' skills of thinking ahead, planning, organizing, coordinating and prioritizing tasks may be real challenges for some students. They may leave work until the last minute, lose important papers or equipment and fail to manage their time efficiently. Poor school achievements may be the result of poor organization rather than lack of ability or low motivation.

In an inclusive classroom, problems with concentration and organization need to be addressed by a range of strategies.

The section headings in this chapter follow the structure of the **Appendix #4: Concentration and Organization Observation Chart.**

The Concentration and Organization Observation Chart may be reproduced and used to informally assess and record difficulties for individual students. The Concentration and

Organization Observation Chart is divided into four sections, each focusing on a specific area. As you assess individuals, specific patterns of difficulty may emerge. The sections in the chart will provide a direct link between the recorded Concentration and Organization Observation Chart and the corresponding sections in this chapter that provide strategies to help the student in those specific area(s) of need. The four sections of the chart have also been reproduced within the main text of Chapter Five.

If you are interested in using the strategies without completing an informal assessment of the student, the sections will easily guide you through the chapter and provide a quick, easy reference tool for specific strategies. This will enable you to select from the intervention strategies, modifications and adaptations listed to help individuals and small groups of students.

The following forms from the Appendix are referred to in this chapter:

Appendix # 4:   Concentration and Organization Observation Chart
Appendix #37:  Student Reward Cards
Appendix #34:  Student Plan for Getting Organized
Appendix #32:  Student Priorities Chart
Appendix #31:  Student Work Planner

| 1. Student is physically restless. |
| --- |
| Student is often active and has a very high energy level. |
| Student fidgets and moves around even when asked to sit still. |
| Student often touches and fiddles with things. |
| Student is often loud and hard to quiet down. |

# Student is Physically Restless

## Section 1 – Concentration and Organization Chart

We all know that physical activity is essential for the healthy development of children and young people. Today, many youngsters do not get enough natural, physical activity outside of school. Perhaps they live in an urban environment where safe, open places to play are limited. Perhaps they like to stay indoors and watch television, play electronic games and so forth. Or, parents may prefer to drive students to school instead of having their children walk or ride a bike.

The increasing problem of childhood obesity is obviously linked to the lack of normal, healthy activity. Another unwanted side effect of limited opportunities for physical activity is the way in which some students need to 'let off steam' inappropriately in the classroom or school yard.

However, even when there are adequate opportunities for physical exercise, some students have an abundance of energy that seems inexhaustible. They never seem to tire and are always moving, often boisterous and usually in a full-speed mode.

One real difficulty for restless students is that often they really don't know what it feels like to be still and less active. For these students, their restless, active, busy state is what feels absolutely normal. Sometimes, they will indignantly deny they are restless, even when they have been touching, pushing and moving around the entire time. (*"But I wasn't fidgeting—I was sitting still."*)

> *"They were always telling me to sit still, but I really thought they were just giving me a hard time. Then one day I saw myself in a home movie of my cousin's wedding, and I can tell you I was really shocked. All the other kids were sitting watching the ceremony, but not me! I was under the chair, then standing up, sitting down, looking all around, pulling weird faces, trying to talk to my Mom, undoing my shirt buttons . . . ."*

Everyone has a need for incoming sensation through the senses of touch, smell, taste, hearing, awareness of body position (proprioception) and vision. Indeed one of the most powerful forms of torture is sensory deprivation, where humans are deprived of incoming sensations.

We all vary in the amount of sensory stimulation needed to maintain a comfortable level. If you do not believe this, take a look around at the next teachers' meeting and see how many of your colleagues need to create some sensory input by fiddling with  paper clips, doodling, tapping their pens and so on!

Students, too, may need a high level of physical sensation to maintain their sensory comfort zones. This need for sensory input may result in them swinging back on their chairs, flicking their pens, rolling bits of paper or a multitude of other, often irritating, mannerisms.

> *" It's weird, but if I have to keep very still and not touch anything, my fingers tingle and I don't know what to do with them. It's not a good feeling, like something is really wrong with my hands. As soon as I can touch something, say a paper clip, the tingling in my fingers stops and I feel OK again."*

There also are students who have a real need for physical contact with others. They will push and shove, wrestle, hug and generally create opportunities to touch other people. Standing in a line can be real trouble for these youngsters. They just cannot resist pulling on the person in front, backing into the person behind them and generally creating a disturbance.

Have you noticed how some students cannot sit still on the floor? They lean back on their arms, stick their legs out and constantly move around. The reason for this may be that these students lack good muscle control of the upper body. Without this muscle control, it is very difficult to maintain a steady, balanced posture when seated on the floor.

# Strategies for Managing Physical Restlessness

## Providing opportunity for physical activity

✻ Recognize that young students, in particular, may need to be physically active most of the day.

✻ Allow for the fact that some students (and adults) need frequent physical activity.

✻ Encourage parents to involve their children in daily physical activities, such as walking to school, playing a sport or playing outside in the neighborhood instead of watching TV or sitting in front of the computer.

✻ Make sure that all students have plenty of opportunities for healthy, physical activity. Some students may need intense, vigorous physical activity to let off steam.

✻ Provide restless students with legitimate reasons to get up from their seats. Have students bring work up to your desk, or send them on errands to other classrooms.

✻ If possible, arrange for some physical activities to be in a natural environment, such as a park or playing field, rather than in a building. This may be more likely to meet the student's need for large, open surroundings and uninhibited movement.

✻ Encourage physically active students to take up a sport where energy and stamina are assets.

✻ Depending on your locality, encourage parents to get the students to walk or cycle to school instead of being driven.

✻ If parents are concerned about safety when students walk to school alone, encourage parents to set up a 'walking train.' One parent sets off at the far end of the route, adding other students along the way. The students all walk to school together under the supervision of the parent. Another parent along the way may be able to relieve the first parent, if the distance warrants it.

✻ Build physical activity into your daily classroom routine.

## Managing physical restlessness

✻ Some physical therapists use a form of deep massage to deal with students' high need for sensory input. Ask specialists in your school about this.

✳ Tolerate students' physical restlessness, if it is not doing any harm.

✳ Provide restless students with items such as a squishy ball, piece of play dough or soft eraser to fidget with to meet their needs for physical sensation.

✳ Provide students with good seating of a suitable height and with good back support.

✳ If students are restless sitting on the floor, allow them to sit on chairs or bean bags instead.

✳ Provide restless students with special cushions to sit on, designed to allow for movement and restlessness.

✳ Seat the student in a position on the floor where he has room to move without disturbing other students.

✳ Ask a physical therapist for advice for any student who has difficulties sitting on the floor. The therapist may be able to provide the student with exercises to strengthen upper-body muscle control.

✳ In situations where the class usually lines up and the restless student causes a disturbance, try allowing the class to move in informal groups to see if it works better.

✳ When it is essential that students sit still and remain quiet, provide clear instructions about what is required. Tell them how long they will need to maintain tight control on their restlessness.

✳ Do not require students to stay physically still for long periods of time, as it is physically impossible for some to comply.

✳ Encourage the students to keep their desks clear of loose items that they will want to touch.

✳ Allow for some 'wind down' time between energetic activity and quiet working time.

## Introducing more settled behavior

✳ Encourage the students to monitor their own activity levels. Many are unaware of how restless they are. Seat the student near a mirror or reflective window. This will help some students become aware of their own restlessness.

✳ Get the student to use a mirror to see what he looks like when he is still. Get him to focus on what it feels like to be physically settled and calm, as the student may not be able to tell the difference without the visual feedback.

✷ Have quiet, calming experiences in your classroom to settle students and help them learn how to vary their activity levels.

✷ Speak and move quietly and calmly yourself. Loud, excitable adults tend to increase restless behavior in students.

✷ Ask parents to enroll their child in yoga or tai chi classes. This will help students to experience the feeling of body calmness.

✷ Have the student try out various ways of talking, such as quiet, loud, slow and fast talk. Use a video or audio recorder to provide feedback. Encourage the student to recognize the different styles of talking, and select the styles to be used in a given situation, such as in the classroom or on the playground.

✷ Use drama to provide the students with experience of what it feels like to have a different activity level. Ask a restless student to play the role of a character who is quiet, restrained and calm. You can sometimes use this as a prompt for behavior in the future by reminding the student of the character: *"Remember what a great job you did being the palace guard? I'd like you to act like the guard again please, Ben."*

✷ Talk to the students about the characters of various animals: the active monkey, the scurrying ants, the calm, slow-moving tortoise, the watchful owl, etc. Create stereotypes for various styles of behavior, put posters up in your class and use these visual prompts to remind students of what style of behavior you desire at the moment: *"Think 'owl' please, John. Watch and listen carefully."*

# Student Is Impulsive and Impatient

## Section 2 – Concentration and Organization Observation Chart

| 2. *Student is impulsive and impatient.* |
| --- |
| Student acts before thinking. |
| Student calls out in class. |
| Student 'forgets' rules and continues to do the wrong thing. |
| Student rushes through school work and makes silly mistakes. |
| Student interrupts when others are speaking. |
| Student pushes in or becomes frustrated when having to wait for turn. |
| Student gets restless and frustrated when having to wait. |
| Student often seems to be in a rush. |
| Student complains if a task or game takes too long. |

Impulsive, impatient students may often get into trouble. They know the rules, and they know the likely punishments perfectly well, but the trouble is, they don't stop and think before they act.

> *"I just reacted so quickly that it was all over in a second. It was only later that I thought, 'Oh no! That was against the rules, and the last time I did that I was in big trouble.'"*

When a student has behaved inappropriately, there is usually no sensible answer to the question *Why did you do that?* The behavior was so impulsive that it wasn't thought through. The student will often feel obliged to say something, making an excuse or blaming others to try to explain the impulsive behavior.

Impulsive students may often have a very poor sense of time. A few seconds feels like hours, and an hour seems like an eternity! They really find it hard to wait their turn or hold back until there is an opportunity to speak. They may forget what they were going to say unless they say it right away.

Impulsive, impatient students often make a lot of careless mistakes with their school work. They quickly begin without checking what they are supposed to do, they start before they have a plan and finish as fast as they can. It is unlikely that these students will stop and check their work before handing it in.

## Strategies for Managing Impulsivity and Impatience

### Creating a calm, thoughtful atmosphere in your class

* Be clear and methodical in your own teaching.

* Plan every lesson well ahead so that you know exactly you are doing.

* Organize equipment ahead of time to avoid the last-minute panic of trying to find what is needed.

* Try not to rush students. Give plenty of time for tasks to be done properly.

* Impose thinking time before getting students to start a task: *"Everyone, take two minutes to look over this assignment. Don't pick up your pencils yet; just look at the paper and think about what you have to do."*

* Impose checking time at the end of the task: *"Everyone, take two minutes to look through your work. Check that you have completed all the questions. Check your spelling."*

★ Introduce tasks so students have to stop and think about the requirements. For instance ask the students to:

- Say how many tasks are on the worksheet.
- Circle the key words in the question.
- Make a chart and check off when parts of the task are complete.
- Estimate the time needed to complete each task and the whole assignment.

★ Use highlighting, bold print, underlining and color to draw the students' attention to important information on worksheets, curriculum materials, assignments and tests.

★ Remind students to stop and think as an important part of following the rules.

★ Use **Appendix #37: Student Reward Cards** to recognize and encourage students' efforts to stop and think.

## Having students practice restraint

★ Use a stopwatch to show impulsive students how they often try to give answers instantly. Encourage them to take a few seconds of thinking time before answering or raising their hands.

★ Have students write down the answer before raising their hands. This can help impulsive students refrain from shouting out, while at the same time, allowing them to instantly record their answers.

★ When asking the students questions in class, allow plenty of time for thinking: *"I'll ask you to raise your hands in a moment. Right now, think about it carefully, so you are ready when I ask for answers."*

★ When asking the students questions in class, invite students to rethink their initial answers: *"Okay now, I can see plenty of hands up. I'll give you a few seconds more to think about your answers before I choose someone."*

★ Look at the response times of people being interviewed on TV or radio to convince your students that good answers are not always instant.

★ Play review games, where students take turns answering the easy questions orally. Don't allow students to call out the answer until you drop your finger to show that three seconds have gone by.

★ Uses games and activities where students have to think and plan to get the best result. Chess, card games, writing rough drafts and so forth can work well.

✳ Provide 'speaker cards' to help students take their turn at speaking in class. Each student receives an allocation of cards that entitle them to speak during group time. If the student wishes to speak, he must hold his card in the air and wait until called upon. When the student has used up his cards, he has also used up his turns to speak and must wait for a new allocation. Some students become better at 'budgeting' their use of the cards.

✳ Play a game where students call out answers to questions orally, but add a twist. For example, when using simple mental arithmetic questions, whenever the answer is *nine*, the students must say *"rhubarb"* instead. If a student says *"nine,"* then he is out of the game. This encourages the student to slow down and think.

✳ Have activities where students are required to make sudden and complete stops in what they are doing. For example, you could play Statues, where on a signal, everyone has to freeze in position and hold it.

✳ If you catch a student just about to do the wrong thing, ask him to *"Stop, think, and make a good choice,"* rather than just telling him to stop what he is doing.

✳ Make clear statements about how much restraint is needed. Do not say, *"Would you mind waiting just one moment,"* if what you mean is, *"I need you to wait until I have finished this. It could take 10 minutes or so."* The impulsive student will wait a moment and then feel quite justified in interrupting you.

✳ Help students to develop restraint by giving positive instructions. Instructions to do something are easier to follow than instructions not to do something. So always try to describe the desired behavior *("Stand still")* instead of saying what not to do *("Stop running").*

✳ If punishment is needed, make it a natural consequence of the behavior, and have it follow as quickly as possible after the incident.

✳ Do not expect parents to curb their children's impulsive behavior at school by giving them punishments at home. Consequences need to follow through quickly and in the context where the mistake occurred.

# Student Finds It Hard to Concentrate

## Section 3 – Concentration and Organization Observation Chart

| 3. Student finds it hard to concentrate. |
|---|
| Student often looks around and fidgets when supposed to be listening. |
| Student loses concentration when working on a task. |
| Student does not see things through to the finish and frequently does not complete the task. |
| Student starts one thing and gets sidetracked with something else. |
| Student pays attention to distractions instead of concentrating on task. |
| Student is inattentive and seems to be in a dream. |
| Student sometimes does not appear to have heard what is said. |
| Student does not respond to time pressures. |
| Student seems vague and unaware of what is going on in the classroom. |
| Student does not follow instructions. |
| Student starts something but then drifts off task. |

Some students are active, restless and easily distracted. These students may be impulsive, always ready to move their attention to whatever new is happening. In some ways, they may seem over-alert, as they are always ready to notice something new. A hundred and one small details seem to divert them from what they are supposed to be doing. Everything attracts their attention, and nothing is filtered out.

On the other hand, some students seem to lack alertness. They may gaze around them, apparently oblivious of what is happening. When asked a question, they may seem startled and unsure of what has gone on before. They seem to tune out completely.

Inattentive students can often seem in a world of their own. They move at much the same speed, regardless of whether they are supposed to be hurrying or not. They may take a long time to begin a task and then work slowly at their own pace. All too often, they may not finish the assigned task. There are some special reasons for students being inattentive and perhaps in a world of their own.

Some very bright students may be deeply involved in their own thoughts—imagining, thinking or creating. These bright students may be bored by the general classroom work and find their inner world a much more engaging place to be.

At the other end of the scale, students with intellectual or language disabilities may be out of their depth with the classroom activities and thus fail to connect with what is going on.

Depressed and worried children and adolescents can also be preoccupied and deep in their own thoughts. School may be of little importance in comparison to the worries with which they may be dealing.

A range of medical difficulties can also cause a student to be inattentive in class. A student may have a hearing problem. Most hearing difficulties occur in selected frequencies, so the student may be able to hear part of every word but have difficulties making sense of what has been said. In this situation, the student often tunes out and stops making any attempt to listen.

Epilepsy is a surprisingly common cause of inattentiveness. Students may have very brief, but frequent, lapses of consciousness, which can be hard to detect in the classroom. Many cases of mild epilepsy probably go undetected and are treated as inattentiveness. Doctors can assess any students suspected of this condition.

Students who are unwell or tired may also be apathetic, vague and slow in class. Obviously, it is important to investigate further if the student seems to be unduly inattentive, especially if it is not typical of the student's usual behavior.

## Strategies for Managing Concentration Difficulties

### Checking for medical problems

* Get the student's hearing checked if there is any doubt.

* If you think that the student may be depressed or anxious, discuss your concerns with the parents. Seek further advice from an appropriately qualified professional, such as a psychologist.

* Ask parents to have a doctor examine any student who seems unusually distractible, inattentive or vague.

### Matching the curriculum to the student

* An inattentive student might be very bright and bored. If this seems likely, provide more interesting and challenging work, and monitor the student's response.

* If the student seems to be struggling with the class work, consider having the student assessed to clarify what type of curriculum would be more appropriate.

## Providing support and monitoring

✳ Provide support and close monitoring to help the student stay with the task. Give quiet reminders when the student is inattentive.

✳ Have the student sit close to the teacher, with a clear view of the teacher's face.

✳ Use the **Appendix #37: Student Reward Cards** to encourage on-task behavior.

✳ Use a range of rewards as incentive for task completion.

✳ Look for examples of strong concentration. Praise the student when this occurs.

✳ Try to ignore irritating but essentially harmless inattentiveness.

✳ Have students monitor their own concentration with the use of note cards. Set a timer, and when it rings, students should ask themselves, *"Was I concentrating when the timer sounded?"* If they were on task, they write *Yes* on the card. If they were not on task, the card is marked *No*.

✳ Keep a collection of reminder cards in your pocket. This reminder card can be used for any goal the student is working towards. This silent reminder card is placed on the student's desk to break into periods where the student seems to be 'miles away.'

✳ Often standing quietly beside a student can be sufficient to remind him to reactivate himself.

✳ Have 'secret codes' to let students know when they need to pay attention or when you think they are doing well. Use a prearranged signal, such as putting a pencil on the student's desk, to signify that the student needs to attend to the task at hand.

✳ Create videos of important lessons, and keep them as references. You can build up a library with colleagues as a resource for students who need to repeat a lesson for any reason.

✳ Some students listen better if they can doodle or manipulate a small ball or eraser when required to listen. Try this to see if it helps your inattentive students listen better.

✳ Some students find it hard to tune in when the teacher transitions between speaking to individuals and speaking to the entire class. Have a signal, such as a bell, to let students know when they should stop what they are doing and listen to what you have to say.

✳ Allow extra time for students who are slow or easily distracted to finish a piece of work to a satisfactory standard.

✶ Give students help in summarizing what has been taught, in case they have missed something.

## Reducing distractions

✶ Have students keep their desktops clear, except for the books and materials needed for a task.

✶ Create personal workstations. A three-sided screen placed on the desk can cut out distractions and help students focus.

✶ Seat the student away from visual distractions such as a corridor window.

✶ Seat the student away from auditory distractions such as the air conditioner, aquarium pump and the like.

✶ Offer students the option of a single desk. Many students prefer this.

✶ Provide blocks of time where students work or read quietly without any interaction with each other or the teacher.

✶ Establish a quiet, working atmosphere in your classroom.

✶ Avoid distracting visual displays such as mobiles. Have a special place to display creative work that does not intrude into work spaces.

✶ Play calming music while students settle down.

✶ Consider using a radio loop. The student wears the earpiece and the teacher has a microphone, so the teacher's voice is delivered directly to the student, cutting out background noise.

✶ Use noise-canceling headsets to cut out distracting background noise.

## Structuring tasks

✶ Break large tasks into smaller sections that are more easily completed in a short timeframe.

✶ Draw a diagram of your lesson plan and mark off steps as you proceed, so students find it easier to connect with what you are doing.

✶ Use graphics to show the 'road map' or diagram of how a task is structured, so students can see how much they have completed and what is still ahead.

✱ Back up verbal instructions with bulleted points on the board, so that once you have finished speaking, students can refer back to the written points, if needed.

✱ Provide an overview of the lesson before you start, and summarize it at the end. Clarify expected learning outcomes, and check that they have been achieved.

✱ Provide a list of questions that you are going to ask at the end of the session. Write the questions on the board for students to refer to. This helps students to listen carefully, as they have specific information that they need to know.

✱ Use theme tunes to signal changes in activity. For instance, have a special tune that is played for the first few minutes of each task, while students get organized and settle down to work. By the time the tune is faded out, all students should be in their seats and working. Another tune signals the last five minutes of the task, when students should be preparing for the next activity.

✱ Have a definite start time when students are asked to start writing. Give a minute or two of thinking time and then a clear signal that writing time has begun.

✱ Provide prompts and reminders to keep on task: *"Ten minutes left. I will give you another reminder when there are only five minutes left to finish."*

## Providing information and training to improve concentration

✱ Brainstorm with the class to determine methods of concentration. Often you will find students use self-talk to remind themselves of priorities.

✱ Teach the students to use self-talk to stay on task: *I will keep going until I finish. . . . If I can concentrate on this for five minutes, I will be finished. . . . I lost concentration there for a minute. Better get back on track.*

✱ Have students create motivating notices to be displayed at their workstations. Slogans such as *Just do it!* or *Work hard! Work smart!* can help students to keep on track.

✱ Help students to practice ignoring distractions. Provide a simple task that requires concentration, and try as many fun ways as you can think of to distract them from the task. Challenge their idea that they 'cannot' concentrate!

✱ Be sure you have eye contact with students, and that students can observe your face as you talk.

✱ Talk to the students about what good listening usually looks like (i.e., looking at the speaker, having an alert expression, responding quickly to questions). Have the students 'act as if' they are listening to experience a contrast between this and what might be their usual style of inattentive behavior.

✷ Introduce activities where alertness and quick reactions are essential. For example, have the students throw a bean bag to each other, calling the name of the next person to make the catch. Make it more challenging by having two or three bags being thrown around, so the action is fast and students have to stay alert.

✷ Provide practice in working quickly with activities that are judged by speed and volume: *"How many words can you write in two minutes?"*

✷ Give the students frequent physical activity. This can get the circulation going and help students to reenergize. It also helps to work off pent-up energy.

✷ Set a timer or stop watch to help students work faster for shorter periods of time.

✷ Use dictation as an activity to help students develop skills in sustained listening and writing without pauses.

## Making it worthwhile for students to listen

✷ Vary your teaching style and your voice. Colorful and engaging styles help students maintain their interest. Be unpredictable, and have fun with what you do.

✷ Do not endlessly repeat yourself. If you do, students will ignore what you say, because they know you will say it again (and again and again!). Make sure students know that they need to listen right now! *"Listen carefully, as I am only going to say this once."*

✷ Have a student repeat what you have just said to give extra emphasis.

✷ To add variety, ask students, instead of the teacher, to read the class announcements.

✷ Allow plenty of student action in your class to stimulate involvement.

## Allowing for some quiet reflection

✷ Some students do need periods of quiet reflection and 'dreaming,' so sometimes allow for this in the program for these students.

✷ Some students work to maintain alertness and focus in the classroom but need quiet, unhurried time at recess. Create a quiet spot as a haven for those students.

# Student Is Poorly Organized

## Section 4 – Concentration and Organization Observation Checklist

| 4.  *Student is poorly organized.* |
| --- |
| Student is often unprepared, because student has not planned ahead. |
| Student leaves things until the last minute. |
| Student loses things such as school work, materials or clothing. |
| Student forgets to bring materials and books when they are needed. |
| Student is messy; does not keep papers, materials and supplies in order. |
| Student misses deadlines for handing in work. |

Some students seem to be in a permanent muddle. Important materials are lost, papers are mislaid and assignments are late. The students' desks, backpacks and lockers are always a mess. These students often fail to demonstrate their potential because of poor organization. They may have very good intentions to stay on top of the work, but because of poor planning and time management, they end up in chaos.

These students often have 'time blindness.' They have a poor sense of time. They misjudge how long a task will take. They do not realize how few days remain before a task must be finished. Often they leave things until the very last minute, hopeful that they will have plenty of time. Sometimes work is finished, but it is lost or forgotten and not handed in on time.

Students also may think that other people's good organization just 'happens' and that their own lack of organization is due to unexpected circumstances. They may also be overly optimistic, always sure that the library will have the book they need right away, that the equipment they need will not be checked out to another student, that the printer will keep working and that they will be able to complete the assignment in record time.

Poorly organized students will often spend too much time on trivial elements of a task, such as decorating the title page, and do not leave enough time for the rest.

# Strategies for Working with Organization

## Monitoring and supporting

✱ Have an adult support the student to ensure that organization is monitored and assisted if needed.

✱ Create groups where students support one another with daily organization.

* Give all students equal opportunity to take responsibility in the class and in the school. If necessary, support the student in the organization of the duties required.

* Assign an 'organization buddy' to help with organization.

* Set aside time each day for the students to organize themselves and their possessions. Keeping desks, backpacks and lockers neat and tidy is a good start.

* Set aside time weekly to more fully organize desks, backpacks and lockers. Students can use this time to discard unnecessary items and organize the remaining materials.

* Insert two minutes of thinking time at the end of the school day. Students must sit still and use the time to think: *What do I need to take home with me? What do I have to remember to do when I get home? What day is it today? Is there anything special I need to remember for tomorrow?*

* Suggest that parents impose a similar thinking time before the students leave home: *Have I got all my stuff? Did I check my assignment book?*

* Check the student's study assignment at the end of the school day to make sure all the important information is written down.

* Where possible, ask rather than tell students: *"What do you need to remember for tomorrow? How are you going to make sure you don't forget? Tell me what material you will need to bring with you."*

* Quickly identify students who are behind schedule or who are late in completing their work. Help these students to catch up before they fall too far behind.

## Organizing the classroom

* Have a clear routine in your classroom, so there is predictability.

* Be very explicit about what is required of the students. Make definite statements, and stick to the rules you make so that students know where they stand.

* Be organized yourself, so that you set a good example.

* Provide students with an organized learning program. Think ahead, and plan appropriate modifications from the start. Try not to change instructions or expectations once students have started on a task.

* Manage class time so that students are not rushed. Allow time for planning, checking, general organization and administration.

✳ Invest time in making your classroom neat and well organized, so students can find and store things quickly and easily. Clean up often and avoid letting things become out of order or cluttered.

✳ Have a definite place (a labeled box or tray) where students place finished work.

✳ Have a planner on the classroom wall, and refer to it often as you indicate what is expected of the students in terms of organization: *"See, here we are today, and your assignment is due in on Friday, the day after tomorrow. So you have just one day left to get it finished."*

## Developing good organization

✳ Brainstorm in the class to share ideas about how to get organized.

✳ Make a poster of things that 'smart thinkers' do to organize themselves, and have it clearly displayed in the classroom. Use visual illustrations to give quick visual prompts.

✳ Have students figure out what has gone wrong in situations where they were poorly organized. Did they misjudge the time needed? Did they lose something? Did they forget?

✳ Listen to the students' excuses about what went wrong with their organization, and then use **Appendix #34: Student Plan for Getting Organized** to help students plan better strategies next time.

✳ Have the students write a reminder list of good strategies to keep on display. Get the student to make the list highly visible with graphics, color and decoration. Find a very prominent place to put the list.

✳ Have the class make a list of how optimistic thinking can help. Have fun with the ideas. Here are some to get you started:

- Papers that are not put in a folder will get stolen by aliens.
- Work left until the last minute turns into the Hulk.
- Lockers can turn into black holes in the universe unless you keep them tidy.

✳ Make organization part of the task requirements: *"Make a folder with four sections. List the materials needed. Write a checklist of all the things you need to do for this task."* Consider grading students for meeting these basic requirements. This will help students see that organization is an important part of what they have to do.

✳ Have students use a task planner on a computer, which provides task-specific reminders several days before something is due.

✱ Encourage students to identify priorities and focus on them. Encourage students to make a list of what needs to be done, and number the items in order of importance. The student then starts with the top priority task first. You can use the **Appendix #32: Student Priorities Chart** to help with this.

✱ Have students challenge themselves to complete an assignment the day before it is actually due, so they have a spare day if needed.

✱ Help students to schedule work so they are able to meet the deadlines. As well as entering the due date, have them select the day they will start, dates when they plan to have completed the various sections of the work and the date they plan to have their final draft ready for revision and editing. You can use the **Appendix #31: Student Work Planner** to help with this.

✱ Ask students to share their timetables for tackling a big task, such as a final test review or a large project. Ask students to check in with you daily to keep you up-to-date on their progress.

✱ Create a group or class timetable for large projects, where all students check off their individual progress. Students lagging behind can see what is happening.

✱ Get your students to 'expect the unexpected,' and build this into their timetable/plan so that they have a margin when the inevitable setback occurs.

✱ Link a routine task (such as putting up your chair at the end of the day) with an organizational task (such as running through a checklist of what to take home). Help students to build organization into their daily routines.

## Managing paperwork and equipment

✱ Keep a list of homework assignments on the class website. Students can log on, view the list and download it if necessary.

✱ Encourage students to submit assignments electronically to avoid work being finished and then lost.

✱ Have students keep one large file that holds every piece of loose paper they are currently working on. Help the student set up the file with appropriate sections.

✱ Have students make themselves a 'Home—School' plastic zip file. It is brightly colored, decorated and easy to find. All notices to take home, all notes from parents to the teacher and other important documents and reminders go into this file. The file is checked by the student (with adult prompting, if needed) at the start of each school day and when the student gets home at night.

✶ Worksheets that are not hole-punched hardly ever get filed. Hole-punch worksheets before they are given out, or have students carry a small hole punch with them.

✶ Have a spare set of basic materials (pencil, ruler, calculator, etc.) that students can use when they cannot find their own.

✶ If students become too dependent on borrowing from you (or another adult in the classroom), ask the students to give you something of their own each time they borrow. When the teacher's item is returned, the student receives his own possession back.

✶ Color code books to help identification.

✶ If the student has an exercise book for each subject, then either hole-punch each book and place them all in a large file, or use an accordion file to keep all the exercise books together.

✶ Teach good filing skills, so students do not lose information that is stored outside of their minds! Provide suitable filing systems, such as alphabetical folders, accordion files, filing cabinets and the like.

✶ Teach good organization of computer files, using proper folders and accurate file naming when saving.

✶ Make sure students have their computers set to save work automatically and at frequent intervals.

✶ Have students get in the habit of backing up everything they do on the computer.

## Concluding Chapter Five

This chapter has brought to light the fact that some students are far more challenged in areas of concentration and organization than others, and their challenges are often endemic. They can't seem to help themselves. Rather than give up on these students and allow them to fail due to their inattention and disorganization, many strategies are presented here that will help not only those students who have real problems in these areas, but also those who could just use a little boost. Everyone has times when it's difficult to concentrate, and all students can benefit from developing habits of organization that will help them throughout their lifetimes. For some students, these strategies may mean the difference between a life of struggle and a successful future.

# Chapter Six
## Teamwork

## Introduction

Teaching is a team effort. In this chapter, we look at how we can work together with professional colleagues to create a school community where inclusion is welcomed as the *fair and reasonable thing to do*.

Inclusion of students without the inclusion of their parents just does not make sense, so we also must explore the importance of understanding parents' perspectives, respecting their needs and including them as important members of the team.

The following forms from the Appendix are referred to in this chapter:

Appendix #25: Teacher: Personal Profile as an Inclusive Teacher
Appendix #28: Teacher Notes: Getting Ready for a Meeting
Appendix #39: Student Notes: Getting Ready for a Meeting
Appendix #42: Parent Notes: Getting Ready for a Meeting
Appendix #29: Teacher: Meeting Record

## Teamwork with Professional Colleagues

### Creating an inclusive school community

Inclusion is the law, but that's just the beginning of the story. A real commitment to meet the needs of all students through an inclusive school program goes beyond the letter of the law. Often it is the small, intuitive, personal choices made by adults and students within a school community that reflect true inclusiveness. Often it is not so much what you do as how you do it!

> *"As soon as we arrived, I could tell it was going to be fine. They did not treat us like we were asking for anything extra, only that they wanted to know all about Zoe, so they could help her fit in with the other kids. The other school made it seem like we were asking too much. They made it sound like they were doing us a big favor."*

School leadership, policy development and ongoing professional training are all important elements in the development and maintenance of an inclusive school community. Individual commitment from every teacher and strong teamwork are the other essential ingredients in an inclusive school.

Effective intervention also needs a coordinated and positive group effort, from planning to implementation and evaluation. Meeting individual needs is an ongoing process that will involve many members of the school community working together.

Parents and students will see the end result of good teamwork and communication skills. Of course, they also notice when teamwork or communication are ineffective!

Here are some things that parents noticed and worried about:

- *"Last year the teacher and I worked it all out. She made quite a few changes to how she taught him, and it worked very well. This year, the teacher did not know anything about what happened last year. I don't think she had even looked in his file or spoken to the teacher from the previous year."*

- *"When we have a meeting with the specialists and the teacher and the school principal everything sounds fine. But really once it gets down to what actually happens in the classroom, it's nothing like we agreed at the meeting."*

- *"We go to lots of meetings and I can tell that the teachers don't see eye to eye with each other. There's one teacher, Mr. Gladstone, who is really keen to help. But whatever he suggests the other teacher says it can't be done, or it's too hard, or it is 'not appropriate,' whatever that means."*

- *"He has two teachers, Mandy on Monday and Tuesday and Ted for the rest of the week. The trouble is they have such different ways of doing things, so what is OK on Monday is all wrong on Wednesday. My son can't cope with that. He has enough trouble dealing with one set of rules."*

- *"The classroom teacher does a very good job, but when she was away, he was always in trouble. Then I found out that the substitute teacher had not been given any information about him or his difficulties."*

- *"My son does have an unusual disability, but last year was fantastic. Faye, his teacher, had received special training in just that area. But this year it's really frustrating. His new teacher was really offended when I asked if Faye could come to the meeting. This teacher says she can handle it herself. I think she's afraid to admit that she does not have the same expertise as Faye."*

## Strategies for Working with Teaching Colleagues

### Creating an inclusive school community

★ Openly endorse the right of every student, parent and colleague to equal and appropriate treatment, not only because it is the law but because it is the *fair and reasonable thing to do*.

✦ Check your own profile as an inclusive teacher. Use **Appendix #25: Teacher: Personal Profile as an Inclusive Teacher.** Seek out professional development opportunities, such as courses, books and conferences to further your knowledge.

✦ Always treat inclusion and intervention as integral and essential parts of everything you do. Avoid implying or thinking that intervention strategies are 'extras' you have to do on top of your 'real' work.

✦ Emphasize that the school community is a single social unit. Every student, every parent and every staff member is included in the group. Celebrate anniversaries, achievements and special occasions together.

✦ Have informal social gatherings to share fun and friendship with everyone connected with your school.

✦ Use *our* instead of *the* to stress the fact that everyone belongs and shares in the school community. *Our school, our library, our helpers.*

✦ Make a celebration of diversity. Highlight the fact that *everyone* is unique and that a mix of abilities, talents, difficulties and differences is normal.

✦ Create a collage of photographs that includes every student and adult in the school. As soon as someone new arrives, include that person's photograph in the group picture.

✦ Do not tolerate 'put downs' of any student, parent or colleague, even in the privacy of the teachers' room or 'teachers only' meetings. Such statements immediately create a division between 'us' and 'them.' Comments made should always be professional, inclusive, respectful and nonjudgmental.

✦ Use 'I statements' when talking about colleagues, parents or students, such as:

   • *"I found it difficult to explain how the program will work."*
   • *"I don't think I have earned his trust yet."*

✦ Avoid using words such as *pushy, angry, anxious, difficult* and *negative,* which place blame on a colleague or parent. Try to rephrase words to show the other side of the story:

   • *Pushy* could mean *she does not trust us to do the right thing.*
   • *Angry* could mean *he is feeling powerless and frustrated.*
   • *Anxious* could mean *she is afraid and needs a lot of reassurance.*
   • *Difficult* could mean *we have not looked at it from his perspective.*
   • *Negative* could mean *she has a sense of hopelessness about this.*

✦ Do not allow prejudice, gossip, bias or exclusion to go unchallenged or unchecked.

## Leadership

✱ Create a 'can do' culture, where finding positive ways of meeting challenges is the norm.

✱ Recognize and celebrate achievements in good teaching, where intervention and inclusive practices are part of the success story.

✱ Encourage team members to ask for help, share expertise and work together to maximize inclusive practices and interventions.

✱ Set up interest groups, advisory groups, mentor systems and goal-directed teams to contribute to inclusion and intervention.

✱ Model inclusive behaviors in your relationships with students, colleagues and parents.

✱ Actively encourage ongoing professional development so that team members can continually improve their skills related to intervention and inclusive practices.

✱ Follow through with team decisions, and support those required to implement them in the classroom.

✱ Deal with interpersonal differences that impact the teachers' abilities to provide interventions for the students.

✱ Make sure administrative systems are in place, so information about students and their needs can be effectively communicated to all teachers.

## Teamwork

✱ Teaching is a demanding job that can be stressful. Support your colleagues with care, concern and practical assistance when the going gets tough.

✱ Ask for support and assistance from your colleagues, supervisors and administrators, if you are finding that your work is too stressful.

✱ Take care of yourself! If you are exhausted, unwell, depressed, anxious or overly stressed, you will not be able to provide the students or your colleagues with the support they need.

✱ Follow through with what has been agreed upon by the group. Do not say one thing in a group meeting and then do something different once the meeting is over.

✱ You do not have to be an instant expert on everything. Talk to colleagues, and share expertise both ways.

* Make time for regular meetings with colleagues. You cannot work together unless you spend time talking together.

* Be flexible and accommodating and a good team player.

* Be prepared to pull your weight. Be generous with your time, effort and expertise to make inclusive education and intervention a success story in your school.

* Communicate with your colleagues and coordinate what you do, so students and parents have continuity between one teacher and another.

* Be particularly careful during transition periods, such as changes from one school year to the next, so that all information is shared with the next teacher.

* Have regular 'show and tell' sessions, where colleagues report back from conferences, present professional papers, describe examples of good practice and generally enhance the team's ability to be inclusive and provide effective intervention.

* Share resources that individual teachers develop in class. You could include:

  * teacher-made materials, such as worksheets that can be copied and used again
  * audiotape and reading book packages
  * resource folders that support students with projects on specific topics
  * classroom posters
  * classroom pets and plants

## Working with Parents

When a student experiences difficulties in school, parent reactions may vary. Some parents will immediately do everything they can to support the teachers, other parents may blame the school, and yet others may appear very anxious, defensive or demanding.

Learning difficulties often create friction and upset at home. The parent may need to deal with a child who is anxious, depressed, angry or distressed because of difficulties in school. Some students may show physical signs of emotional disturbance, such as bedwetting, poor sleeping or poor eating. Others may become emotionally volatile or withdrawn in response to their day-to-day difficulties in school.

Parents may become genuinely concerned that their child faces a future with seriously limited prospects for employment, independence and a fulfilling life. Family patterns can give a dramatically different slant on the situation.

. . . . . . . . . . . . . . . . . . . . . . . . . . . . . . . .

Some parents may fear that failure at school may push their child towards substance abuse, suicide or anti-social behavior. Sometimes, the level of the student's distress is not seen or even suspected by teachers at school.

- *"My brother was exactly the same [as my son] when he was at school. He ended up on the wrong side . . . juvenile detention and then jail . . . never has had a proper job . . . in and out of jail all his life. I just hope and pray that Joel won't go the same way."*

- *"Sometimes I feel real guilty. . . . It was in my family and now I've passed it on to my kids."*

- *"He's Mr. Cool in school. He would hate for the other kids to see him upset. But at home he is cranky, says he is 'hopeless' and that he 'would be better off dead.' He really scares me sometimes."*

- *"They say I worry too much. But I don't know what else to do. If I don't worry about her, who will?"*

A student's difficulties at school can also create friction within the family. Parents can blame each other, and siblings can resent the extra attention given to the brother or sister with learning difficulties.

> *"Eric just won't accept that his son isn't at the top of the class, so there's no let up. 'Make him do extra work . . . make him try harder . . . tell him to do it again.' Eric just won't listen to me and give the kid a break. The other kids get fed up too. 'When are you going to help me? It's not fair he gets all the help.' To be honest, it's all getting too much for me to cope with."*

## Parents as part of the team

The law states that parents must be informed and involved in all aspects of their children's education. Indeed, how could one imagine that the student is included if the parent is *excluded*?

Parents are the real experts with their own child. Not only do they know the student better than anyone else, they also care more than anyone else. Their influence on the student is likely to be much stronger than the teachers' and their involvement will be lifelong. On the other hand, teachers have professional expertise and experience. It is obvious that a partnership between these two expert groups is going to be part of the future.

But how does this partnership between school and parents work in practice?

Parents sometimes find that dealing with school is a challenge. Maybe their personal school experiences were negative. Perhaps they lack the skills or confidence needed to deal with

. . . . . . . . . . . . . . . . . . . . . . . . . . . . . . . .

teachers, systems and situations. Some parents may not understand their child's rights and may feel ashamed of the demands that are placed on teachers; other may have unrealistic expectations of what teachers and school systems can provide.

Even if parents lack skills or understanding, doing nothing may not be an option for them. Parents often have a strong drive to help their child and will often find a way to do the best they can. They may search the Internet and come up with unreliable information. They may be sucked into inappropriate therapies or try to invent their own do-it-yourself program at home.

Likewise, teachers find that working in partnership with parents demands skill, tact, time and patience. Teachers need to be flexible to work with a wide range of parents, all with different expectations, skills and circumstances. It is all too easy to misjudge parents on the basis of preconceived ideas, prejudices or limited understanding. The following expressions of parental concern provide a little insight into how some parents react to their children's difficulties and the teacher's role.

- *"I still feel like I am a kid waiting to be told off by the teacher."*

- *"I ask the teachers how I can help, but they say he is doing fine and that they can handle it. But I want to be sure I have done all I can, so I've just bought this very expensive computer program. It was more than we could afford, but the salesman said it will definitely make him an A student."*

- *"They say he has developmental delay, so I can't understand why he is still doing little kids' stuff if he needs to catch up."*

- *"When they tell me all the trouble he is having, I feel real bad, like he is making a lot of extra work for the teachers . . . and they are busy people. I've told him . . . don't keep bothering the teacher."*

- *The teachers tell me all this stuff about him, like it's my fault. I tell them I'm not educated myself and I can't be there to see what he is doing in class. It's hard enough when he comes home from school and he's got all that work to do . . . it's way beyond me. My reading isn't so good and they teach things differently now."*

- *"The teachers never told me about the special summer camp. I guess they knew I wouldn't be able to afford it. But my boss knew about the camp and told me about it. He said the company had a special fund to help employees' families, and so the kids went. . . . It was great for them."*

## Communication between home and school

Inclusive education and intervention only work effectively when *everyone* is well informed.

. . . . . . . . . . . . . . . . . . . . . . . . . . . . . . . . . .

Teachers need to understand the big picture before they have enough information to plan an effective program in school. What can the parents tell the teacher about the student? Are there family circumstances that make a difference? What are the parents' priorities? What are the student's main concerns? Why isn't inclusive education working as well as you had hoped? How can the intervention program be improved?

Parents, too, need to have information. How are the teachers helping my child? How does that work? What can I do to help? How is my child doing? What will happen next year?

The exchange of information between home and school may be inadequate for a variety of reasons, such as poor communication skills, lack of time, discontinuity of teachers or poorly established communication channels.

Parents may feel frustrated and anxious, because they do not understand what teachers are doing to help their child. A good inclusive education program is often seamless. Students and adults work together, and special intervention and strategies are an integral part of the classroom. The downside of this is that parents may not 'see' the program at all, as there are no visits to the special education room and no separate work folders or time spent working alone on 'special' work.

- *"Those teachers are all so educated…half the time I don't make any sense of what they are saying to me. 'Oh don't you worry, Mrs. Goldstein,' they say. 'We got the IPP and the AYZ and the ABC, so it's all fixed just fine.'"*

- *"I kept asking him, 'Did you get any extra help today?' and he kept saying, 'No, I just stayed in the classroom like I always do.' So I went up to the school, ready to have a real fight. But then the teacher shows me her class record. Every day the teacher's helper has been working with him in the class. It is all written down, there's a file of work he's already done and there's plenty more to come. So they have been doing a real good job, but they hadn't told me the detail, and Tom didn't see it as anything special. I had to apologize to the teacher for thinking she wasn't doing her job."*

- *"Every year the teachers say, 'It will click. Don't worry. He is making progress.' But I can see that he is so far behind the other kids that he will never catch up."*

- *"The teacher says to write a note, but my writing and spelling is shameful . . . so I don't do that. I just tell him to tell the teacher . . . but I reckon he forgets."*

## Strategies for Working with Parents

### The parents' perspective

✱ Recognize that a family's cultural and religious values and traditions may play a significant part in the parents' perspective.

. . . . . . . . . . . . . . . . . . . . . . . . . . . . . . . . . .

✳ Remember that parents often see a different side of their child compared to the one you see at school. Always talk to them about how things are at home and their personal concerns about the student.

✳ Anxiety is a normal and healthy reaction to a problem. It stimulates action and problem solving. Work with anxious parents to deal with the problems they perceive.

✳ Do not dismiss parents' anxieties as unfounded because you think the problem is minor. Respect parental concerns, and do all you can to address them.

✳ Parents will be particularly anxious if they do not know or understand the full picture. Provide as much information as you can and help to interpret it, so that parents have an accurate picture of the situation and what is being done to work with the problem.

✳ Parents, too, have a lot of information about their child. Ask parents to discuss their child and to help you to see things through the eyes of the student and the family.

✳ Sometimes, parents have had unfortunate experiences in previous encounters with professionals. You do not have to judge or defend your colleagues, but you do need to understand the issues that the parents are dealing with. So say to them: *"Things do not always go well. Looking back, what have been the worst situations for you or for your child?"*

✳ Other times, parents have had very positive experiences with professionals. Knowing what has worked well in the past and what the parents find most helpful is an important part of future planning. So ask parents: *"What has worked really well in the past? ... When did you feel things were going well?"*

✳ Remember that there may be a family history that colors the parents' reactions to difficulties with learning.

✳ Do not take parental concern or questioning about a student's progress as a personal attack on your professional skills as a teacher. Parents have a right to ask questions, express concern and obtain as much information as they can about their child.

✳ Let parents know that you hear and understand their perspective. Rephrase what they have told you, and reflect it back to them: *"So your main concern is with her reading."* Sometimes they will need to correct you, if you have misunderstood.

✳ Do not make the parents feel that they are to blame for the student's difficulties.

✳ Make sure that parents have the support they need to understand and support their child. Provide extra counseling, discussion and practical help to ease tensions, if they exist.

★ Talk to parents about the pressures that the student's learning difficulties place on the family. Do what you can to relieve the pressure. For example, make sure homework does not require excessive parental involvement, and provide parents with information about community support groups.

★ Talk to parents about their thoughts concerning their child's future, so that you understand their hopes and fears.

★ Work with the parents to find out about positive avenues that may be available to the student in future years.

★ Share with parents the positives as well as the negatives about the student.

## Parents as part of the team

★ Do whatever you can to make parents feel that *your* school is *their* school, too. Consult and involve parents in the day-to-day life of the school.

★ Invite the parents to bring a support person (relative, neighbor, social worker, friend) when they attend meetings at school.

★ Ask parents to select a person on the school staff with whom they feel comfortable. Ask that person to attend school meetings for support and as the parents' advocate.

★ Make sure that the parent knows the name and function of each person on the professional team. Provide a written list of names and contact details for the parent.

★ When a large number of professionals meet together with parents, make sure that the professionals include the parents in the discussion and do not leave them on the sidelines.

★ Have one member of the meeting monitor the discussion and 'translate' any professional exchanges that the parents may not understand: *"IEP stands for Individualized Education Program, so that means it is an individual program that we will work out especially for Sarah Jane."*

★ Help parents to work with you rather than seek outside help (such as possibly dubious 'educational' products or perhaps poorly qualified 'therapists'). Provide the parents with the guidance and resources to enable them to work successfully with their child.

★ Some parents are unable to contribute to the team in any practical way. This does not mean that they do not want to know what is going on and have a say in how things proceed, so include them in the information loop, even if they do not actively participate.

✳ Parents are not necessarily educational experts. Parents often need help to understand the ongoing nature of their child's difficulties, the reasons the student's program is modified and the purpose of the activities provided.

✳ Conversely, some parents are very well informed. Accept the information that they bring to you with interest and respect. They may have done some excellent research and have a lot to contribute.

✳ Even if you think parents are misinformed, you still need to understand what it is they believe to be true, so you can work with them to clarify the issues.

✳ Invite parents to join the teaching staff at professional conferences where members of the public are able to attend.

✳ As a teacher, accompany parents to public meetings that relate to the student's needs.

✳ Share professional information with parents. Copy a journal article that might be of interest, lend a book or record a relevant TV program.

✳ As well as meeting your legal requirements related to parents, create as many opportunities as you can for parents to be involved in the student's program. Invite parents into the classroom, offer them training sessions in how to help and talk to parents often about their child.

✳ Do not hold back information (for example, about a special program) because you judge that these parents will not be interested, cannot afford the option, will not be prepared to travel or cannot put in the extra time or similar reasons. Always provide the information, and let the parents decide whether it is suitable for them.

# Communication between Home and School

## Listening

✶ Communication is a two-way street. *You need to be a good listener* so that parents can communicate with you. Good listening involves a range of skills.

### Effective Communication

| Communication Skill | Examples of Good Communication | Examples of Poor Communication |
|---|---|---|
| **Positive Nonverbal Language** | **Examples of Positive Nonverbal Language** | **Examples of Negative Nonverbal Language** |
| **Appropriate eye contact** | You look at the person you are speaking to. You make eye contact (unless this is culturally inappropriate or seems to make the parent uncomfortable). | You look around the room while they talk. You glance at your watch or computer screen. You look at papers on your desk |
| **Warm and responsive facial expression** | You smile appropriately, you look interested and your face reacts to what is said. | You look bored. You yawn. Your face does not register the appropriate emotion. |
| **Body posture reflects interest and involvement** | You lean slightly forward. You look relaxed and open. | You look defensive: your arms are folded tightly across your chest. You look aggressive: you point your finger at them to make a point. You look disinterested: you fiddle with papers or pens. |
| **Respectful and caring attitude** | **Examples of respectful and caring attitude** | **Examples of disrespectful and uncaring attitude** |
| **You are aware of cultural, religious or racial differences.** | You offer refreshments that meet religious dietary requirements. | You offer refreshments that violate religious dietary requirements. |

| | | |
|---|---|---|
| **You know something about the family circumstances.** | You remember what the parents told you previously about their family. You have taken time to get some background information. | You clearly know nothing about the family. You have forgotten what they told you last time. You have not even looked at the child's file. |
| **You use the person's preferred name.** | The parent has said his name is 'Robert,' and you call him that. | You call the parent 'Bob.' You forget his name or call him the wrong name. |
| **You value the parents' time.** | You are on time when you arrange to meet with parents. | You are late. You forget the appointment. |
| **Empathetic listening** | **Examples of good empathetic listening** | **Examples of non-empathetic listening** |
| **You make time and provide opportunity for the parent to talk.** | You ask the parent to come into a quiet room to talk. You arrange to meet later when you can listen properly. | You expect the parent to talk to you while you are supervising students. You hold a discussion in a busy corridor where other parents are waiting. |
| **Your phone is on silent.** | You pay full attention to the parent and their concerns. | Your phone rings and you take the call. |
| **You have arranged not to be disturbed.** | You pay full attention to the parents and their concerns. | You talk to people who come into your room during the meeting. |
| **You reflect the speaker's feelings.** | *"I can see you are feeling very worried about the new schedule."* | *"I think the new schedule will be excellent—no problem at all."* |
| **You express interest by maintaining brief verbal remarks.** | *"That's tough . . . I see . . . did he really . . . amazing . . . oh dear . . . mmm . . ."* | You interrupt and/or talk over the parent. |
| **You rephrase what has been said.** | *"So you are pretty sure that the other kids were mostly to blame."* | You shift to a new topic as if you have not heard what the parent said. |

| You summarize what has been said. | "Basically, there are two main issues. We need to look at her reading program and sort out the problems with the math times table." | You do not clarify what has been discussed. "Well it was good to meet you. Thank you for coming." |
| You accept the parent's situation without judgment. | "I know that often you both have to work late. A lot parents find that is difficult. It's not so easy being a parent sometimes." | "Of course, if you can't be bothered to get home in time . . . . Most parents in this school can." |
| You give the parents time and space to speak. | You do not always rush in to speak when the parent pauses. You can sit quietly and wait. People will often tell you a lot more if you do this. | You cut the parent off as they speak. As soon as there is a gap in what the parent says, you start to talk. You dominate the meeting and talk most of the time. |
| **Good questioning** | **Examples of good questioning** | **Examples of poor questioning** |
| You ask questions that relate to what the parent has just said. | The parent has just said that they are pleased with the student's progress. You ask, "So what do you think was the reason it worked so well?" | The parent has just said that they are pleased with the student's progress. You ask, "Did I give you that form for the school camp?" |
| You ask questions that reflect an awareness of the parent's viewpoint. | "I know you prefer Kylie to sit next to Kim, but we would like her next to Jo. Would that be okay?" | "We are going to try to sit Kylie next to Jo. Is that okay?" |
| You ask open questions that allow the parent scope to answer. | "How do you think things have gone since John started the program?" | "John has done very well on the program. Are you pleased?" |
| You use questions to increase the flow of information. | "Tell me more about . . . . Can you explain . . . . What was the background to that . . . ?" | You close topics too soon before you have all the information. You do not ask enough questions. |

# Language

✴ For parents to be included, everyone must speak the same language. Avoid using jargon or 'buzz' words that will immediately put parents at a disadvantage. Use plain language that everyone can understand.

✴ Identify the parents' preferred language for communication and use that, if possible. If not, have an interpreter available.

# Contact

✴ Find out the best way to contact the parents. Would they rather you telephoned them at home or at work? What time is best? Do they prefer email or a written note?

✴ Identify the parent's preferred place for a meeting. Many parents do not like you to visit them at home. Other parents will be pleased for you to call.

✴ Let parents know how to contact you and your colleagues. Should they telephone the school office with a request that you call them back? Should they email you? Should they write a note?  Make sure that the parents have the full range of contact details that will work for them.

✴ When needed, set up a regular two-way system of communication for regular exchange of information, such as a 'Home—School' book that travels between home and school each day with the student, for daily updates from the parent and the teacher.

# Meetings

✴ Parents may never have been to a formal meeting before. Explain what to expect, and offer reassurance and assistance if they seem anxious or uncertain.

✴ Before any meeting, it is a good idea to give everyone the chance to think ahead and plan what they want to say. **Appendix #28: Teacher Notes: Getting Ready for a Meeting, Appendix #39: Student Notes: Getting Ready for a Meeting** and **Appendix #42: Parent Notes: Getting Ready for a Meeting** are forms created for teachers, students and parents. You can use these to help everyone be equally prepared.

✴ Prepare an agenda, and circulate it before the meeting. This can range from a simple list of discussion points to a formal agenda.

✴ Ask a person to chair the meeting to make sure that the agenda (however informal) is covered and that everyone has a fair chance to speak.

✴ If several family members attend a meeting, you may need to help get a balance if one dominates the discussion: *"John, Rachel has told us her concerns. How do you feel about Sam?"*

✱ Allow enough time for a meeting. There is nothing worse for parents than to feel that time is limited and the teacher is in a hurry.

✱ Finish meetings in an orderly way. Signal when the time is running out, and invite everyone to have their final words.

✱ If you do run out of time, set a date and time for another meeting to continue the discussion.

✱ It is important to have a written record of every meeting. Parents often get left out of this process! Invite the parents to make a contribution to the minutes of the meeting or to write and submit their own record. **Appendix #29: Teacher: Meeting Record** can be used by the teacher, parent or student.

✱ It is useful to compile all the meeting records and to look for discrepancies in people's understanding of the meeting and its outcome. Obviously, any differences need to be dealt with quickly.

## Honesty

✱ Provide parents honest and regular feedback about their child's progress. False reassurance does more harm than good.

✱ Parents will be particularly anxious if they do not know or understand the full picture. Provide as much information as you have, and help them to interpret it, so they have an accurate picture of the situation and what is being done to work with the problem.

✱ Keep parents well informed about the intervention and inclusion strategies you are using in the classroom. Because effective and truly inclusive strategies are often virtually 'invisible,' parents may not know what is being done unless they are told explicitly.

✱ Always admit it if you do not know something or you have made a mistake: *"I am really not sure about that. I will find out and let you know. . . . Right now things are not going well, so we will need to look at making some changes to his program. . . . I'm afraid I made a mistake, so I will . . . ."*

## Concluding Chapter Six

This chapter has stressed the importance of teachers working with professional colleagues and parents to establish good communication regarding students' programs and their well-being. Everyone has different pieces of the puzzle, and it behooves all team members, including parents, to work together and support each other. It's crucial to make no prejudgments or assumptions as to what another member of the team is thinking or feeling. Openness, cooperation and implementing strategies for sharing information will create an atmosphere of trust, make everyone's job easier and support the final goal of helping the student thrive.

# APPENDIX: TABLE OF CONTENTS

# APPENDIX – SECTION ONE

# Observation Charts

Form #1

# READING OBSERVATION CHART

| | DOES NOT APPLY | SOMETIMES APPLIES | USUALLY APPLIES | SEE PAGE |
|---|---|---|---|---|
| **1. Student feels negative about reading.** | | | | |
| Student is reluctant to read; will not read without prompting; complains when reading. | | | | |
| Student avoids reading, 'loses' book, tries delaying tactics. | | | | |
| Student becomes angry or upset with reading. | | | | |
| Student tries to avoid reading in front of fellow students. | | | | |
| **2. Student is disadvantaged by poor reading.** | | | | |
| Student demonstrates difficulty reading materials or textbooks suitable for age group. | | | | |
| Student needs additional time to complete reading tasks compared to peers. | | | | |
| Student does not finish reading assignments in the allotted time. | | | | |
| Student runs out of time in examinations because of slow reading. | | | | |
| **3. Student has difficulties with reading.** | | | | |
| Student needs additional time to acquire basic reading skills. | | | | |
| Student achieves less than other students in reading. | | | | |
| Student needs more support than others when learning how to read. | | | | |
| **4. Student does not understand how reading 'works.'** | | | | |
| Student thinks that reading happens automatically. | | | | |
| Student does not realize that skilled readers have to work hard at times. | | | | |
| Student does not think about own reading strategies. | | | | |
| **5. Student has difficulties with phonics.** | | | | |
| Student has difficulties remembering letter shapes. | | | | |
| Student makes errors when sounding out single letters. | | | | |
| Student makes errors when sounding out letter blends. | | | | |

| | DOES NOT APPLY | SOMETIMES APPLIES | USUALLY APPLIES | SEE PAGE |
|---|---|---|---|---|
| **6. *Student has difficulties with phonological awareness and word building.*** | | | | |
| Student makes errors when trying to hear sounds in words. | | | | |
| Student makes errors when blending sounds together. | | | | |
| Student makes errors reading new words. (See Appendix #6: Diagnostic Phonics Assessment.) | | | | |
| **7. *Student has difficulties recognizing words at sight.*** | | | | |
| Student makes errors when attempting to read everyday words. | | | | |
| Student can read words in a familiar book but cannot read the same words out of context. | | | | |
| Student relies on pictures to get sense of story. | | | | |
| Student makes many errors and self-corrections when reading. | | | | |
| Student confuses words of similar appearance, such as *bread* and *bird*. | | | | |
| Student makes errors when copying words. | | | | |
| Student reads word by word. | | | | |
| Student puts in different words but keeps the meaning of the story. For example, reads *Jane got a present for her birthday* instead of *Jane got a parcel for her birthday*. | | | | |
| **8. *Student has difficulties with reading fluency.*** | | | | |
| Student's oral language is hesitant and lacks fluency. | | | | |
| Student stammers when speaking and reading. | | | | |
| Student cannot find the right word when reading. | | | | |
| Student's reading is hesitant and stilted. | | | | |
| Student takes a long time to recognize words. | | | | |
| Student sounds out the same words over and over again. | | | | |
| Student does not use punctuation to guide reading. | | | | |
| Student reads so slowly that the amount of practice is limited. | | | | |

| | DOES NOT APPLY | SOMETIMES APPLIES | USUALLY APPLIES | PAGE |
|---|---|---|---|---|
| **9. Student has difficulties making sense of what is read.** | | | | |
| Student puts in words that do not make sense. For example: *Jane got a playing for her birthday.* | | | | |
| Student makes up words. For example: *Jane got a purrel for her birthday.* | | | | |
| Student makes errors answering reading comprehension questions. | | | | |
| **10. Student may have visual difficulties.** | | | | |
| Student rubs eyes when reading. | | | | |
| Student tilts head when reading. | | | | |
| Student uses finger to keep place when reading. | | | | |
| Student covers one eye with hand when reading. | | | | |
| Student complains of headache when reading. | | | | |
| Student skips words and lines when reading. | | | | |
| Student reads for only a short period of time before needing a break. | | | | |
| Student chooses books with large print. | | | | |
| **11. Student has advanced reading skills.** | | | | |
| Student's reading is advanced compared to peer group. | | | | |
| Student complains that reading is boring, even though the student reads well. | | | | |
| Student prefers factual books to fiction. | | | | |

# Form #2

## WRITTEN LANGUAGE OBSERVATION CHART

| | DOES NOT APPLY | SOMETIMES APPLIES | USUALLY APPLIES | SEE PAGE |
|---|---|---|---|---|
| **1. Student feels negative about writing.** | | | | |
| Student complains when asked to write. | | | | |
| Student avoids writing whenever possible. | | | | |
| Student's writing is very brief in comparison to peers' work. | | | | |
| Student expresses difficulty in knowing how to start or knowing what to write. | | | | |
| **2. Difficulties with written language impact classroom achievement.** | | | | |
| Student's oral contribution in class is not reflected in written work. | | | | |
| Student does not do well in written assignments, tests and exams. | | | | |
| Student has problems in getting ideas down on paper. | | | | |
| Student writes sentences that are brief, incomplete, disjointed or hard to follow. | | | | |
| Student does not use a wide vocabulary to express ideas. | | | | |
| Student often writes the same words and sentences over and over again. | | | | |
| Student often uses the same format in every type of writing. | | | | |
| Student has difficulties in sequencing sentences in a logical order. | | | | |
| **3. Student has spelling difficulties.** | | | | |
| Student makes many spelling errors. | | | | |
| Student makes phonological errors in spelling, such as *beg/bec*. | | | | |
| Student does not use the correct letters for sounds in words, such as *train/tran*. | | | | |
| Student makes errors in the use of spelling rules. | | | | |
| Student has repeated spelling errors with common words, such as *what/wot*. | | | | |
| Student's work is full of spelling corrections made as the student writes. | | | | |
| Student successfully learns words for a spelling test but then forgets them. | | | | |

| | DOES NOT APPLY | SOMETIMES APPLIES | USUALLY APPLIES | SEE PAGE |
|---|---|---|---|---|
| **4. Student has handwriting difficulties.** | | | | |
| Student does not always form letters correctly. | | | | |
| Student's letters and words are often too close together, have irregular spacing or are too widely spaced. | | | | |
| Student prints instead of using cursive writing. | | | | |
| Student's writing begins neatly but quickly becomes messy. | | | | |
| Student takes longer than peers to complete writing tasks, and work is still untidy. | | | | |
| Student's hand gets tired or sweaty after a few minutes of writing. | | | | |
| **5. Student finds it difficult to copy accurately.** | | | | |
| Student makes errors when copying words. | | | | |
| Student needs additional time to complete copying in comparison to peers. | | | | |
| **6. Student has difficulties with punctuation.** | | | | |
| Student makes errors in punctuation when writing spontaneously. | | | | |
| Student makes more errors than peers when doing formal punctuation. | | | | |
| **7. Student has difficulties with proofreading and editing.** | | | | |
| Student overlooks errors when proofreading. | | | | |
| Teachers often comment, *"Check your work carefully."* | | | | |
| Student may alter correct words during proofreading activities. | | | | |
| Student may replace one error with another one during proofreading. | | | | |
| Student is not able to describe or demonstrate strategies for proofreading. | | | | |
| Student's editing of drafts leaves a significant number of unresolved problems. | | | | |
| Student is not able to describe or evaluate personal writing strategies. | | | | |
| Student does not seek editorial advice or assistance. | | | | |
| **8. Student has advanced writing skills.** | | | | |
| Student sometimes produces work of exceptional quality. | | | | |
| Student expresses a love of writing and will write by choice at home or school. | | | | |
| Student has accurate and advanced spelling skills. | | | | |
| Student uses a wide range of vocabulary and expression. | | | | |
| Student uses punctuation accurately and to good effect. | | | | |
| Student can vary writing style to meet various requirements. | | | | |
| Student shows exceptional imagination and creativity in writing. | | | | |

Form #3

# MATH OBSERVATION CHART

| | DOES NOT APPLY | SOMETIMES APPLIES | USUALLY APPLIES | SEE PAGE |
|---|---|---|---|---|
| **1. Student feels negative about math.** | | | | |
| Student expresses dislike of mathematics. | | | | |
| Student lacks confidence in own ability to solve math problems. | | | | |
| Student does not think mathematically in everyday situations. | | | | |
| Student expresses difficulty with mathematics. | | | | |
| Student's math difficulties impact the student's classroom achievement. | | | | |
| Student needs additional time to complete math tasks compared to peers. | | | | |
| **2. Student has difficulties in understanding the number system.** | | | | |
| Student makes errors when counting. | | | | |
| Student makes errors when working with place value. | | | | |
| Student makes errors in addition and subtraction. | | | | |
| Student does not understand the relationship between addition and subtraction (e.g., cannot use the missing addend to solve subtraction). | | | | |
| **3. Student has difficulties with the four operations.** | | | | |
| Student uses tangible objects to count without real understanding. | | | | |
| Student has difficulty applying standard algorithms. | | | | |
| Student makes errors in addition. | | | | |
| Student makes errors in subtraction. | | | | |
| Student makes errors in multiplication. | | | | |
| Student makes errors in division. | | | | |
| **4. Student has difficulties with recall.** | | | | |
| Student relies on calculator for basic number facts every time they are needed. | | | | |
| Student makes errors when saying multiplication tables. | | | | |
| Student forgets algorithms. | | | | |
| Student does not solve math problems mentally. | | | | |

| | DOES NOT APPLY | SOMETIMES APPLIES | USUALLY APPLIES | SEE PAGE |
|---|---|---|---|---|
| **5. Student has difficulties with math problems.** | | | | |
| Student can solve basic math facts but makes errors when choosing which operation to use in a word problem. | | | | |
| Student gets confused about what method to use to solve a word problem. | | | | |
| **6. Student has difficulties with spatial reasoning.** | | | | |
| Student does not use concrete math materials effectively. | | | | |
| Student's written numbers and symbols are untidy. | | | | |
| Student's math work is unorganized and difficult to follow. | | | | |
| Student expresses confusion when working with spatial math skills. | | | | |
| **7. Student has advanced skills in math.** | | | | |
| Student demonstrates advanced mathematical thinking. | | | | |
| Student finds standard class work too easy. Can handle more difficult work. | | | | |
| Student expresses an interest in math and seeks out interesting math challenges. | | | | |
| Student makes negative statements about class math. | | | | |

# Form #4

# CONCENTRATION AND ORGANIZATION OBSERVATION CHART

| | DOES NOT APPLY | SOMETIMES APPLIES | USUALLY APPLIES | SEE PAGE |
|---|---|---|---|---|
| *1. Student is physically restless.* | | | | |
| Student is often active and has a very high energy level. | | | | |
| Student fidgets and moves around even when asked to be still. | | | | |
| Student often touches and fiddles with things. | | | | |
| Student is often loud and hard to quiet down. | | | | |
| *2. Student is impulsive and impatient.* | | | | |
| Student acts before thinking. | | | | |
| Student calls out in class. | | | | |
| Student 'forgets' rules and continues to do the wrong thing. | | | | |
| Student rushes through school work and makes silly mistakes. | | | | |
| Student interrupts when others are speaking. | | | | |
| Student pushes in or becomes frustrated when having to wait for turn. | | | | |
| Student gets restless and frustrated when having to wait. | | | | |
| Student often seems to be in a rush. | | | | |
| Student complains if a task or game seems to take too long. | | | | |
| *3. Student finds it hard to concentrate.* | | | | |
| Student often looks around and fidgets when supposed to be listening. | | | | |
| Student loses concentration when working on a task. | | | | |
| Student does not see things through to the finish and frequently does not complete the task. | | | | |
| Student starts one thing and gets sidetracked with something else. | | | | |
| Student pays attention to distractions instead of concentrating on task. | | | | |
| Student is inattentive and seems to be in a dream. | | | | |
| Student sometimes does not appear to have heard what is said. | | | | |
| Student does not respond to time pressures. | | | | |
| Student seems vague and unaware of what is going on in the classroom. | | | | |
| Student does not follow instructions. | | | | |
| Student starts something but then drifts off task. | | | | |

| | DOES NOT APPLY | SOMETIMES APPLIES | USUALLY APPLIES | SEE PAGE |
|---|---|---|---|---|
| **4. Student is poorly organized.** | | | | |
| Student is often unprepared because student has not planned ahead. | | | | |
| Student leaves things until the last minute. | | | | |
| Student loses things such as school work, materials or clothing. | | | | |
| Student forgets to bring materials and books when they are needed. | | | | |
| Student is messy, does not keep papers, materials and supplies in order. | | | | |
| Student misses deadlines for handing in work. | | | | |

# APPENDIX – SECTION TWO

# Literacy Resources

Form #5

## 100 MOST FREQUENTLY USED WORDS

| | Set 1 | ✓ | | Set 2 | ✓ | | Set 3 | ✓ | | Set 4 | ✓ |
|---|---|---|---|---|---|---|---|---|---|---|---|
| 1 | the | | 26 | or | | 51 | will | | 76 | number | |
| 2 | of | | 27 | one | | 52 | up | | 77 | no | |
| 3 | and | | 28 | had | | 53 | other | | 78 | way | |
| 4 | a | | 29 | by | | 54 | about | | 79 | could | |
| 5 | to | | 30 | word | | 55 | out | | 80 | people | |
| 6 | in | | 31 | but | | 56 | many | | 81 | my | |
| 7 | is | | 32 | not | | 57 | then | | 82 | than | |
| 8 | you | | 33 | what | | 58 | them | | 83 | first | |
| 9 | that | | 34 | all | | 59 | these | | 84 | water | |
| 10 | it | | 35 | were | | 60 | so | | 85 | been | |
| 11 | he | | 36 | we | | 61 | some | | 86 | call | |
| 12 | was | | 37 | when | | 62 | her | | 87 | who | |
| 13 | for | | 38 | your | | 63 | would | | 88 | over | |
| 14 | on | | 39 | can | | 64 | make | | 89 | its | |
| 15 | are | | 40 | said | | 65 | like | | 90 | now | |
| 16 | as | | 41 | there | | 66 | him | | 91 | find | |
| 17 | with | | 42 | use | | 67 | into | | 92 | long | |
| 18 | his | | 43 | an | | 68 | time | | 93 | down | |
| 19 | she | | 44 | each | | 69 | has | | 94 | day | |
| 20 | I | | 45 | which | | 70 | look | | 95 | did | |
| 21 | at | | 46 | they | | 71 | two | | 96 | get | |
| 22 | be | | 47 | do | | 72 | more | | 97 | come | |
| 23 | this | | 48 | how | | 73 | write | | 98 | made | |
| 24 | have | | 49 | their | | 74 | go | | 99 | may | |
| 25 | from | | 50 | if | | 75 | see | | 100 | part | |

# Form #6

# DIAGNOSTIC PHONICS ASSESSMENT: NONSENSE WORD READING

**Purpose:** This assessment provides a representative sample of the phonic patterns that students will encounter as they develop reading skills. Students are assessed on their knowledge of letter sounds and their ability to blend sounds together.

**Administration:** Ask the student to 'sound out' each word and then say the whole word. It is important that you hear the student do both parts of the task (sounding the word out AND saying the whole word) to make sure that students are not guessing at words by sight.

| Sample words | Sounds | Whole word | Teacher's notes: Introduction |
|---|---|---|---|
| | | | Say to the student, *"Look, here are some nonsense words. They don't mean anything, but we can still read them. I am going to say the sounds of the letters, and then I am going to say the word. Listen!"* Point to each letter as you sound it out, and then say the word. |
| tob | | | **t-o-b, tob** |
| guk | | | **g-u-k, guk** |
| fab | | | Say to the student, *"You try this one. Say the sounds, and then say the word."* Coach the student until the student gets it right. Then continue with the rest of the assessment. <br> ✓ if the student gives the correct sound for each letter in the nonsense word. <br> ✓ if the student says the whole word correctly. |
| **STAGE 1** | ✓ | ✓ | **Three-letter words: Consonant–vowel-consonant** <br> *The nonsense words in this section include every letter of the alphabet.* |
| | | | Teachers: Use this column to make notes and record observations |
| bam | | | |
| dep | | | |
| fiv | | | |
| jox | | | |
| kuz | | | |
| gik | | | |
| han | | | |
| lub | | | |
| med | | | |
| nif | | | |
| pog | | | |

| | | | |
|---|---|---|---|
| ruk | | | |
| quat | | | |
| sen | | | |
| tib | | | |
| von | | | |
| wug | | | |
| yad | | | |
| zed | | | |
| **STAGE 2** | **Sounds** | **Whole word** | **Two consonants slide together**<br>**Two consonants make a new sound**<br>**Final e** |
| steb | | | |
| snop | | | |
| frade | | | |
| crast | | | |
| flug | | | |
| chite | | | |
| brin | | | |
| prab | | | |
| blat | | | |
| yend | | | |
| plete | | | |
| chim | | | |
| shab | | | |
| thop | | | |
| **STAGE 3** | **Sounds** | **Whole word** | **Two vowels make a new sound**<br>**Vowel and consonant make a new sound**<br>**Silent letters** |
| neek | | | |
| tain | | | |
| harb | | | |
| maub | | | |
| soun | | | |
| mawkay | | | |
| hoak | | | |
| poin | | | |
| weam | | | |
| rirt | | | |
| noomer | | | |

| terb | | | |
|------|--|--|--|
| kneat | | | |
| gnorb | | | |
| **STAGE 4** | **Sounds** | **Whole word** | **Three consonants slide together**<br>**Four letters make a new sound**<br>**Words end in *'y' or 'ing'*** |
| shrit | | | |
| ging | | | |
| scrab | | | |
| pight | | | |
| abtion | | | |
| strunning | | | |
| hatty | | | |
| **STAGE 5** | **Sounds** | **Whole word** | **Two patterns combine**<br>**Compound words with prefixes and suffixes** |
| fadyen | | | |
| boinhard | | | |
| scribby | | | |
| unkeamed | | | |
| preteeking | | | |
| connotion | | | |

# Form #7

## SPELLING LOG

| Target word: | | | | | | | | | | | | |
|---|---|---|---|---|---|---|---|---|---|---|---|---|

| Daily practice and test until 6 consecutive ✓ | date | date | date | date | date | date | date | date | date | date | date | date |
|---|---|---|---|---|---|---|---|---|---|---|---|---|
| ✓ if correct  ▪ if incorrect | | | | | | | | | | | | |
| Weekly practice and test until 4 consecutive ✓ | date | date | date | date | date | date | date | date | date | date | date | date |
| ✓ if correct  ▪ if incorrect | | | | | | | | | | | | |
| Monthly practice and test until 3 consecutive ✓ | date | date | date | date | date | date | date | date | date | date | date | date |
| ✓ if correct  ▪ if incorrect | | | | | | | | | | | | |

| Target word: | | | | | | | | | | | | |
|---|---|---|---|---|---|---|---|---|---|---|---|---|

| Daily practice and test until 6 consecutive ✓ | date | date | date | date | date | date | date | date | date | date | date | date |
|---|---|---|---|---|---|---|---|---|---|---|---|---|
| ✓ if correct  ▪ if incorrect | | | | | | | | | | | | |
| Weekly practice and test until 4 consecutive ✓ | date | date | date | date | date | date | date | date | date | date | date | date |
| ✓ if correct  ▪ if incorrect | | | | | | | | | | | | |
| Monthly practice and test until 3 consecutive ✓ | date | date | date | date | date | date | date | date | date | date | date | date |
| ✓ if correct  ▪ if incorrect | | | | | | | | | | | | |

Form #8

# 100 MINUTES READING CHART

To be a good reader you have to practice! This chart will help you to see just how much time you spend reading.

Maybe your parent or teacher will agree to give you a small prize or reward if you read for 100 minutes.

Here's what to do. The chart below has 100 squares, one for every minute that you read. If you read for 4 minutes, color in 4 squares. If you read for 10 minutes, color in 10 squares. You can make patterns and use whatever colors you like.

Every time you read, color in more squares, and very soon you will see that you have done 100 minutes of reading.

**Is every square colored in? Fantastic!! You have read for 100 minutes!**

## Form #9

# NEW IDEAS FOR WRITING

## You can turn real facts into new ideas!!

| Try this! | Real fact | New idea |
| --- | --- | --- |
| **Exaggerate**<br>Make it extreme | | |
| **Substitute**<br>Change the detail | | |
| **Reverse**<br>Switch things around | | |
| **Elaborate**<br>Make it fancy | | |
| **Hypothesize**<br>Guess | | |
| **Try this!** | **Real fact** | **New idea** |
| **Exaggerate**<br>Make it extreme | | |
| **Substitute**<br>Change the detail | | |
| **Reverse**<br>Switch things around | | |
| **Elaborate**<br>Make it fancy | | |
| **Hypothesize**<br>Guess | | |
| **Try this!** | **Real fact** | **New idea** |
| **Exaggerate**<br>Make it extreme | | |
| **Substitute**<br>Change the detail | | |
| **Reverse**<br>Switch things around | | |
| **Elaborate**<br>Make it fancy | | |
| **Hypothesize**<br>Guess | | |
| **Try this!** | **Real fact** | **New idea** |
| **Exaggerate**<br>Make it extreme | | |
| **Substitute**<br>Change the detail | | |
| **Reverse**<br>Switch things around | | |
| **Elaborate**<br>Make it fancy | | |
| **Hypothesize**<br>Guess | | |

## Form #10

### PUNCTUATION CHECKER

Before you finish your work, check your punctuation using this
checklist.

| Things to look for: | Checked |
|---|---|
| Sentences end with the correct punctuation. | |
| Sentences begin with a capital letter. | |
| Proper nouns begin with a capital letter. | |
| Question marks are used where needed. | |
| Quotation marks are used where needed. | |
| Commas are used correctly. | |
| Paragraphs are used correctly. | |
| **Personal watch list.**<br>*Write down any punctuation that you forget to use correctly.*<br>*Take **extra** care to look for these every time you check your work.* | |
| | |
| | |
| | |
| | |
| | |
| | |

Use this chart and create your own!

| Things to look for: | Checked |
| --- | --- |
|  |  |
|  |  |
|  |  |
|  |  |
|  |  |
|  |  |
|  |  |
|  |  |
|  |  |
|  |  |
|  |  |
|  |  |

# APPENDIX – SECTION THREE

## Math Resources

Form #11

# COUNTING CHART

Name:_____

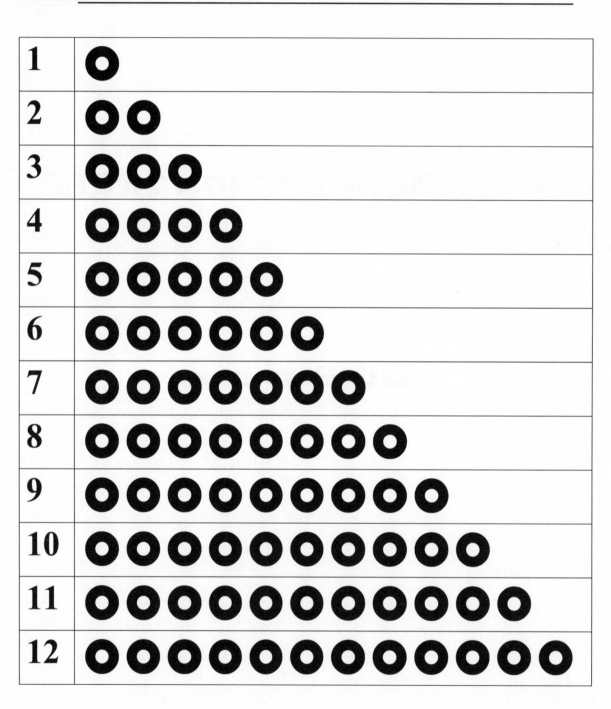

Form #12

# ADDITION CHART

| | | | | | | | | | | |
|---|---|---|---|---|---|---|---|---|---|---|
| **1** | 1+0 | | | | | | | | | |
| **2** | 1+1 | 2+0 | | | | | | | | |
| **3** | 1+2 | 2+1 | 3+0 | | | | | | | |
| **4** | 1+3 | 2+2 | 3+1 | 4+0 | | | | | | |
| **5** | 1+4 | 2+3 | 3+2 | 4+1 | 5+0 | | | | | |
| **6** | 1+5 | 2+4 | 3+3 | 4+2 | 5+1 | 6+0 | | | | |
| **7** | 1+6 | 2+5 | 3+4 | 4+3 | 5+2 | 6+1 | 7+0 | | | |
| **8** | 1+7 | 2+6 | 3+5 | 4+4 | 5+3 | 6+2 | 7+1 | 8+0 | | |
| **9** | 1+8 | 2+7 | 3+6 | 4+5 | 5+4 | 6+3 | 7+2 | 8+1 | 9+0 | |
| **10** | 1+9 | 2+8 | 3+7 | 4+6 | 5+5 | 6+4 | 7+3 | 8+2 | 9+1 | 10+0 |

Form #13

# SUBTRACTION CHART

| 10 | 10-0 | | | | | | | | | |
|----|------|------|------|------|------|------|------|------|------|------|
| 9 | 10-1 | 9-0 | | | | | | | | |
| 8 | 10-2 | 9-1 | 8-0 | | | | | | | |
| 7 | 10-3 | 9-2 | 8-1 | 7-0 | | | | | | |
| 6 | 10-4 | 9-3 | 8-2 | 7-1 | 6-0 | | | | | |
| 5 | 10-5 | 9-4 | 8-3 | 7-2 | 6-1 | 5-0 | | | | |
| 4 | 10-6 | 9-5 | 8-4 | 7-3 | 6-2 | 5-1 | 4-0 | | | |
| 3 | 10-7 | 9-6 | 8-5 | 7-4 | 6-3 | 5-2 | 4-1 | 3-0 | | |
| 2 | 10-8 | 9-7 | 8-6 | 7-5 | 6-4 | 5-3 | 4-2 | 3-1 | 2-0 | |
| 1 | 10-9 | 9-8 | 8-7 | 7-6 | 6-5 | 5-4 | 4-3 | 3-2 | 2-1 | 1-0 |

Form #14

# MULTIPLICATION CHART

| | 1 | 2 | 3 | 4 | 5 | 6 | 7 | 8 | 9 | 10 |
|----|----|----|----|----|----|----|----|----|----|-----|
| 1 | 1 | 2 | 3 | 4 | 5 | 6 | 7 | 8 | 9 | 10 |
| 2 | 2 | 4 | 6 | 8 | 10 | 12 | 14 | 16 | 18 | 20 |
| 3 | 3 | 6 | 9 | 12 | 15 | 18 | 21 | 24 | 27 | 30 |
| 4 | 4 | 8 | 12 | 16 | 20 | 24 | 28 | 32 | 36 | 40 |
| 5 | 5 | 10 | 15 | 20 | 25 | 30 | 35 | 40 | 45 | 50 |
| 6 | 6 | 12 | 18 | 24 | 30 | 36 | 42 | 48 | 54 | 60 |
| 7 | 7 | 14 | 21 | 28 | 35 | 42 | 49 | 56 | 63 | 70 |
| 8 | 8 | 16 | 24 | 32 | 40 | 48 | 56 | 64 | 72 | 80 |
| 9 | 9 | 18 | 27 | 36 | 45 | 54 | 63 | 72 | 81 | 90 |
| 10 | 10 | 20 | 30 | 40 | 50 | 60 | 70 | 80 | 90 | 100 |

## Form #15

# MATH CHECKLIST: ADDITION

### (single-digit numbers)

Student's name:_____

Date:_____

*Use this chart to observe and record the student's method of solving the problem.*

*Provide the student with a pencil, paper and counters or blocks. Ask the student to complete the addition problem, and observe the working method.*

## Addition:  4 + 5

| Strategy | Student response | ✓ |
|---|---|---|
| Uses counters or blocks | Student uses blocks or counters. | |
| Uses fingers | Student uses fingers. | |
| Draws lines or dots to count | Student draws and counts lines or dots. | |
| Does not use support | Student says the answer without counting. | |
| Counts each, counts all | 1, 2, 3, 4    1, 2, 3, 4, 5    1, 2, 3, 4, 5, 6, 7, 8, 9 | |
| Counts whole group once | 1, 2, 3, 4, 5, 6, 7, 8, 9 | |
| Counts on from first number | 5, 6, 7, 8, 9 | |
| Counts on from largest number | 6, 7, 8, 9 | |
| Works from a known fact | 4 + 4 = 8,  8 + 1 = 9 | |
| Retrieves known fact | 9 | |

**Notes on student's subtraction strategies:**

Form #16

# MATH CHECKLIST: SUBTRACTION

## (single-digit numbers)

Student's name:_____

Date:_____

*Use this chart to observe and record the student's method of solving the problem.*

*Provide the student with a pencil, paper and counters or blocks. Ask the student to complete the subtraction problem, and observe the working method.*

## Subtraction:   8 – 3

| Strategy | Student's response | ✓ |
|---|---|---|
| Uses counters or blocks | Student uses blocks or counters. | |
| Uses fingers | Student uses fingers. | |
| Draws lines or dots to count | Student draws and counts lines or dots. | |
| Does not use support | Student says the answer without counting. | |
| Counts all and then counts back | 1, 2, 3, 4, 5, 6, 7, 8 ,        7, 6, 5 | |
| Counts back from largest number | 7, 6, 5 | |
| Counts up from the lowest number | 4, 5, 6, 7, 8 | |
| Works from a known fact | 8 - 2 = 6,  6 - 1 = 5 | |
| Retrieves known fact | 5 | |

**Notes on student's subtraction strategies:**

**Form #17**

# MATH CHECKLIST: MULTIPLICATION

Student's name:_____

Date:_____

*Use this chart to observe and record the student's method of solving the problem.*

*Provide the student with a pencil, paper and counters or blocks. Ask the student to complete the multiplication problem, and observe the working method.*

## Multiplication:  4 x 5

| Strategy | Student's response | ✓ |
|---|---|---|
| Uses counters or blocks | Student uses blocks or counters. | |
| Uses fingers | Student uses fingers. | |
| Draws diagram of scattered lines or dots | Student draws and counts lines or dots. | |
| Draws diagram of orderly lines or dots | Student draws and counts lines or dots. | |
| Does not use support | Student says the answer without counting. | |
| Counts up in fives | 5, 10, 15, 20 | |
| Counts up in fours | 4, 8 ,12, 16, 20 | |
| Recites times table | 1 x 5 = 5, 2 x 5 =10,  3 x 5 =15,  4 x 5 = 20 | |
| Works from a known fact | 5 x 5 = 25,  25 - 5 = 20 | |
| Retrieves known fact | 20 | |

**Notes on student's subtraction strategies:**

## Form #18

# MATH CHECKLIST: DIVISION

Student's name:_____

Date:_____

*Use this chart to observe and record the student's method of solving the problem.*

*Provide the student with a pencil, paper and counters or blocks. Ask the student to complete the division problem, and observe the working method.*

## Division:  15 ÷ 3

| Strategy | Student's response | ✓ |
|---|---|---|
| Uses counters, blocks | Student uses blocks or counters. | |
| Uses fingers | Student uses fingers. | |
| Draws diagram: scattered lines or dots | Student draws and counts lines or dots. | |
| Draws diagram: orderly lines or dots | Student draws and counts lines or dots. | |
| Does not use support | Student says the answer without counting. | |
| Counts off groups of 3 | 1, 2, 3,    1, 2, 3,    1, 2, 3,    1, 2, 3 | |
| Counts in 3's | 3,6, 9, 12, 15 *or 15,12,9,6,3* | |
| Works from a known fact | 5 + 5 + 5 = 15 | |
| Retrieves known fact | 5 | |

**Notes on student's division strategies:**

Form #19

# MATH CHECKLIST: ADDITION

(two, two-digit numbers, no regrouping)

Student's name:_____

Date:_____

*Use this chart to observe and record the student's method of solving the problem.*

*Provide the student with a pencil, paper and counters or blocks. Ask the student to complete the division problem, and observe the working method.*

$$14$$
$$+\,25$$

Two-digit addition:

| Strategy | Student's response | ✓ |
|---|---|---|
| Deals with 14 and 25 as whole numbers | 14 + 25 = | |
| Counts on from 14 | 15, 16, 17 . . . | |
| Counts on from 25 | 26, 27, 28 . . . | |
| Works with columns | 4 + 5 =    1 + 2 = | |
| Starts to work on right-hand column first | Works on 4 + 5 =, then 1 + 2 = | |
| Adds columns by counting | Counts on to obtain total for each column | |
| Starts to work on right-hand side of sum | | |
| Adds columns, uses known facts | Writes answer in without counting | |

**Notes on student's addition strategies:**

Form #20

# MATH CHECKLIST: ADDITION

### (two, two-digit numbers, with regrouping)

Student's name:_____

Date:_____

*Use this chart to observe and record the student's method of solving the problem.*

*Provide the student with a pencil, paper and counters or blocks. Ask the student to complete the addition problem, and observe the working method.*

$$\begin{array}{r} 27 \\ + 35 \\ \hline \end{array}$$

## Two-digit Addition with Regrouping:

| Checkpoints | Observations |
|---|---|
| Is the student using the method taught in your class correctly? | |
| Is the student using counting to calculate the answers for each column? | |
| How does the student handle the regrouping of $7 + 5 = 12$? | |
| How does the student deal with the tens column? | |
| **Notes on student's addition strategies:** | |

**Form #21**

# MATH CHECKLIST: SUBTRACTION

## (two, two-digit numbers, no exchanging)

Student's name:_____

Date:_____

*Use this chart to observe and record the student's method of solving the problem.*

*Provide the student with a pencil, paper and counters or blocks. Ask the student to complete the subtraction problem, and observe the working method.*

**Subtraction using two, two-digit numbers:**

$$\begin{array}{r} 28 \\ -\ 13 \\ \hline \end{array}$$

| Strategy | Student's response | ✓ |
|---|---|---|
| Deals with 28 and 13 as whole numbers | 28 – 13 = | |
| Counts down from 28 | 27, 26, 25 . . . | |
| Counts up from 13 | 14, 15, 16 . . . | |
| Works with columns | 8 - 3 = ,  2 - 1 = | |
| Subtracts columns by counting | Counts to obtain answer for each column | |
| Starts to work on right-hand column first | Works on 8 – 3 =,  then  2 -1 = | |
| Subtracts using known number facts | Writes answer in without calculating | |

**Notes on student's subtraction strategies:**

Form #22

# MATH CHECKLIST: SUBTRACTION

### (two, two-digit numbers, with exchanging)

Student's name:_____

Date:_____

*Use this chart to observe and record the student's method of solving the problem.*

*Provide the student with a pencil, paper and counters or blocks. Ask the student to complete the subtraction problem and observe the working method.*

## Subtraction using two, two-digit numbers with exchanging:     32
##             -15

| Checkpoints | Observations |
|---|---|
| Is the student using the method taught in your class correctly? | |
| Is the student using counting to calculate the answers for each column? | |
| How does the student handle 2 - 5? | |
| How does the student deal with the tens column? | |

**Notes on student's subtraction strategies:**

# APPENDIX – SECTION FOUR

## Teaching Resources

## Form #23

# TEACHER CHECKLIST FOR MASTERY LEARNING

Student's name: _____

Date: _____

Write a clear description of the task:

| | Monday | Tuesday | Wednesday | Thursday | Friday | Saturday | Sunday |
|---|---|---|---|---|---|---|---|
| ✓ | | | | | | | |
| ✓ | | | | | | | |
| ✓ | | | | | | | |
| ✓ | | | | | | | |
| ✓ | | | | | | | |
| ✓ | | | | | | | |
| ✓ | | | | | | | |
| ✓ | | | | | | | |

| | |
|---|---|
| Has the student succeeded on three consecutive days? | **YES:** Wait one week and check again. The next check will be on _____[date].<br><br>**NO:** If the student cannot achieve three successes after a reasonable period of instruction and practice, then the task is too difficult and should be revised. |
| Is the student able to succeed one week later? | **YES:** Wait four weeks and check again. The next check will be on _____[date].<br><br>**NO:** Go back and practice some more until the student gets another three successes in a row, then try the one-week wait again. |
| Is the student able to succeed four weeks later? | **YES:** Congratulations!! The student has mastered the task.<br><br>**NO:** Go back and practice some more until the student gets another three successes in a row, then try the one-week wait again. |

## Form #24

# TEACHER CHECKLIST FOR SUCCESSFUL LEARNING

For the student to have the best chance of successful learning, all the items should be checked **Yes**.

| | Yes | Not sure | No |
|---|---|---|---|
| The student understands the purpose of the learning. | | | |
| The student knows the learning goal(s). | | | |
| The student expectations are realistic. | | | |
| The student understands how the current lesson connects to previous learning. | | | |
| The student is confident that he will be able to learn what is being taught. | | | |
| The student is not criticized, punished or ridiculed if a mistake is made. | | | |
| The learning is at the correct level of difficulty. It is not too hard or too easy for the student. | | | |
| Complex tasks are broken down into small sequential steps. | | | |
| Teaching is explicit. | | | |
| Teaching is carefully structured. | | | |
| The teacher has shown the student what to do. | | | |
| The teacher asks questions to guide learning. | | | |
| The student can see his progress. | | | |
| The student is encouraged to evaluate his own learning. | | | |
| The student is provided with guided practice. The teacher monitors and guides the student toward success. | | | |
| The student continues to practice until the student is 100 percent sure of what to do. | | | |
| Mistakes are used as information. The student and teacher look at mistakes to understand what went wrong. | | | |
| The student is encouraged to think aloud, so the teacher can understand the student's learning process. | | | |

# Form #25

## TEACHER: PERSONAL PROFILE AS AN INCLUSIVE TEACHER

*This personal checklist will help you determine areas in which you feel you are doing well and areas where you may want to make some positive changes.*

| | No | Sometimes or maybe | Yes |
|---|---|---|---|
| **Organizing an inclusive classroom** | | | |
| I always make detailed plans for my daily teaching. | | | |
| My daily teaching plan includes accommodations and modifications for students with special needs. | | | |
| I keep careful records of intervention and inclusive strategies that have been used in my class. | | | |
| I keep accurate, up-to-date records of each student's progress. | | | |
| **Teaching in an inclusive classroom** | | | |
| I deal with most student behavior problems successfully. | | | |
| I am flexible and use a range of teaching strategies to support students who have learning difficulties. | | | |
| I have developed a good collection of resources to help me meet the needs of all my students. | | | |
| Most students make good personal progress in my class. | | | |
| I willingly accommodate students with difficulties in my class by modifying and adapting the curriculum and the assignments. | | | |
| I have a positive and inclusive attitude towards all students in my class, regardless of their learning or behavioral difficulties. | | | |
| I enjoy teaching students of all abilities. | | | |
| I am patient and supportive when students find learning difficult. | | | |
| I am patient and supportive when students have emotional or behavioral problems. | | | |
| When my students with special needs become adults, I think they will look back and remember my class positively. | | | |
| **Working with colleagues and parents** | | | |
| My colleagues and I support each other in assisting students with learning difficulties and disabilities. | | | |
| I am prepared to seek help from colleagues. | | | |
| I know whom to ask when I need additional support or materials to support a student with special needs. | | | |
| When I meet with parents, our discussions are usually constructive and positive. | | | |
| I understand when parents are upset, angry or worried about their student's difficulties and can offer positive, practical solutions. | | | |
| I meet frequently with my colleagues to discuss how our students are doing and what further support is needed. | | | |
| I think parents of students with special needs feel that I respect their views and that I am doing my best for their child. | | | |
| **Professional development for inclusive teaching** | | | |
| My school offers enough training and support opportunities for developing inclusive teaching skills. | | | |
| I keep up to date with new ideas in inclusive teaching. | | | |

Form #26

# TEACHER CHART FOR PLANNING AN INCLUSIVE PROGRAM

Student's name: _____

Date: _____

General Education Teacher:

_____

Special Education Teacher:

_____

Other Team Members:

_____

| Barriers to successful inclusion and learning | Specific strategies to be implemented | Person responsible | Resources needed |
|---|---|---|---|
| Student has physical or sensory special needs. | | | |
| Student has trouble understanding basic classroom instructions and/or assignments. | | | |
| When a topic is taught to the class, the student often has trouble grasping the ideas. | | | |
| Student has difficulties reading worksheets and curriculum materials . | | | |
| Student reads very slowly. A lot of class time is taken up with reading class work, assignments or tests. | | | |
| Student has difficulties in understanding what has been read. | | | |
| Student has difficulties expressing in writing. | | | |

| Barriers to successful inclusion and learning | Specific strategies to be implemented | Person responsible | Resources needed |
|---|---|---|---|
| Student has difficulties with locating the key information when researching a topic. | | | |
| Student has difficulties organizing information and ideas into a logical sequence. | | | |
| Student has difficulties with spelling and punctuation. | | | |
| Student has difficulties copying things down quickly and accurately. | | | |
| Student's understanding of math concepts and methods is below the expected level for the student's age. | | | |
| Student is slow and inaccurate with mental math. | | | |
| Student does not participate in class activities and discussion or ask for help when it is needed. | | | |
| Student has difficulties concentrating on what is being taught. | | | |
| Student does not finish the tasks and assignments in the allotted time period. | | | |
| Student's poor organizational skills are a barrier to successful learning. | | | |
| Student is anxious, frustrated or negative towards learning because of difficulties. | | | |
| Behavioral, social or emotional problems (not related to learning difficulties) interfere with student's progress. | | | |

Form #27

# TEACHER GUIDE TO WRITING STUDENT GOALS

Student's name: _____

Date: _____

| | |
|---|---|
| **AREA OF CONCERN** Note area of concern. | |
| **ACHIEVEMENTS** What can the student already achieve in this area? | |
| **GOAL** What is the goal set for the student? | |
| **METHOD** How are you going to work towards this goal? | |
| **TIMEFRAME** When do you expect to reach this goal? | |
| **ASSESSMENT** How will you assess whether or not the student has reached the goal? | |

. . . ■ . ■ . ■ . ■ . ■ . ■ . ■ . ■ . ■ . ■ . ■ . ■ . .

# Form #28

## TEACHER NOTES: GETTING READY FOR A MEETING

Teacher: _____ Student: _____ Date: _____

What positive things you would like to say about the student?

What are your main concerns about the student?

What strategies seem to work best for the student?

Are there any strategies or situations that seem to increase or emphasize the problems?

Why do you think the student is having these difficulties?

What plans do you have for intervention or support over the next two months?

What are the school's longer term plans for meeting the student's needs?

Is there any information that you want to give the parents?

Are there any questions that you would like to ask the parent[s]?

Are there any questions that you would like to ask your professional colleagues?

What assistance do you need to meet the student's needs?

How do you think the student views the situation?

What do you hope the meeting will achieve?

Additional areas to address:

## Form #29

# TEACHER: MEETING RECORD

(Provide copies to everyone attending the meeting.)

Date of the meeting: _____ Student's name: _____

People in attendance:

_____

_____

_____

Record keeper: _____

What was discussed at the meeting?   Make a note of who spoke and what they said.

List the decisions. Make a note of what was agreed to and who is responsible for the implementation.

# APPENDIX – SECTION FIVE

# Student Support Resources

## Form #30

# STUDENT GUIDE TO MAKING CHANGES

Let's look at the things you are good at and things that maybe you are not so good at. See if there are any changes that would be good to make.

## How do you rate yourself with **friendliness?**

**Very low**                                    **Average**                                    **Very high**

OOOOOOOOOOOOOOOOOOOOOOOOOOOOOOOOOOOOOOOOOO

How could you make your rating go higher?

Write three ways you could improve your personal rating for friendliness.

1. _____

2. _____

3. _____

## How do you rate yourself in **reading?**

**Very low**                                    **Average**                                    **Very high**

OOOOOOOOOOOOOOOOOOOOOOOOOOOOOOOOOOOOOOOOOO

How could you make your rating go higher?

Write down three ways you could improve your personal rating for reading.

1. _____

2. _____

3. _____

# How do you rate yourself on **concentration?**

**Very low**                                    **Average**                                    **Very high**

○○○○○○○○○○○○○○○○○○○○○○○○○○○○○○○○○○○○○○○○○○○○

How could you make your rating go higher?

Write down three ways you could improve your personal rating for concentration.

1. _____

2. _____

3. _____

# How do you rate yourself on **personal organization?**

**Very low**                                    **Average**                                    **Very high**

○○○○○○○○○○○○○○○○○○○○○○○○○○○○○○○○○○○○○○○○○○○○

How could you make your rating go higher?

Write down three ways you could improve your personal rating for organization.

1. _____

2. _____

3. _____

# How do you rate yourself with **spelling and writing?**

**Very low**                                    **Average**                                    **Very high**

OOOOOOOOOOOOOOOOOOOOOOOOOOOOOOOOOOOOOOOOOOOO

How could you make your rating go higher?

Write down three ways you could improve your personal rating for spelling and writing.

1. _____

2. _____

3. _____

# How do you rate yourself in **math?**

**Very low**                                    **Average**                                    **Very high**

OOOOOOOOOOOOOOOOOOOOOOOOOOOOOOOOOOOOOOOOOOOO

How could you make your rating go higher?

Write down three ways you could improve your personal rating for math.

1. _____

2. _____

3. _____

How do you rate yourself in _____?

**Very low**                     **Average**                     **Very high**
○○○○○○○○○○○○○○○○○○○○○○○○○○○○○○○○○○○○○○○○○

How could you make your rating go higher?

Write down three ways you could improve your personal rating for this subject.

1. _____

2. _____

3. _____

How do you rate yourself in _____?

**Very low**                     **Average**                     **Very high**
○○○○○○○○○○○○○○○○○○○○○○○○○○○○○○○○○○○○○○○○○

How could you make your rating go higher?

Write down three ways you could improve your personal rating for this subject.

1. _____

2. _____

3. _____

# Form #31

## STUDENT WORK PLANNER

| Task to be done: | Date to be completed | ✓ Done |
|---|---|---|
| **Getting organized: Things to do to get started**<br>*For example:*<br>*Visit the library and get reference books.*<br>*Make a folder.*<br>*Highlight key words in question.* | | |
| | | |
| | | |
| | | |
| | | |
| | | |
| **Stages of work to be done:**<br>*For example:*<br>*Take notes from all the references.*<br>*Write an outline.*<br>*Discuss the outline with the teacher.*<br>*Write the introduction.* | | |
| | | |
| | | |
| | | |
| | | |
| | | |
| | | |
| | | |
| | | |
| | | |
| | | |
| **Wrapping up: Final stages before completion**<br>*For example:*<br>*Proofread and edit the final draft.*<br>*Prepare the cover sheet.*<br>*Hand in for grading.* | | |
| | | |
| | | |
| | | |
| | | |

Form #32

## STUDENT PRIORITIES CHART

**Step 1:** Write a list of all the things you have to do today.
**Step 2:** Number the items on the list in order of importance.
**Step 3:** Check the items off as you finish them.

| Order of importance | What do I have to do today? | Done ✓ |
|---|---|---|
|  |  |  |
|  |  |  |
|  |  |  |
|  |  |  |
|  |  |  |
|  |  |  |
|  |  |  |
|  |  |  |
|  |  |  |
|  |  |  |
|  |  |  |
|  |  |  |
|  |  |  |
|  |  |  |
|  |  |  |
|  |  |  |
|  |  |  |
|  |  |  |
|  |  |  |
|  |  |  |
|  |  |  |

# Form #33

# STUDENT GUIDE TO SETTING GOALS

*Note to teachers: Work through this sheet with the student to help select and clarify personal goals.*

## Long-Term Goals
*My dream is that when I am an adult:*

*I will be working as a*_____

*I will be living in*_____

*I will have*_____

## Medium-Term Goals
*By this time next year, I hope that:*

*I will have improved in*_____

*I will have succeeded at*_____

*I will have started to*_____

## My Achievements
*You may need to talk to your teacher about what to put in this section.*

Write down three things you have already achieved. For example: *I can already sound out words with single sounds. I can already read all the Level 1 books. I can already add two single numbers together.*

*I can already*_____

*I can already*_____

*I can already*_____

## My Short-Term Goals for the Next Four Weeks
*Ask your teacher to help you with this.*

Talk to your teacher and choose some goals that you think you can achieve. For example: *In the next four weeks, I am aiming to read three Level 2 books. In the next four weeks, my goal is to learn how to sound out words with **ch, sh** and **ee** in them. In the next four weeks, I will try to learn how to add two double-digit numbers together.*

**Goal #1** *In the next four weeks, I am aiming to*_____

**Goal #2** *In the next four weeks, I am aiming to*_____

**Goal #3** *In the next four weeks I am aiming to*_____

*If I achieve these goals my reward(s) will be:*

**Goal #1** _____

**Goal #2** _____

**Goal #3** _____

Form #34

# STUDENT PLAN FOR GETTING ORGANIZED

Use this chart to keep a record of what went wrong with your organization strategies. Maybe you forgot to take the correct book to class, or perhaps you did not allow yourself enough time between classes.

Write down the excuse or reason you messed up. Then write down a solution for next time.

| Date | My excuse. What went wrong? | How can I fix it next time? |
|------|------------------------------|------------------------------|
|      |                              |                              |
|      |                              |                              |
|      |                              |                              |
|      |                              |                              |
|      |                              |                              |

Form #35

## STUDENT SELF-EVALUATION

### How hard did I try?

☐ I tried pretty hard.

☐ I was OK.

☐ I could have tried harder.

### How did the work turn out?

☐ I am pleased with what I did.

☐ I think that what I did is OK.

☐ I am disappointed with the work.

# What are the best things about this piece of work?

_____

_____

_____

# What would I like to change?

_____

_____

_____

### How does this work compare?

☐ It is better than anything I have done before.

☐ It is about the same as my other work.

☐ It is not as good as my other work.

### What will my teacher think?

☐ My teacher will be really pleased.

☐ My teacher will think it is OK.

☐ My teacher will say I could have done better.

Form #36

# STUDENT: WHAT I THINK ABOUT SCHOOL

Name: _____

| | No | Sometimes Maybe | Yes |
|---|---|---|---|
| I enjoy coming to school. | | | |
| I like the way my teacher teaches me. | | | |
| The other students in my class are friendly. | | | |
| The work in my class is easy for me. | | | |
| I feel worried about my school work. | | | |
| Reading is difficult for me. | | | |
| Spelling and writing are difficult for me. | | | |
| Math is difficult for me. | | | |
| My teacher helps me if I do not understand. | | | |
| I like reading. | | | |
| I like spelling and writing. | | | |
| I like math. | | | |
| Other students hassle or bully me. | | | |
| I am well organized. | | | |
| It is OK to ask the teacher if you need help. | | | |
| I concentrate well in school. | | | |
| I try my best in school. | | | |
| The other students are smarter than I am. | | | |
| My family is proud of how I do in school. | | | |
| I wish the teachers gave us easier work. | | | |
| I wish the teachers gave us harder work. | | | |
| We have fun in our class. | | | |
| We do interesting things in our class. | | | |
| I get in trouble when it is not my fault. | | | |
| Other students think I am smart. | | | |
| I worry about getting into trouble at school. | | | |
| I follow the rules in school. | | | |
| The other students in school are kind to me. | | | |
| The teacher is fair to everyone in our class. | | | |
| I think I need more help with my school work. | | | |
| I think I will get a good school report this year. | | | |

**Three wishes for school:  I wish that . . .**

1. _____

2. _____

3. _____

## Form #37

# STUDENT REWARD CARDS

Photocopy this page, and use the cards to recognize and reward students' efforts with concentration, organization and perseverance. The blank cards can be used to write your own messages. You can offer a small prize once a student has collected a number of these cards. Write the student's name on each card to personalize it.

The cards may be decorated with glitter, stickers and sequins to make them look very special!

| | |
|---|---|
| ***You stayed on task until you finished today. Well done!***<br><br>*Awarded to* .................................................. | ***You ignored the distractions very well. Fantastic job!***<br><br>*Awarded to* .................................................. |
| ***I noticed you listened very well today. Great work!***<br><br>*Awarded to* .................................................. | ***You remembered to bring everything you needed today. Congratulations!***<br>*Awarded to* .................................................. |
| ***That was a tough task, but you did it. Well done!***<br><br>*Awarded to* .................................................. | ***You are so well organized. You are a great example to others!***<br><br>*Awarded to* .................................................. |
| ***You did not stop once. You just kept working. I love it!***<br>*Awarded to* .................................................. | ***You waited your turn so well today. That's terrific!***<br>*Awarded to* .................................................. |
| <br><br><br>*Awarded to* .................................................. | <br><br><br>*Awarded to* .................................................. |

# Form #38

## STUDENT GUIDE TO 'I CAN DO'

**Note to teachers**: *Look over this sheet, and work through both sections with the student. Use the items as discussion points to help the student develop a* **CAN DO** *attitude.*

What you say to yourself makes a BIG difference to whether or not you succeed.

Check out these statements and decide if you think they will help you succeed—or not.

| You are out on the sports field for a training session with the coach. This is what you say to yourself: | **Yes!** This will help me to succeed! | **No!** This will not help me succeed. |
|---|---|---|
| *This is too hard! I can't do it. I give up!* | | |
| *Practice is boring, but it's got to be done.* | | |
| *This is too hard to learn. I'm not doing it.* | | |
| *This is hard to learn. I'll ask the coach for some help.* | | |
| *I've tried this move three times already. Maybe I need to do it five or six times before I get it right.* | | |
| *I don't like practicing. It's boring, and I'm not doing it.* | | |
| *I am not giving up. I will keep going until I succeed.* | | |
| *I won't be able to do that. No way.* | | |
| *That looks hard, but I can give it a try.* | | |
| *Just do it!* | | |
| *I can't!* | | |

Like everyone in your class, you will find some learning difficult and some learning easy. Having a CAN DO attitude will make it easier for you to handle the difficult work successfully.

Look at each of these, and decide whether A or B is the CAN DO attitude.

| **You have tried the math problem twice, and you still cannot figure it out.** |
|---|
| **A.** You give up and put your math book away. |
| **B.** You give it one more try and then ask the teacher for help. |
| **The book you have to read for class is taking a long time to get through.** |
| **A.** You put in some extra time, and you ask someone to read some of it to you. |
| **B.** You put the book away and forget about it. |
| **The assignment your teacher has set looks really difficult.** |
| **A.** You get started and give it a try. You check in with your teacher for help if needed. |
| **B.** You don't get started, because it looks too hard. |
| **The teacher has asked for volunteers to help but has not told you what you will have to do.** |
| **A.** You think it might be difficult or boring, so you do not put your hand up. |
| **B.** You think it might be interesting. At least it is worth finding out. You put your hand up. |

# I CAN DO!

Here are some CAN DO statements that you can copy, cut out and put where you see them often. How about on your book covers, your wall by your desk, your computer or your school desk?

## WHEN THE GOING GETS TOUGH, THE TOUGH GET GOING.

## JUST DO IT!

I DON'T GIVE UP, 'CAUSE I'M A HERO!

*I never give up and never give in!*

*If I can dream it, I can do it.*

*If at first I don't succeed, I try, try again.*

## DON'T QUIT: WINNERS NEVER QUIT!

**Think big. You can do it!**

If I think I can, I can!

. . . . . . . . . . . . . . . . . . . . . . . . . . . . .

## Form #39

# STUDENT NOTES: GETTING READY FOR A MEETING

**Your name:** _____

**Date:** _____

What are the good things about school right now?

How do you think you are doing at school?

Are you worried about anything at school?

Is anything at school upsetting you or making you angry?

What sorts of things would make school better for you?

What sorts of things would make school worse for you?

Can you think of ways you can deal with any of the problems you are experiencing?

What would you like the teachers to do to help you?

Is there anything you want to tell the teachers?

Are there any questions you would like to ask the teachers?

What sorts of things do you enjoy outside of school?

How can your family help you best?

Who is the person at school you feel you can talk to best if you have a problem?

Soon you will be having a meeting with your teachers and family. What do you hope will happen at the meeting?

. . . . . . . . . . . . . . . . . . . . . . . . . . . . .

# APPENDIX – SECTION SIX

## Parent Resources

# Form #40

# PARENT GUIDE TO READING AT HOME

Learning to read is an important skill, and most students take several years to master the basics. Reading at home can really help your child develop good reading skills.

- Make reading practice a part of your daily routine. Choose a regular time and place, and whenever possible, stick to this.

- Talk to your child's teacher about your child's progress and how you can help with reading practice at home.

- For younger children, or those older students who find reading difficult, practicing early in the day (before school) might be better than after school, when the child is tired.

- If you are free during the day, you may be able to go into school to help your child with extra reading practice.

- Try to make the reading sessions relaxed and pleasant for both you and your child. If your child gets anxious about reading, progress will be slower. Sitting together in a comfortable chair, or even cuddled up on the bed, can be a good place to practice reading where you both feel relaxed.

- Reading time at home can sometimes be a very stressful situation. If upsets seem unavoidable, see if another family member, family friend or tutor can help your child.

- Make sure that the child's reading material is suitable. It needs to be easy enough to read with enjoyment and suitable to your child's interests. Talk to the teacher if you feel that your child has a book that is too easy or too hard, or not interesting.

- Students who find reading difficult generally need a highly structured program, where books are read in a sequence of difficulty and where there is a lot of repetition. Talk to the teacher about this if you are unsure.

- Read for a specific period of time. Ten minutes of reading is long enough for a younger student. This time can be increased gradually up to about 20 minutes for the older student. Knowing that the reading session will end at a definite time helps to encourage the reluctant reader.

- For the very reluctant reader, start with very short, easy reading sessions, and gradually increase the time.

- For the reluctant reader, provide an incentive for reading. For instance, provide a small reward for every 10 minutes of reading, and if necessary, you can add a bonus for good attitude.

- Remember to teach, not to test. When you teach, you help your child to succeed by providing as much help as needed and by praising and encouraging. (When you test, the child does not get any help, and they are judged while reading.)

- Make sure that the reading book is easy enough for your child to read with only a little assistance. Make sure that the book is of interest to your child.

- If your child wants to read a book that is much too difficult, read the book aloud, or take turns reading a page, or read along together.

- If your child gets stuck on a word, silently count to four before you help.

- Sound the word out, and say it to your child; e.g., *"m-a-tch, match."* Do not add extra comment, just demonstrate the sounding out and saying the word, and then allow your child to continue.

- If the word cannot be sounded out, just tell your child the word and allow him to continue.

- If your child makes a mistake on a word but continues reading and picks up the story, simply continue.

- If your child gets confused, take the child back to where the errors began. Read the section out loud, and then let your child read it again. If necessary, read along with your child until you arrive at an easier part that the child can read without help.

- When your child has finished reading, go back over any words for which you provided help. Have your child practice sounding out the words, and reread the sentence in which the errors occurred.

- Let your child prepare to read before a final 'performance.' Look at the pictures, read the title and discuss what the story might be about. Read the story to your child, and encourage your child to practice reading it. Allow your child to practice until he feels ready to read 'for real.'

- Some children like the idea of a 'performance.' Your child may like to read the story to another adult or record the story for another family member, friend or younger sibling.

- Some children like to use a scoring system, where the progress is measured by reducing errors and increasing speed. You can use a stopwatch or kitchen timer to determine how the speed increases with each practice session.

- Audio cassette tapes can be used for practice. The child can listen to the story on tape until ready to read it alone or can read along with the tape during practice.

- Always encourage reading comprehension by discussing the selections that your child has read, including the pictures and information obtained.

- Having your child ask you questions about the reading is a very good way of developing comprehension. Asking an adult questions takes pressure off the child.

# Form #41

## PARENT GUIDE TO MATH AT HOME

Parents can play an important part in helping their children develop confidence and good skills in math. But that does not mean you have to give them sheets of sums or drill them with times tables. Math is a real-life subject, so help your children notice and use the math that is all around you at home and in the neighborhood. You will provide your children with a strong basis and a good start for the school math curriculum.

Here are some ideas to help your children work with numbers and math at home.

- Point out the math around them. How much does that box of cookies weigh? How much does it cost to get into the movies? What is the latest score in the game?

- Involve your children in practical activities that use math. Cook with them and show them how to follow the instructions and measure the ingredients. Does the fence need fixing? Let them help you measure the fence. Take them with you to the hardware store to purchase the materials you need.

- Give children an allowance, and teach them how to budget and save.

- Use sports to teach math. How many runs does the home team need to get ahead? How far from the record was that time?

- Teach your children how to compare prices and find good buys at the store.

- Have them look at the sales receipts from your shopping trip. Which item cost the most? What was the total cost of your shopping? Did you pay more than the price advertised by the store down the road?

- Keep a calendar and a clock at home, and show your children how to use both. Encourage the children to check off on the days on the calendar as they wait for a birthday or special day. Show them how to use the TV guide and the clock to catch their favorite programs.

- Have the children take part in planning a family outing. Incorporate as many math skills as possible. How long will the journey take? What time will you leave? Discuss money. How much will it cost to go into the show? What much gas will the car need? What is the price per gallon?

- Play family games for fun in the car. Look at the license plates of the cars around you. Who can find the largest number on a plate? Who is the first to see a number 2, or three numbers that add up to 10? Who can see a license plate that has only odd numbers on it? Who can find a plate that has only even numbers?

- Talk to the teacher about the sort of math your children are doing in school. If you do help with school math assignments, be sure you are using the same method your child is learning in class.

# Form #42

## PARENT NOTES: GETTING READY FOR A MEETING

Your name: _____ Child's name: _____ Date: _____

What positive things would you like to say about your child?

What are your main concerns about your child?

What seems to work best for your child?

Does anything seem to increase or emphasize your child's problems?

Why do you think your child is having these difficulties?

What do you hope the school will be able to do for your child?

Is there anything you can tell the teachers to help them understand your child better?

Are there any questions you would like to ask the teachers?

What have you found outside of school to help your child?

What help do you need from the teachers or other professionals?

How do you think your child views the situation?

What do you hope the meeting will achieve?

# Notes

# Notes

# Notes

# Notes

# Notes

# Notes

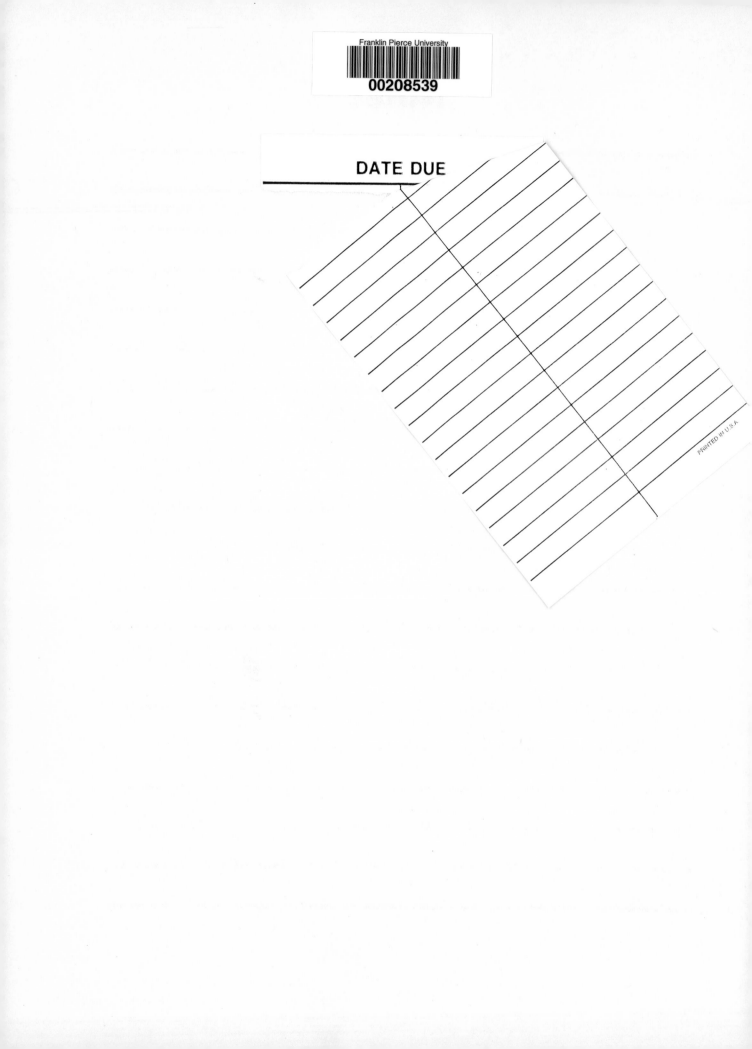

DATE DUE